The One and Indivisible
French Republic

COMPARATIVE MODERN GOVERNMENTS

General Editor: Max Beloff

Gladstone Professor of Government and Public Administration,
University of Oxford

The One and Indivisible French Republic

JACK HAYWARD
Senior Lecturer in Politics, University of Keele

W · W · NORTON & COMPANY · INC ·

NEW YORK

Contents

Tables

Figures

Abbreviations

APPCA	*Assemblée Permanente des Présidents de Chambres d'Agriculture*
CDP	*Centre Démocratie et Progrès*
CFDT	*Confédération Française Démocratique du Travail*
CFTC	*Confédération Française des Travailleurs Chrétiens*
CGC	*Confédération Générale des Cadres*
CGPME	*Confédération Générale des Petites et Moyennes Entreprises*
CGT	*Confédération Générale du Travail*
CID-UNATI	*Comité d'Information et de Défense – Union Nationale des Artisans et Travailleurs Indépendants*
CNIP	*Centre National des Indépendants et Paysans*
CNJA	*Centre National des Jeunes Agriculteurs*
CNPF	*Conseil National du Patronat Français*
CRS	*Compagnies Républicaines de Sécurité*
DATAR	*Délégation à l'Aménagement du Territoire et à l'Action Régionale*
DGRST	*Délégation Générale à la Recherche Scientifique et Technique*
EEC	European Economic Community
ENA	*Ecole Nationale d'Administration*
ESC	Economic and Social Council
FDES	*Fonds de Développement Economique et Social*
FNSEA	*Fédération Nationale des Syndicats d'Exploitants Agricoles*
IFOP	*Institut Français de l'Opinion Publique*
MODEF	*Mouvement de Défense de l'Exploitation Familiale*
MRP	*Mouvement Républicain Populaire*
NATO	North Atlantic Treaty Organization
OAS	*Organisation Armée Secrète*
ORTF	*Office de Radiodiffusion-Télévision Française*

PDM	*Progrès et Démocratie Moderne*
PSU	*Parti Socialiste Unifié*
SDECE	*Service de Documentation Extérieure et de Contre-Espionnage*
SNI	*Syndicat National des Instituteurs*
SOFRES	*Société Française d'Enquêtes par Sondages*
TPG	*Trésorier Payeur Général*
UDCA	*Union de Défense des Commerçants et Artisans*
UDR	*Union des Démocrates pour la République*
UNAF	*Union Nationale des Associations Familiales*
UNEF	*Union Nationale des Etudiants de France*

Acknowledgements

This book owes an immeasurable debt to all those who have enabled its author to maintain close contact with French political and administrative activity over nearly a quarter of a century. Its content should make clear that a scholarship received from a Fourth Republic government in 1952 has bought no complaisance towards its Fifth Republic counterpart twenty years later.

I wish to thank, in particular, Professor Martin Harrison and the editor of the series in which this book is published, Professor Max Beloff, for the extremely thorough criticism to which they subjected the whole of the first draft. I am also grateful to Mrs Ann Millward, Mrs Arlene Holmes and Mrs Sheila Pye, who at various stages typed parts of the manuscript and helped with the preparation of the index.

Editor's Introduction

The series of which this volume forms part is intended as a contribution to the study of contemporary political institutions in a number of countries both in Europe and in the rest of the world, selected either for their intrinsic importance or because of the particular interest attaching to their form of government and the manner of its working. Although we expect that most readers of such a series will be students of politics in universities or other institutions of higher or further education, the approach is not wholly that of what is now technically styled 'political science'. Our aims have been at once more modest and more practical.

All study of government must be comparative, in that the questions one asks about one system will usually arise from one's knowledge of another, and although we hope that anyone who has read a number of these volumes will derive some valuable general ideas about political institutions, the notion that politics is a suitable subject for generalization and prediction is alien to the empirical spirit that animates the series.

The authors are concerned with government as an important practical activity which now impinges upon the life of the citizen in almost every sphere. They seek in each individual country to ask such questions as how laws are made and how enforced, who determines and in what manner the basic domestic and foreign policies of the country. They seek to estimate the role not only of elected persons, presidents, ministers, members of parliament and of lesser assemblies but also of the officials and members of the armed forces who play a vital role in different ways in the different societies.

But government is not something carried out for its own sake; ultimately the criterion of success and failure is to be found in its impact upon the lives of individual citizens. And here two further questions need to be asked : how does government conduct itself in regard to the citizen and what protection has he through the courts or in other ways against arbitrary action or mal-administration? The second question is how the citizen can in fact make his influence felt upon the course of government, since most of the countries that will be discussed in these volumes claim to be democratic in the broadest sense. And this inquiry leads on to a discussion of political parties and the various interest-groups or pressure-groups which in modern states form the normal vehicles for self-expression by citizens sharing a common interest or common opinions. To understand their working, some knowledge of the role of the press and other mass-media is clearly essential.

The study of such aspects of politics has recently been very fashionable and is sometimes styled the behavioural approach or the investigation of a political culture. But our authors have kept in mind the fact that while the nature of a country's formal institutions may be explained as the product of its political culture, the informal aspects of politics can only be understood if the legal and institutional framework is clearly kept in mind. In the end the decisions are made, except where anarchy or chaos prevails, by constituted authority.

We would like to feel that anyone suddenly required for official or business or cultural purposes to go to one of these countries hitherto unknown to him would find the relevant volume of immediate use in enabling him to find his way about its governmental structure and to understand the way in which it might impinge upon his own concerns. There is a great deal to be said for a guide-book even in politics.

Nevertheless no attempt has been made to impose uniformity of treatment upon these volumes. Each writer is an authority for his particular country or group of countries and will have a different set of priorities; none would wish to treat in the same way an old-established and highly integrated polity such as that of France or the United Kingdom and a vast and heterogeneous political society still searching for stable forms such as India.

1 The Unwritten Constitution

France's unwritten constitution is partly constituted by the débris of its numerous written constitutions. Because the latter can be dismissed as periodical literature, the current document is regarded as merely a treaty provisionally settling the allocation of power to suit the victors in a political struggle. The constitution is only a partisan procedural device setting out the formal conditions according to which the government is entitled to rule. It is not endowed with the sacredness or permanence attributable to a constitution that symbolizes fundamental agreement about political values as well as about political procedures. In France, there is no clear separation between the prevailing institutional arrangements and the supporters of the government currently in power. Each régime is fragile because its legitimacy is always open to question and its duration depends on the hegemony of the political forces that established it. As a result, it has been impossible to institutionalize opposition because governments regard their opponents as dedicated to all-out war against the order established after the last constitutional crisis. It is necessary to situate the fifth republic in relation to its antecedents, so that we can assess what is enduring and what is new about the form of government that was instituted in 1958.

The main theme of this book is the perennial dialogue between French unity and French diversity, between a divided nation and a unitary state. The fifth republic is the most recent reassertion of the authoritarian tradition in French political history, exemplified by the absolute monarchy and the Napoleonic empires, against the régimes, such as the third and fourth republics, that sought to circumscribe public power by subordinating government to an indecisive legislature that accurately reflected French diversity. During the period from 1789–99, bedevilled by civil and foreign wars, France tried out a variety of political systems, culminating in a seizure of power by Napoleon Bonaparte that concluded a decade of revolutionary experiment. The failure of the first republic to find an acceptable institutional expression for the replacement of hereditary monarchy by popular sovereignty was to promote a search for a way of reconciling stability and effectiveness with freedom and democracy that has still not been concluded. Each of the régimes that followed left behind a legacy of constitutional experience that collectively incorporate the values which shape day-to-day French political behaviour. The first republic's main contribution was the development of government by a single chamber assembly elected by universal suffrage. Together with the assertion of the civil and political rights of the citizen, government by assembly provided a continental model of liberal democracy which contrasted strongly with the parliamentary government that developed in Britain. However, the two constitutional monarchies (1815–48), the third republic (1870–1940) and the fourth republic (1946–58) sought to import and adapt the British model as the French misunderstood it. The constitutional monarchies, in particular, did not learn the lesson of the failure of George III's attempt to govern personally and thought that British practice involved an active, politically implicated head of state; while the conspicuous absence of the religious, economic, social and political solidarity that allowed Britain to achieve the simplicity of a two-party system led to unstable republican government, the third republic having reduced the president to the role of master of constitutional ceremonies. The fourth republic curtailed the power of the second chamber and increased the importance of the prime minister and of the political parties, to come into line with the twentieth-century British model. However, the reversion to government by assembly and weak coalitions that disintegrated when faced with each new controversial problem left the régime vulnerable.

The 1958 challenge to the indivisibility of the republic – could Algeria be given independence? – provided General de Gaulle with his long-awaited opportunity to 'restore the state'. This meant reverting to the Napoleonic concentration of power in the hands of the chief executive and a reduction in the ability of parliament to paralyse government. It involved a reorganization of the administrative, military and judicial system of the country in the most authentic Napoleonic style. However, it was not possible to make all the necessary changes straightaway. The direct popular election of the president was postponed until 1962 and the president's supporters in parliament and in the country were gradually organized into a party that achieved an unprecedented measure of comprehensiveness and cohesion on the right of the political spectrum.

De Gaulle resuscitated the Napoleonic plebiscite as a means of appealing to the French people over the heads of their parliamentary representatives and used it with success until the rejection of his 1969 referendum, which he interpreted as a personal repudiation. Above all, he provided France with the remodelled political institutions of the fifth republic, embodying his vision of a truly sovereign state authority. The success he and his successor have achieved and the fragility of the fifth republic both derive from the fact that the new institutions he established are a natural extension of one side within the French political tradition but of one side only. The fifth republic has concentrated on giving the executive every facility to govern while denying to the 'oppositions' the constitutional means to oppose short of rendering the country ungovernable. This has stimulated the proliferation of extra-constitutional and illegal forms of opposition by groups motivated by sectional interest or ideology whose activities range from being a minor irritant to being a threat to the whole organization of French society. However, rather than describe the variegated dimensions of French diversity, I have concentrated on exploring the attempt to impose more discipline and uniformity on the insubordinate members of the French nation, which appears to be the main aim of France's political leadership.

The preoccupation with state sovereignty

In seeking to identify the source of legitimate political authority, Alexis de Tocqueville concluded : 'It is with the doctrine of the sovereignty of the people that we must begin. The principle of the sovereignty of the people, which is to be found, more or less, at the bottom of almost all human institutions, generally remains concealed from view. It is obeyed without being recognized, or if for a moment it be brought to light, it is hastily cast back into the gloom of the sanctuary.'[1] Sovereignty was bound to be an especially sensitive issue in France, where the power to decide has always been bitterly contested. However, to single out state

3

sovereignty as the salient feature of the French political tradition involves a great oversimplification. For France is a country of counterbalancing contradictions. It combines anarchic individualism and centralized statism. Revolutionary responses and rhetoric are coupled with the conservative traditionalism of entrenched vested interests. Instability and continuity coexist in extreme forms. Nevertheless, to clarify such familiar paradoxes, we assert the thesis that the attitude of the French élite towards politics has been dominated by a belief in the need for a strong, unified, centralized authority, capable of containing the centrifugal forces that constantly threaten the integrity of the state. It will be our task to develop and qualify this assertion.

It was the sixteenth-century French forerunner of political science, Jean Bodin, who first systematically expounded a theory of state sovereignty, a concept alien to the mainstream of medieval political thought. The sixteenth and seventeenth centuries marked a rapid modernization of the royal administration and army, the breakdown of medieval pluralism being associated with the reassertion of sovereign authority embodied in an absolute monarch. The concept of sovereignty involved a revival of the Roman Law notion of *imperium*. In the republican period it had referred to the supreme power of the citizens; in the consular period to the authority conferred on the emperor by the senate representing the citizens; whilst in the imperial period it had described the omnipotence and omnicompetence of the emperor, who was above the law. Written in a period of civil war, such as nearly a century later was to inspire Hobbes' *Leviathan*, Bodin's *Les Six Livres de la République* defended the pragmatic view of those in France (the party known as *politiques*) who argued that the state's role was to maintain order, not to establish true religion. Against the warring factions of Catholic and Huguenot, Bodin returned to the Roman Law assertion of the state as perpetual and absolute power and to the claim that the only constraint on the sovereign was his ability to limit his own sovereignty. The unique attribute of sovereignty was the power to make binding law, the sovereign's commands being entitled to unconditional obedience. Bodin's concept of sovereignty, a legal fiction formulated in the service of the nascent nation-state, an entity inclusive of all its provincial and sectional parts and exclusive of all more universal communities, was to prove influential long after his works ceased to be read.

It was Bodin who, by describing sovereignty as 'one' and 'indivisible',[2] prepared the way for the French revolution's subsequent assertions of national, parliamentary and popular sovereignty as embodied in the one and indivisible republic. However, it required the mediation of Rousseau's *Social Contract* to transfer sovereignty from the monarch to the people, whilst reiterating that 'sovereign authority is one and simple and cannot be divided without being destroyed'.[3] Despite Rousseau's warning of the dangers of representative government and his assertion of the inalienable nature of sovereignty, the 'general will' was displaced by the people's elected deputies as the repository of national sovereignty. The principal architect of this transformation of popular into parliamentary sovereignty in 1789 was Sieyès, just as in 1799 he paved the way for Bonaparte's seizure of power. So central a figure in the establishment and demise of the first republic's representative system of government merits a brief comment on his contribution to the French conception of political authority : the advocacy of government by assembly.

The attack on the *ancien régime* was inspired by a wish to substitute a political order based on nationwide uniformity and equality for the provincial, estate and corporate particularisms and privileges that had survived as the enfeebled vestiges of feudal polycentrism. After having asserted in *What is the Third Estate?* of January 1789 that 'the right to be represented is single and indivisible', Sieyès, who proposed the transmutation of the third estate into a national assembly, presented a motion in June 1789 that 'representation being one and indivisible, no deputy of whatever order or class he may be chosen, has the right to exercise his functions separately from this assembly'.[4] He went on to develop a theory of representation to allow the assembly to take over the people's sovereignty. It was based (like Burke's more famous British version) on the contention that the deputies represented the nation and not their constitutents. The exercise of legislative power had been delegated to the assembly by the people, whose sovereignty was reduced to the right to elect their legislators. In a speech in September 1789, Sieyès affirmed: "The people or the nation has only one voice, that of the national legislature; it

5

can only speak through its representatives.'[5] Thus was the threat of direct democracy *à la* Rousseau exorcised.

Sieyès' standpoint was enshrined in Title 3 of the 1791 (monarchical) constitution which proclaimed:

Article 1.   Sovereignty is one, indivisible, inalienable and imprescriptable; it belongs to the nation; no section of the people nor any individual is entitled to appropriate it.
Article 2.   The French constitution is representative. . . .
Article 3.   The legislative power is delegated to a national assembly. . . .

In the republican constitution of 1793, the emphasis shifts from the nation to the people. Its first article proclaims: 'The French republic is one and indivisible.' However, whilst reiterating the principle of popular sovereignty in Article 25 of the Declaration of the Rights of Man and in Article 7 of the constitution, it goes on to proclaim: 'The legislative body is one, indivisible and permanent.' The sovereign power was successively transferred between 1789–99 by successive *coups d'état* from the king to the nation, from the nation to the people, from the people to the assembly and from the assembly, via an attempt at a 'dictatorship of the notables' led by Sieyès, to the popular dictator Napoleon. On the 19 Brumaire (10 November) 1799, the day after the coup, the consuls of the republic – who included Sieyès and Napoleon – took an oath to 'the sovereignty of the people; to the French republic, one and indivisible; to equality, liberty and the representative system'.[6] However, Napoleon was to establish a Caesarist régime in which, in the words of Sieyès, concerned now to strengthen the executive against the legislature, 'authority comes from above and confidence from below'. In 1814, shortly before he lost his imperial throne, Napoleon lectured the legislative body on his superior representativeness, just as in 1869 Louis Napoleon was to secure overwhelming public support in a plebiscite shortly before the end of the second empire. Such has been the pattern ever since in France: the fragility of a power impersonating popular sovereignty.

France having attempted government by assembly and one-man rule, it remained for Benjamin Constant to sketch out a liberal type of representative government inspired by British constitutional monarchy, in which sovereignty would be constitutionally curbed. Like Sieyès, Constant supported the middle-class reaction that led to the *Directoire* in 1795 and the installation of Napoleon in 1799. However, he spent the period 1800–14 in outspoken opposition to Napoleon before joining him during the Hundred Days, being charged with the task of preparing a liberal constitution. In his *Réflexions sur les Constitutions* of May 1814, Constant wrote : 'None of our constitutions have assigned limits to the legislative power. The sovereignty of the people, absolute and unlimited, was transmitted by the nation, or at least in its name, as is customary, by those who dominated it, to representative assemblies. The result was the most unheard of arbitrariness.'[7] A year later, in his *Principes de Politique*, Constant went on to develop a theory of 'limited and relative' sovereignty, declaring in an anticipation of J. S. Mill's *On Liberty* : even if authority is 'the whole nation, less the citizen that it oppresses, it would be no more legitimate'.[8]

The French had been both fascinated and repelled by the notion of sovereignty. It is the harbinger of modernization, order and security but also of conflict, arbitrary power and despotism. Constant pointed out how Rousseau tried to evade the dilemma of sovereignty :

Terror-stricken at the sight of the immensity of the social power he had created, he did not know into whose hands he should deposit this monstrous power and found no safeguard against the danger inseparable from such sovereignty except in an expedient that renders its exercise impossible. He declared that sovereignty could not be either alienated, delegated or represented. This was tantamount to stating that it could not be exercised; it was to annihilate the principle he had just proclaimed.[9]

This unresolved problem of the location of sovereign power has continued to bedevil French attempts at creating an effective and acceptable form of government. All these attempts have required violation in practice of the ambiguous fundamental principles, either in the direction of parliamentary omnipotence or of executive dominance. Constant gave the French a characteristic liberal warning : 'When sovereignty is not limited, there is no way of protecting individuals from governments. It is in vain that you seek to subordinate governments to the general will. They always dictate that will. . . .'[10] Unfortunately, France has been deaf to this message, liberalism having shrunk into a narrow and feeble doctrine when it reached France. Constant's ideas have ever since suffered a guilt-by-association with the July monarchy's reign of the 'absolute bourgeoisie'.

Extreme statism has led by reaction to its antithesis : the out-right repudiation of the state, although this usually takes the form of inconclusive protest. It has been stressed that in France, on the right as well as on the left, in political parties as well as among pressure groups, protest is the norm.[11] It is a type of protest that is generally quietist in deed but verbally vociferous; intransigently negative, moralistically ideological and demagogically defeatist. Albert Camus' *The Rebel* provided the most celebrated mid-twentieth century formulation of this philosophy, as had Alain under the third republic. In the mid-nineteenth century, Proudhon, France's greatest anarchist, gave eloquent expression to a traditional hostility towards the coercive, centralized power of sovereign governments :

To be governed is to be kept under surveillance, inspected, spied upon, directed, regimented, regulated, enrolled, indoctrinated, sermonized, checked, numbered, valued, censured, commanded, by creatures who have neither the right, nor the wisdom, nor the virtue to do so. . . . To be governed is to be at every action, at every trans-action, noted, registered, inventoried, taxed, stamped, measured, enumerated, licensed, assessed, authorized, penalised, endorsed, admonished, obstructed, reformed, rebuked, punished. It is, under pretext of public utility and in the name of the general interest, to be placed under contribution, manoeuvred, ransomed, exploited, monopolized, extorted, pressured, mystified, robbed; then, at the slightest resistance, the first word of complaint, to be repressed, fined, vilified, harassed, hounded, manhandled, bludgeoned . . .; and to crown all, cheated, ridiculed, outraged, dishonoured. That is govern-ment; that is its justice; that is its morality.[12]

This extreme distrust and defiance of authority and the consequent propensity to direct action makes Proudhon as characteristic a spokesman of the French working classes as the Fabians are of intellectual British socialism, with its reliance on gradualist reform based upon influencing a rather passive govern-ment.

Although Proudhon's practical alternative to state domination was voluntary association, the civic culture in France has been too weak to provide a viable alternative, despite the proliferation of many competing groups, each articulating the overlapping demands of a voluble and self-consciously diverse society. The prevailing mass apathy is linked with a negative conception of freedom, liberty being conceived as fundamentally a matter of non-commitment, an antipathy towards authority so complete that any involvement with it is shunned. The result has been subordination to a remote and bureaucratic authority, Frenchmen responding with free thought and servile conduct, except for occasional outbursts of revolt, such as May 1968, followed by another demonstration of their lack of capacity to participate. The intransigent few provoke the restoration of traditional authority, whilst most Frenchmen take refuge in parochialism, content if they can secure a personal enclave of freedom in an over-regulated society. This relapse into docility is the characteristic French reaction to the suspension of written and unwritten rules during a crisis in which a short spasm of change can be terminated and an extended freedom from change can be secured. The sovereign state can be tolerated because it preserves the *status quo*.

Acquiescence in immobilism and the threat of insurrection

After the traumatic experiences it underwent in the revolutionary decade of 1789–99 when the two main French political traditions, Jacobinism and Bonapartism took shape, France experimented with a variety of constitutional devices. For most of the third republic, however, despite the fact that the legitimacy of the régime was under challenge by intransigent minorities, it was possible for government to function in a routine fashion, giving full play to the representative tradition of parliamentary sovereignty. This 'representative' emphasis, by reaction against the executive and administrative domination of the *ancien régime* and of the first and second empires, was modelled on the 1792 Convention. Nevertheless, despite Sieyès' famous stricture on second chambers – if they disagree with the first chamber they are obnoxious and if they agree with it they are superfluous – the indirectly elected senate shared parliamentary sovereignty with the chamber of deputies. A century after the Convention, however, it was possible for parliament to exercise its sovereignty in the social context of a bourgeoisie no longer struggling for ascendancy, but triumphant.

9

Although based, like Bonapartism, on the doctrine of popular sovereignty, Jacobinism had – under the guidance of Sieyès – rapidly translated this into a doctrine of parliamentary sovereignty nominally not unlike that attributed to Britain in the mid-nineteenth century. Members of the national assembly were representative of the nation and not of their constituents. The deputies, in particular, chosen by direct manhood suffrage, were the authentic spokesmen of the popular will and the custodians of political legitimacy. Their constituents had sectional interests which were to be expounded and defended in dealings with the administration and with ministers. This was the price of re-election. The mass electorate were, however, expected passively to rely upon the notables whom they had selected to represent them in the national parliament, to decide matters of national policy on their behalf. Thus emerged what has been dubbed the 'deputy-centred republic',[13] in which, unlike Britain, power was really concentrated in parliament. Undisciplined by party, members of the French parliament were also independent, in practice, both of a predominantly peasant electorate and of the government.

Although rent by the bitter anti-clerical and anti-militarist struggle of the Dreyfus Affair, the third republic had achieved, at the turn of the century, an immobilist symbiosis between the liberal-representative and the authoritarian-administrative traditions. Behind the protective tariff wall erected by Méline, the peasant, the artisan, the small shopkeeper of the predominantly small-town and rural French society flourished. An anarcho-syndicalist industrial proletariat was making anti-capitalism an increasingly important issue, whilst a united socialist party emerged to challenge the hitherto dominant radical party for the left-wing vote. However, what has been described as 'the coexistence of *limited* authoritarianism and *potential* insurrection'[14] continued to characterize the prevailing style of authority in the latter half of the third republic. Power was concentrated in parliament, itself paralyzed by class, ideology and sectional and local cleavages. Gambetta's claim in 1875 that the new constitution would 'consecrate the union between the bourgeoisie and the proletariat' proved an illusory hope. Successive governments devoted themselves to preserving stability; the radicals in particular acquiring a reputation for self-restraint in office that was connected with the frequency with which they occupied it. The same behaviour was required of the prefect who, as the local agent of the centralized political system, had as his prime function the maintenance of the *status quo*.

The stability of the French administrative substructure tended to go unnoticed by contrast with the instability of French governmental superstructure. However, as Alexis de Tocqueville pointed out over a hundred years ago:

We have had several other revolutions in France since '89, revolutions which changed the whole structure of the government of the country from top to bottom.... Usually, in fact, the majority of the population was almost unaffected by them; sometimes it hardly knew a revolution was taking place. The reason is that since '89 the administrative system has always stood firm amid the débâcles of political systems.... For though in each successive revolution the administration was, so to speak, decapitated, its body survived intact and active.[15]

While for the most part the bureaucracy helped to prop up the *status quo*, it had shown in the past and was to demonstrate once again in the post-second world war period, that it, rather than the business bourgeoisie, was the main modernizing force in France.

Heroic leadership: the crisis imposition of change

A régime organized to minimize the impact of change postpones and accumulates a backlog of overdue business. Developments in the political system's environment make increasingly pressing demands for attention. If they are neglected, they may threaten the régime with revolt or abrupt innovation. During the ensuing crisis it is frequently possible to carry out the changes which the political system has hitherto rejected. The crisis might take the relatively anodyne form of a government reshuffle – the characteristic method of the third and fourth republics – but it might lead to the collapse of the régime, as in the case of the settler-military revolt over the Algerian issue in May 1958. At such times, France appeals to 'one of those men who spring from events and are the spontaneous offspring of peril' as Pompidou expressed it, in presenting his general policy declaration to the assembly on taking office as prime minister in 1962. The appeal to the heroic

leader involves a reassertion of the latent need for assertive executive action within the political system to impose changes precluded
by the routine operation of a representative system that inhibits
ambitious reforms.

Writing at a time when France had subordinated itself by
plebiscite to the coup d'état of *Napoléon le Petit*, Tocqueville
presented a superb portrayal of his countrymen's equivocal
attitude to strong leadership :

Ordinarily the French are the most routine-bound of men, but
once they are forced out of the rut and leave their homes, they
travel to the ends of the earth and engage in the most reckless
ventures. Undisciplined by temperament, the Frenchman is always
readier to put up with the arbitrary rule, however harsh, of an
autocrat than with free, well-ordered government by his fellow
citizens, however worthy of respect they be. At one moment he is
up in arms against authority and the next we find him serving the
powers-that-be with a zeal such as the most servile races never
display. So long as no one thinks of resisting, you can lead him
on a thread, but once a revolutionary movement is afoot, nothing
can restrain him from taking part in it. That is why our rulers
are so often taken by surprise; they fear the nation either too much
or not enough, for though it is never so free that the possibility of
enslaving it is ruled out, its spirit can never be broken so completely
as to prevent its shaking off the yoke of an oppressive government.[16]

When the routine working of the political system fails, the nation
turns to someone who is immune from the discredit shared by
those closely identified with the *système*.

The heroic leader is usually someone who has not been involved
directly in politics : a general like Napoleon or de Gaulle. On the
other hand he might be a solitary rebel against the conventional
political system, like Clemenceau or Mendès-France.[17] It is vital
for such leaders to mobilize mass support against the stranglehold
of the traditional élites and of the political parties and sectional
interests who have monopolized the mediatory role between the
people and the government. They do this by seeking to personify
an underlying national consensus, exalting national pride and
stimulating hero-worship. In the early 1960s, with de Gaulle no
doubt in mind, the heroic leader's freedom of action was characterized thus : 'During crises, individual initiative prevails and
people eventually come to depend on some strategic individual's

arbitrary whim.'[18] Successive Gaullist political parties had ample cause to suffer the humiliating relegation to the passive role of supporters which this style of leadership imposed upon them. However, once the emergency is over, the heroic leader seems out of place, less an object of gratitude than a flagrant reminder of the incapacity of the political class to cope with serious problems successfully. Having fulfilled his function as 'agent of social change *in* the system and the preserver *of* the system',[19] he lacks the routine legitimacy to survive under crisis-free circumstances. He may seek to keep up a sense of impending crisis to sustain his flagging authority, as de Gaulle did by using the bogy of a return to the fourth republic or the threat of a totalitarian takeover by the communists. Although the May 1968 'events' temporarily sustained him by creating the feelings of mass fear and panic peculiarly propitious to maintaining the national saviour in power, public notice of the termination of the heroic leader's task was signified in the plebiscite less than a year later.

The May 1968 crisis represented the escalation of student unrest into an all-out attack on authority in all French institutions. Michel Crozier has explained that, because of the bureaucratic character of French organizations, change, when it finally comes, is comprehensive. 'To obtain a limited reform in France, one is always obliged to attack the whole "system", which is thus constantly called into question. ... Reform can be brought about only by sweeping revolution. Reformers, in any case, cannot succeed without counting on the pressure generated by revolutionary or quasi-revolutionary movements.'[20] Another leading French disciple of Tocqueville, Raymond Aron, recalled in his study of the May 'events' that in the early 1950s he had said in a lecture : 'From time to time France carries out a revolution, but never carries out reforms.' He was corrected by de Gaulle's comment : 'France only undertakes reforms in the wake of revolutions.'[21] That this should continue to be true under the fifth republic, whose founder prided himself on the imperious and sovereign fashion in which he exerted his authority, by contrast with the despised fourth republic, is an earnest of its enduring character.

A Gaullist deputy admitted, in an assembly debate on the 1969 referendum, that in France governments only acted under extreme pressure :

13

Our citizens sometimes contribute to this awareness of the need for action by methods which should be condemned but whose effectiveness one cannot objectively deny. A few windows are broken in a prefecture or even a subprefecture; then a series of measures awaited for years, sometime vainly demanded in the national assembly, suddenly begins to be implemented. The paving stones are dug up and a few cars are set on fire : the entire French educational system is totally reformed. . . . France thus progresses by reprimands that brutally bring it to its senses, at the cost of unrest which paralyses it and from which it emerges as from a dream. . . .[22]

The political system excluded mass participation at the national level except of a very remote and indirect kind. Despite its modernizing protestations, it slowed down the tempo of economic change to preserve the social and political equilibrium, arousing frustrations not merely among student activists but in many quarters. Farmers, shopkeepers, artisans and workers were all accustomed to using extra-legal and 'outrageous' forms of pressure on government. Each sectional interest has been prepared to use a strategy of blackmail against the authorities, openly flouting the law through forms of direct action which expose the pretence of national consensus upon which the government prides itself. When they cannot repress these challenges, the authorities are compelled to surrender. At such times, recourse to negotiation, and the modest reconciliation of conflicting interests with public policy, is more effective than the promulgation of grandiloquent edicts.

Unheroic consensus: the search for reconciliation

The new stalemate into which Gaullism was sinking in the period 1963–8, following the double victory of autumn 1962 in which the constitution was amended to the president's advantage and a stable majority was returned to the national assembly, was spectacularly interrupted by the May 1968 crisis.* However, instead of imparting to the fifth republic a new heroic impetus, it marked an interlude in the transition to a different style of political leadership. Georges Pompidou had, as prime minister, played a major part in organizing the domestic scene whilst President de Gaulle concentrated his innovative energies in the field of foreign policy.

* See below, p. 209.

However, he emerged in the crisis as the leader capable of settling the immediate grievances by economic concessions and restoring the government's authority by a parliamentary general election, not by recourse to a presidential plebiscite. After leading the Gaullist candidates to an overwhelming victory in June 1968, Pompidou said in a complacent broadcast : 'Now we can take a breather.' The heroic leader's response to the May crisis was entirely different. He saw it as a summons to new endeavour and ten days later, when he sacked Pompidou, he is supposed to have said to him : 'Now Pompidou, you can take a breather.' However, in the referendum of 27 April 1969, a majority of the French people said that they wanted to 'take a breather' from the heroic exertions imposed upon them by de Gaulle.

The search for political equilibrium through the avoidance of conflict is the hallmark of the post-Gaullist fifth republic. It is content to settle for an unheroic consensus based upon the general acceptance of the existing constitution and institutions. An attempt to establish a perpetual peace between the republics was made, facilitated by the re-emergence in major ministries of such familiar fourth republic figures as Maurice Schumann and René Pleven. To have elected the president of the senate, Alain Poher, as president of the republic in preference to Pompidou would have savoured too much of a return to pre-Gaullist immobilism. The new régime, which took some time to readjust to the departure of its hero, seems securely based on a collaboration between the president, his chosen government and a stable parliamentary majority. They have declared themselves dedicated to the reconciliation of the conflicts that are generated by the process of economic change through full consultation with (and where necessary concessions to) the party and pressure group representatives of the people, rather than bypassing them through the direct mobilization of the nation for spectacular achievements at home and abroad. The National Plan, described by de Gaulle as an 'ardent obligation', is deflated into an instrument of medium-term market research and industrial development. Whilst it had never been obligatory, even the ardour has now evaporated. Whereas de Gaulle had been determined to bestride the world like a colossus, Pompidou endeavours to bestride the EEC. The emphasis has been switched from ambitions for France to the aspirations of Frenchmen.

The fifth republic, having weathered the challenge of May 1968 to the social system, and the departure of de Gaulle in April 1969, has survived intact. Backed by an unprecedentedly large and loyal majority in parliament, its political leaders were intent in 1972 on preserving the institutional legacy bequeathed by de Gaulle. A central feature of that heritage is the constitution, whose preamble reasserts the principle of national sovereignty and whose First Title, labelled 'sovereignty', begins: 'France is an indivisible, secular, democratic and social republic.' This reaffirmation of the continuity of the French political tradition must now be explored in greater detail, notably by demonstrating the way in which the principle of the indivisibility of the state affects the organization of French government.

2 Modernizing Centralism and Traditional Localism

France is a state-nation rather than a nation-state. The nation is an artefact of the state. The political régime has retained a precedence over the political community that is derived from but extends far beyond its historic precedence. France is a unitary state superimposed upon a multinational society, the authority of Paris having been established under the monarchy, expanded by the Napoleonic empires and reinforced by the republics. Despite the incomparable assimilative power that France had shown over the centuries, the obsession with national unity betokens an uneasy sense that the peoples which make up France may have been swallowed but are not wholly digested. A secretary-general of the Gaullist UDR could complacently recall Michelet's claim that 'French France had attracted, absorbed, amalgamated the English, German and Spanish Frances with which it was surrounded. She had neutralized each by the other and converted them all into her substance. . . . She had southernized the north and northernized the south.' However, successive French régimes have regarded the legitimacy of their authority as questionable, the monolithic character of the political and administrative state apparatus being necessary to coerce into a semblance of consensus and order the disparate and divided fragments of the national mosaic. A succession of revolutionary reconstitutions of the central authority have left it particularly vulnerable.

This obsessive vigilance against potential dissidents is particularly associated with the Jacobins. These intransigent advocates of the one and indivisible republic naturally favoured a centralized system of local government and administration. Sieyès, the leading architect and exponent of the new departmental organization, commended centralized state authority on the ground that it would make France a '*single whole*, uniformly submitted in all its parts to the same legislation and a common administration'. 'I know of no better means to make all parts of France into a unit and all the peoples that divide it into a single nation.'[1] At each subsequent onslaught on centralized state authority in France, the Jacobin creed has been successfully reiterated. When the constitution of the second republic was being drawn up, Lamennais – supported notably by Tocqueville and Barrot – sought to base the new political system on the autonomy of the commune and resigned from the constitutional committee in protest when his proposal was defeated. As Proudhon, another great victim of the second republic's march from the revolution of 1848 to the coup d'état of 1851, put it with exasperated overemphasis: 'The commune will be sovereign or a subordinate agent, everything or nothing.'[2] This characteristic escalation into the opposite extreme to the Jacobin insurrectionary Paris Commune of 1792–4 was part of the inspiration for the ephemeral 1871 Paris Commune after which the third republic established the local administrative institutions which have survived largely intact for nearly a century.

State idealism and comprehensive central control

National uniformity, conceived as a comprehensive code of standardized rules imposed on all and sundry by Parisian officials as the guardians of republican virtue, is the keynote of the relationship between the French government and its citizens. The political ministers make the general rules but in implementing them the officials decide on the exceptions in particular cases. These concessions to necessity are part of a local political system which state idealists conceive as 'a kind of morality play, with the Public Interest defending the castle against a horde of savage, ruthless mercenaries of the selfish interests'.[3] To maintain the appearance of impartiality, the agents of the state take refuge in bureaucratic impersonality. They 'deal with categories and not cases'.[4] The objects of these regulations have no choice except to conform, to 'pull strings', to bribe or to revolt. It is by threatening revolt that the exceptions to the general rules are often obtained which make centralized authority tolerable. Without such concessions to the countervailing power of the local communities, the strict interpretation of the rules would shatter the semblance of national unity which is the shibboleth on which state authority is based.

Lamennais, in his famous anathema against centralization, declared that it led to 'apoplexy at the centre and paralysis at the periphery'. Whilst French local authorities are subordinate parts of the administrative system of the country, the integrated prefectoral system has sought to avoid the dangers of both centralization and decentralization by deconcentrating state authority. Although ministerial directives flow from the centre, the field services of the ministries, under the aegis of the prefect, are relatively accessible. They are able to respond more quickly and enjoy a limited measure of discretion in meeting local circumstances by comparison with the functional type of field administration characteristic of Britain and the United States, where there are no prefects to personalize central authority.

The French system denies in practice that one can realistically distinguish between matters of local and countrywide concern. Particularly in an increasingly urbanized and industrialized society, interdependence is such that an integrated type of state authority is required. This conception of a comprehensive system of central administrative control based upon a hierarchical chain of command is paralleled by the integration of local and central politics. The same individuals occupy key offices at the communal level (as mayor), departmental level (as councillor or president of the departmental council), national level (as deputies, senators and ministers) and seek to belong to the constellation of consultative institutions that encompass the decision-makers. Such a high degree of political and administrative centralization was possible because it corresponded in administrative, electoral and community terms to a traditional rural symbiosis.

This symbiosis is characterized by the dual source of executive legitimacy and the central monopoly of rationality. The two leaders who dominate French local government, the centrally nominated prefect in the department and the locally elected mayor in the commune, exemplify in their different ways the enduring triumph of bureaucracy and democracy. Both prefect and mayor derive a dual legitimacy from central government consecration and local representation. This duality of role, involving a conflation of the Bonapartist and democratic ways of legitimizing sovereign power, is aimed at integrating the hierarchical imperatives of the central government and the demands of the local community. Although he is nominated by and is absolutely dependent upon the central government, the prefect can only effectively run his department with the acquiescence of the local notables, the mayors of the communes and the departmental councillors. To win this support, he must in return espouse their causes and so he is converted into the conciliator and champion of local interests as the price for which the local leaders will prevent opposition to his authority. The prefect occupies a strategic point in the administrative system which enables him to mediate and arbitrate between the rival claims of central government and local community. As we shall see, the mayor plays a similar role in the commune. When he is both deputy and mayor of a large town, he rather than the prefect may be regarded locally as the leader, with privileged access to the central government. He will be the person best capable of reconciling conflicting interests. Thus the multiplicity of government grants are not merely the instruments of central control but the result of local pressures, or as it has been described, 'the exchange of subsidies for local votes'.[5] This has led to the phenomenon of *saupoudrage* – the dispersion of public investment grants in egalitarian, unselective profusion, giving a little of everything to everyone – which is politically rational in the present system but economically irrational.

A salient feature of the French type of local politics and administration, which approximates to still life in its ability to survive change, is the central claim to a monopoly of information and rationality. 'The French tend to take for granted the essential irresponsibility of local elected bodies and accordingly insist on administrative safeguards against it. . . .' 'If they were efficient they defied the government, if they were inefficient they endangered the safety of the state.'[6] Some 37,700 communes, whose units varied in population from under a hundred to over a million people, with councils whose total membership amounted to some 468,000 people – nearly 1 per cent of the population and somewhat under 2 per cent of the electorate – were the basic areas of local administration and local pressure. The patent irrationality of such a system condemned the communes to the control and tutelage of the agents of the central government who alone could be entrusted with ascertaining and acting on the requirements of the general interest. In the words of an 1801 circular: 'General ideas should come from the centre.' At that time, the ministry of the interior was responsible for all matters other than foreign affairs, defence, finance and justice. Its prefects could act as the unquestioned embodiments of the central will. The only serious contender as the personification of central rationality was the treasurer and paymaster general (TPG) who represented the ministry of finance in each department. However, the refusal of the ministry of finance to deconcentrate decision-making and the tendency to retain a narrowly financial rather than an economic approach has prevented its field services emerging as the focus of local and regional administrative control. So, although the TPG shares in the financial supervision over the elected local authorities and collects all taxes, the prefect exercises both a political and a budgetary tutelage. He remains the personal representative of every minister and of the government as a whole in his department.

The logic of centralization, that private action must conform to a standardized state pattern, leads to the proliferation of regulations to cover all acts of public life. As the type of economic rationality represented by a regionalized form of national economic planning becomes the official criterion for policy decisions and for allocating public funds, the old incremental improvisation, the case-by-case approach has to be curtailed. The field services of the central ministries and the prefects, thanks to their control of technical and economic expertise and their direct access to the decision-makers, take over the new function of guiding local and regional economic development, conceived as part of the overall strategy determined in Paris. The myriad powers of detailed intervention, authorization, supervision and coordination which the prefect, in particular, possesses can be mobilized for the task of reconciling the demagogic demands of the many communes and cantons under his jurisdiction, prior to negotiating on his department's behalf at the regional and national levels. However, the vicious circle of centralization is completed by the prefect adopting the same strategy as the elected representatives of the towns and villages. He makes large and irresponsible demands on behalf of his department, based on an addition of the separate claims of his constituents. These demands are backed by the threat that he will not be able to control the outburst of discontent that would follow rejection. This leaves the central government free to choose between the claims made upon it and the prefect can blame Paris for the failure to meet the just requests of each and every local community. The interposition of a regional prefect between the departments and the state was aimed partly at making possible a genuine deconcentration of administration and partly at providing a regional impetus for modernization so that development rather than stability was stressed.

Prefect, mayor and paralyzed periphery

(i) THE PREFECT : It is customary to trace the office of prefect to Richelieu's royal *intendants* through whom 'sovereign authority assumes the mundane guise of administrative work and royal absolutism becomes centralized administration'.[7] However, the *intendants* were more like the forerunners of the regional prefect, and their tax assessment and collecting emphasis brings to mind the treasurer and paymaster general. Whilst in England parliament was successfully asserting its right to control the crown, in France a centralized administration was being established. The administrative élite is as much the salient feature of French government as the parliamentary élite has been of British government. It was in the latter half of the seventeenth century, under Colbert, that the *intendants* became institutionalized as the administrative instrument of political modernization, the resistance to change being countered by greater centralization. The mercantilist policy of mobilizing the state's economic resources for the promotion of national power under Louis XIV converted the *intendants* into the main agents of state economic policy, just as three centuries later de Gaulle's regional prefects were intended to spear-head the process of political and economic modernization in provincial France.

After an ephemeral revolutionary experiment in local democracy, Napoleon as first consul resurrected the Roman title of prefect to describe the 'mini-emperors' who were to rule the departments as his agents, mobilize the local resources for the central government's purposes, and ensure universal obedience to his will. The prefect was to be a heroic local leader, restoring consensus after successive revolutionary crises, imposing the changes dictated by his Paris masters, acting as an electoral agent for the parties in power, exercising a paternalistic despotism over the department allocated to him. Above all, he embodied the sovereign state's discretionary prerogative and public security powers for the preservation of law and order which were developed particularly in the 'police state' of the second Napoleonic empire. From the third republic onwards, the restraints of administrative law, the anti-authoritarian political environment, and the developing public service and welfare functions which required coordination rather than coercion, made the prefect appear less of an arbitrary hierarch and more of an urbane mediator between central and local government.

It has been left to an Englishman to provide the classic description of that strategically pivotal product of the French genius for combining opposites, the prefect :

He is the intermediary between the government and the population, between the politicians and the electorate. He is the administrator who is part politician, and the politician who is a first-class administrator. He is the representative of the state in the department, and the protector of departmental interests against the ministries. He makes the mayors obey the law and he fights other officials in the departments, and sometimes their ministries as well, on behalf of the mayors. He is the executive instrument of the government, and at the same time the initiator of departmental policy. . . . Sometimes he acts as the general representative of the state, exercising what almost amounts to prerogative power. Sometimes he acts under specific statutory authority; sometimes his powers are delegated to him by a minister. Sometimes he acts as the general administrator of the department, sometimes as chief executive of the department, sometimes as *tuteur* of the communes, sometimes as chief of police. . . . The personalization of executive responsibility in the prefect, the crystallization of local political activity round the prefect and the mayors, and the balance of forces between administrators and politicians at a local level, are the backbone of French local government.[8]

To combine all these conflicting roles, the prefect must lay convincing claim to represent a timeless, all-embracing state authority similar to that asserted nationally by de Gaulle.

However, the prefect has gradually become less an incarnation of central authority and more an architect of concerted action between all the prevailing social and political forces who are willing to 'play the game'. The current approach is to present the general interest as not being something conceived at the centre and imposed unamended in the provinces. Rather, it is an agreed compromise, worked out with the interested parties under the guidance and leadership of the prefect. Recourse to this bargaining, negotiating style of decision-making is somewhat spasmodic and reversion to the more traditional manner is frequent. Nevertheless, a real attempt is being made to move away from chain-of-command legalism to the more informal and manipulative techniques of *animation* in a context of *participation*. The aim is to give the field services of the ministries and the local notables a feeling that they are being consulted on matters concerning them rather than being commanded by an inaccessible and unresponsive hierarchical superior. The administrative environment is not regarded as a collection of passive subjects to be regulated but a complex and potentially explosive constellation of 'social partners' who have to be softened up in advance and generally handled with circumspection. Their spokesmen may, as the occasion requires, be played off against each other, promised present or future benefits from public funds, flattered or browbeaten.

Compared to the more traditional, negative, regulatory functions of the prefect, the assertion of formal power is frequently neither appropriate nor feasible in the task of securing the positive collaboration on local development projects of official or unofficial 'partners'. Consequently, the prefect must persuade, influence and manipulate through his contacts, rather than cajole, command or coerce those who have the capacity to obstruct him in his activities. In the process of conciliation and compromise, central rationality is often a casualty. It disintegrates when brought face to face with local realities. The prefect tries to reconcile his old role as the solitary, unbending, ostentatious embodiment of the sovereign state's pre-eminence with his new role as the receptive, supple, surreptitious coordinator of public and private activities, to preserve local harmony, organize local economic development and promote the national purposes of the central government. The prefects grapple with the arduous problem of adapting their style of authority to the new norm of unheroic partnership. However, in times of crisis – which in France are either actual, impending or potential – the prefect is expected by the government to resume his traditional role as defender of 'state authority'.

In discharging both his functions of fostering and maintaining order and of stimulating and organizing development, the prefect needs the help of the local notables : not merely those elected to office in the departmental and municipal councils but also those elected to the chambers of commerce, of crafts and of agriculture, the leaders of business, farm organizations and trade unions. A vital aspect of being acknowledged as a representative figure is the access one is known to have to the prefect and his staff. The prefect can give the semi-official status of notable to those whom he nominates to the myriad consultative committees that are the formal channels by which the prefect communicates with his local environment. However, the prefect-made notable would be of no use as an intermediary if he did not enjoy the support of his constituents, so the choice available to the prefect is limited. He must either select the existing political, economic and social leaders as his collaborators, or, if they prove unsatisfactory partners because of their political opposition or divergent aims, discreetly seek to undermine their authority and secure their replacement by more pliable men.

(ii) DEPARTMENTAL COUNCILS : To an even greater extent than is the case with the senate, the *conseils généraux* or departmental councils suffer from a rural bias that not only makes them unrepresentative; it also reduces their will and capacity to adapt to industrial society. It forces them into a client relationship with the prefect who, it is hoped, will secure for them the central government grants on which they are dependent to keep up appearances. About a third of French departments have reached such a state of anaemia that they are no longer capable of providing sufficiently dynamic local leadership to run their affairs. If the office of prefect were abolished, they would regress even further. Paternalistic centralization has made itself indispensable by draining the departments (or allowing them to be drained) of the local élites capable of managing without close administrative supervision and support. In fact, the more underdeveloped the department, the greater is the dependence of the local community upon the expertise and leadership of the prefect, who works through the economic notables rather than the democratically elected political representatives.

The vital decisions concerning the department are increasingly taken not by the departmental council but by the prefect after consulting one of his numerous advisory committees. He uses these new notables as instruments in his task of aggregating the divergent interests which have previously been articulated separately by the groups represented. The primacy of the prefects is seen to advantage in the departmental equipment commissions. Created in December 1961, they are the bodies through which the major public investment projects are decided and coordinated, within the limits fixed by the central ministries and the regional prefect. The local authorities only have minority representation on these commissions, although they will have to contribute to the cost of the projects adopted. Accustomed to their subordinate role as cogs in the state machine, the local councillors sometimes protest but readily acquiesce in this transfer of power to central government nominees. They rely on their departmental prefect to defend them at the regional administrative conference.* However, in the urbanized and industrialized departments, a person who is both the deputy and mayor of the largest town can successfully challenge the prefect for local leadership. In the most dormant rural departments, the president of the departmental council may retain an important representative role, particularly when as deputy or senator he can secure the all-important direct access to Paris.[9] The department is less a locus of decision-making than the traditional place for mediation between central administration and local interests.

The departmental councillors are identified with the dawn of the third republic, the petrified structure of today having been established in 1871. The councillors formed a functional part of that largely pre-industrial society but like the senate they have survived as an immobilist obstacle in a modernizing society. Their unchanging nature is reflected in repeated re-election, often on the first ballot, although the low poll by French standards (43 per cent abstentions in 1964 and 1967, 38 per cent in 1970) indicates that it is indifference rather than contentment that accounts for continuity. Having successfully excluded the forces of change, the departmental councils lie stranded, allowed to perform their ritual but deprived of real power. By giving priority to the avoidance of conflict within the department and between it and the

* See below, p. 41.

government, the parochial commitment to 'keeping politics out' plays into the hands of the prefect, who is much happier to operate in a noncontroversial situation where administration rather than politics is on the agenda. The departmental council meets only from two days to two weeks twice a year, helped by a departmental commission of four to seven members which meets at least once a month. Although the president of the departmental council personifies democratic legitimacy in the department, he is seldom able to challenge the executive leadership of the prefect, embodiment of administrative legitimacy. The prefect attends the meetings of the departmental council, which are held in the *prefecture*. He will try to prevent the council from straying into political criticism of the government and if necessary he will quit the meeting, thereby depriving its proceedings of legal force. His staff prepare the departmental budget. Provided he obeys the convention that funds should be shared 'equally' throughout the department he will seldom have much opposition to fear, regardless of the council's party complexion.

Considering how powerless these councils are, there is still a substantial measure of competition for election to membership. In the March 1970 elections – half the cantons hold elections every three years – there were some 6,000 candidates contesting the 1,769 seats. They included 168 deputies, 75 senators and 14 ministers, as well as a dozen ex-ministers and over a hundred ex-members of parliament. The Gaullist deputies elected in 1968 were particularly keen to secure a firmer local foothold by winning a seat on the departmental council, while Gaullist ministers could similarly strengthen the links with their constituency which the constitution had endeavoured to sever. All fourteen ministers were successful : ten were re-elected on the first ballot (including the independent republican ministers of finance and transport and the centrist ministers of justice, agriculture and labour); two were elected for the first time on the first ballot; and two were elected on the second ballot. Gaullist inroads on these departmental bastions of the third and fourth republic parties remain limited. The semi-stalemate result of the 1970 elections left the disparity between votes and seats on the one hand, and party representation in local and national office on the other, almost intact (see table 1). Of the 94 departmental council presidents elected in 1970, the socialists held 21 (a loss of 4), the

Table 1
Distribution of Seats on Departmental Councils in
*Metropolitan France by Political Party**

Party	Seats Won		Total		% of Vote in 1970
	1967	1970	Seats	%	
Communist	175	144	319	9·6	21·2
PSU	25	22	47	1·4	1·5
Socialists and radicals	642	555	1,197	36·0	19·6
Democratic centre	155	141	296	8·9	7·5
Pro-government centre (CDP)	—	42	42	1·3	1·4
Anti-government right	} 238	96	} 621	18·7	12·5
Pro-government right		287†			3·4†
Non-party/local action	154	—	154	4·6	—
Independent republicans	94	110	204	6·1	4·9
UDR	219	206	425	12·8	17·8
Extreme right	7	6	13	0·4	0·3
Total	1,709	1,609	3,318	100	100

* These ministry of interior figures should be treated with caution because of the problem of classification involved. For the 1970 election, 'local action' and 'non-party' councillors have been allocated
a particular political orientation, a rather subjective exercise into which bias enters. The accuracy
of these figures is always challenged by the various party organizations, as are the commune election
figures discussed below (p. 35).
† The especially large disparity between the low number of votes given to 'pro-government right'
candidates and the high number of seats won is due to the fact that they are often elected in under-
populated rural areas.

radicals and 'other left' won 20 (a gain of 3), the centre held 29
(a loss of 4), the independent republicans won 7 (a gain of 2)
and the UDR won 13 (a gain of 5), but the minister of the interior
claimed that 41 presidents were pro-government. However, this
apparent politicization should not conceal the fact that about 10
per cent of those elected as departmental councillors are non-
party. About two-thirds of them are municipal councillors (half
being mayors) and share in the tranquillizing 'rhetoric of
apolitism' which is such a feature of the public life of the rural
commune.[10]

(iii) THE RURAL MAYOR: In 1884, Waldeck-Rousseau, minister of
the interior in the Ferry government, persuaded parliament to
pass two Acts that laid the foundations for the articulation of
grass-roots grievances: the Act legalizing trade unions and the
Act democratizing commune government (with the notable exclusion of Paris). Approximately 37,700 communes form the basic
units of French local government, each headed by an elected

mayor who personifies authority as much in his town or village as does the prefect in the department or the president of the republic in the state as a whole. At their level, they each exercise a paternalistic style of authority, purporting to embody community consensus and eschewing overt politics in favour of an uncontroversial application in particular situations of the 'general interest'. There is some uncertainty as to whether this apolitical pursuit of consensus, coupled with the legal subordination of the communes to the central government, means that the mayor and his municipal council are powerless. The large number of micro-communes, the overwhelming and increasing majority of which are too feeble in terms of population and finance to be viable as autonomous local authorities (see table 2), lack the competent full-time staff that would enable them to hold their own vis à vis the prefect. They accept the political and financial tutelage of the prefect, that is his 'right to review the *wisdom* and the *desirability*' of decisions[11] as a routine matter and become accustomed to consulting the field services of the ministries and the sub-prefect before coming to a decision. Thus the prefect's influence greatly exceeds his formal power of intervention, such as his ability to suspend or dismiss a mayor; dissolve the municipal council; act in default; check the legality of all decisions and annul them; and exercise stringent

Table 2
The Number of Communes According to Size and Population, 1968

Population Size	Number of Communes	%	Number of Councillors
Less than 100	3,877	10·3	9
101–500	20,130	53·4	11
501–1,500	9,308	24·7	13
1,501–2,500	1,803	4·8	17
2,501–3,500	723	1·9	21
3,501–10,000	1,188	3·1	23
10,001–30,000	482	1·3	27
30,001–40,000 ⎫ 40,001–50,000 ⎭	100	0·3	31 33
50,001–60,000 ⎫ 60,001 or more ⎭	97	0·2	35 37*
Total	37,708	100·0	—

* The three exceptions are: Paris, with 90 councillors; Marseille, 63 councillors; and Lyon, 61 councillors.

control over the commune's budget, which includes the right to strike out any source of revenue he deems inexpedient or against the public interest. Such powers are used sparingly, being more effective in conditioning the local councils to accept the prefect's guidance in the knowledge that he can have recourse to coercion if necessary. He would not wish to provoke an irate municipality into collective resignation or into an embarrassing 'administrative strike' but he may dissolve the council if he believes the subsequent election will yield a more tractable majority.

The mayor, like the prefect, is both the agent of the central government and the representative of the local community, although he generally plays down the former role and often thinks of himself as in opposition to the state rather than as its servant. Nevertheless, in practice, thanks to the mayor's functional amalgam of politics and administration, the majority of rural mayors accept their subordination to the central government officials, particularly the sub-prefect, the tax collector and the public works engineer. The commune's budget is generally drawn up in conjunction with the sub-prefect and the local tax collector, so that even in the case of this key function, government officials are able decisively to influence the taxing and spending policies of the commune at the preparatory stage. Thereby, potential sources of conflict are ironed out before the prestige of either side is risked by an open dispute. The fact that over half the staff of the communes are part-time and that the rural communes in particular lack competent personnel, compels dependence upon the central specialists who are located in their area. The country-wide network of public works engineers are particularly important. They have the dual function of advising on and carrying out, for a fee, local authority road and building projects and supervising the local authorities' public works programmes. Outside the larger towns, this places them in a monopolistic position from the technical standpoint. It also provides a powerful weapon of central control to ensure standardized service, as well as a channel of communication between the ministry of regional planning, public works and housing and its clientèle.[12]

Under the guidance of officialdom, control is exercised by the mayor rather than the municipal council, which consists mainly of leisured notables who regard their election as a recognition of social status and economic success. The mayor runs municipal affairs in a personal manner, unlike his British counterpart. Whereas British local politics are essentially committee politics, in France 'there is no history of independent *ad hoc* authorities, with legal status and statutory powers' providing particular local services.[13] When these specific functions were absorbed into the general local authority system in nineteenth-century Britain, they gave rise to a collective, committee-based leadership, whereas in France it was the cult of personality in the shape of the mayor, the embodiment of the commune's one and indivisible consensus, that became established : 'If the council is unanimously and actively satisfied with mayoral decisions, this signifies that the commune is ideally united. The municipal council's function is thus primarily symbolic. A mayor does not expect or desire the council to function as a legislative body; rather, he wants the municipal council to ratify decisions that he has already reached',[14] thereby placing him in a strong bargaining position vis à vis the other agents of the central government with whom he will have to negotiate. He can use the commune's united support to secure the satisfaction of demands made on the government, just as he uses such success in conflicts with central authority to reinforce community cohesion under his leadership. The electoral influence of both mayor and prefect also conditions local bargaining.

The close collaboration between the mayor and the prefect, reflected at the national level by the links between the thirty thousand strong *Association des Maires de France* and the ministry of the interior, facilitated by the many active mayors in both chambers of parliament, tends to reinforce stability at the price of inhibiting change. The strong tendency for national office-holders to combine this function with local office is popular (see table 3) although it is regarded with less favour in the case of

Table 3
The Desirability of Combining the Office of Mayor
With Other Local or National Office (%) *

	Desirable	Undesirable	No Importance	Don't Know
Departmental councillor	61	15	13	11
Deputy	54	24	11	11
Minister	48	30	11	11

* Source: SOFRES, February 1971

ministers than of deputies, especially in rural communes.* In 1969, out of 283 senators, there were 168 mayors, five ex-presidents of the Paris municipal council and 160 departmental councillors, 29 of whom were presidents. The traditional elected and nominated oligarchs in the departments and communes naturally seek to preserve the system upon which their influence is based. They have successfully resisted attempts to reform the local taxation system and the structure of local government – notably by the government forcing an amalgamation of communes and threatening the existence of the department with the creation of a fully fledged region. Whilst within his circumscribed commune the mayor's capacity to innovate is greater than that of any elected person other than the president of the republic, he seldom does innovate because he places the harmony of the community above all other purposes and fears that change will be disruptive. His leadership is therefore passive in character, except in the larger towns where developments beyond his control compel him to sponsor innovation.

(iv) URBAN POLITICS : It is important to contrast urban and rural politics because 'the traditional battle between the town and countryside . . . is in many ways the fundamental division in all French politics'.[15] Each republic has witnessed conflicts between a revolutionary, minority urban France and a mainly reactionary rural France, repeatedly summoned to restrain and repress a restless Paris commune.

The demographic and industrial transformation of France since the second world war has involved a decisive shift of population away from the generally apolitical, passive consensus of the declining rural communes to the frequently assertive, controversial politics of the urban metropolis which has accepted the disruptive challenge of modernity.

Table 4 shows the dominant position of Paris, despite the rapid expansion of some of the largest cities. It has not been the eight officially designated counter-magnets to Paris, selected in connection with the preparation of the Fifth Plan : Lille, Metz-Nancy, Strasbourg, Lyon-St Etienne, Marseille, Toulouse, Bordeaux and Nantes-St Nazaire, which have provided the best examples of

---

* On the interrelationship between local and national elected office, see below, chapter 3, p. 71.

Table 4
The Six Largest French Cities in 1968 and their Growth, 1962–8

City	Population	% increase, 1962–8
Paris and suburbs	8,182,000	+ 8
Lyon	1,083,000	+15
Marseille	964,000	+15
Lille-Roubaix-Tourcoing	881,000	+ 7
Bordeaux	555,000	+11
Toulouse	440,000	+20

urban municipal dynamism. Two medium-sized towns, Grenoble in the south-east (whose population increased by 27 per cent between 1962–8), led by an 'outsider' engineer turned pragmatic socialist mayor, and Rennes in the north-west, headed by a non-Breton, university professor mayor of centrist convictions, are the most striking demonstrations of what municipal leadership can achieve when freed of the toils of rural consensus politics or central red tape. They have shown what would be possible in a restructured local government system in which the anti-urban, anti-industrial, rural and artisan France of the 37,700 communes was finally replaced by a modern system of some two thousand new communes which have the potential for autonomous local management and development. However, so drastic a surgical operation, envisaged by techno-bureaucrats as part of a radical reconstruction of French local and regional government in which the number of regions would also be reduced from twenty-two to twelve,[16] is too 'modernist' either for the left or the right, although successive Gaullist governments have sought to promote some form of amalgamation between communes. About one-sixth of French communes are involved in some type of joint board, notably the numerous, *ad hoc, syndicats à vocation multiple* and urban *districts*, which are piecemeal and timid attempts to grapple with the problem of reducing the number of communes. Four conurbations out of the eight counter-magnets – Bordeaux, Lille, Lyon and Strasbourg – were selected in 1966 for the imposition of compulsory cooperation on adjacent communes, ranging from twenty-seven in the case of Bordeaux to eighty-nine in the case of Lille. This involved the transfer of the major financial, secondary education, transport, town planning and public works decisions to an 'urban community' council, indirectly representative of the inhabitants.

In the towns, as well as in the villages, power tends to be concentrated in the hands of the mayor, especially when he is both the town's deputy and mayor, like Chaban-Delmas of Bordeaux and Gaston Defferre of Marseille for decades under the fourth and fifth republics, or Edouard Herriot of Lyon under the third and fourth republics. However, the mayor shares power to some extent with the assistant-mayors (sixteen in number in Marseille), who are responsible for the work of particular committees, and with the secretary-general (who in the case of Marseille is always a member of one of the *grands corps*, for example a prefect). The weekly meetings of the mayor and his assistants – who are elected along with him by the council – effectively run the town, with the secretary-general sometimes being extremely influential and at other times being reduced to a purely subordinate role. The council is generally content to ratify the decisions of its executive.

As in the rural communes, the urban mayors have an ambivalent attitude towards their relationship with the central government. On the one hand, they claim that they are at the mercy of the ministries of finance and of regional planning, the *Caisse des Dépôts et Consignations* (the major public source of loan funds for local authorities), as well as the prefect, who can determine whether their programme will be carried out, particularly through control over grants. However, this sense of impotence seems to vanish in practice, because it is recognized that there is scope for substantial variations in performance, depending notably upon the mayor's ingenuity. At the price of assuming a substantial debt burden, a town like Rennes can achieve nationwide renown for its achievements. Furthermore, the political complexion of the municipality influences the housing, education and tax policies pursued, although this is not reflected in local election campaigns. These campaigns centre on drawing up a list of candidates that represent the target socio-occupational, ideological and neighbourhood clientèle which are to be attracted. The willingness of the councillors to respond to any requests for help from organized interests or individuals on a personal and piecemeal basis substitutes for a programme. Such susceptibility to pressure is a natural result of the lack of a party politics capable of aggregating demands. It leads to direct relations between the executive and the many supplicants for its favours. This is true both of national and local government in France.

The absence of a clearly partisan character in the bulk of French communes makes it virtually impossible to provide accurate and objective local election results. Especially in the rural communes, there is a strong inclination, both among the notables and the general public, to strive for one united list and avoid any contest. This is also reflected in the qualities the public consider that a mayor should possess. They stress his experience in handling local problems and accessibility to his constituents, while little importance is attached to his political convictions. There is no great difference as between urban and rural areas in the importance attached to various types of municipal function, although the former favour the development of public services more than the defence of local interests against the central government, to which rural communes attach great importance. Pride of place is given to the satisfactory provision of local services, party politics being almost entirely ignored. Nevertheless, in the 193 larger towns (over 30,000 inhabitants), where the 1971 elections were more highly politicized, the results were of some significance, despite the far greater stability than prevails in elections to the national assembly. The lists of 162 outgoing mayors were re-elected. The communist party – which had held thirty-nine of these towns, mainly located in the red belt around Paris – gained six new towns, while the UDR – which held twenty-eight towns – gained control of only two further towns. However, whereas the left-wing parties increased their share of the poll in these towns from 37·6 to 39·8 per cent (compared with 1965) the UDR and its allies greatly improved their performance from 30·6 to 38·9 per cent at the expense of the centre.[17]

If the July 1971 Local Government Act is at all successful in achieving its aim of reducing the number of communes, future local elections are likely to be a rather simpler affair. Deliberately postponed until after the March 1971 elections, because the government's proposals were bound to be highly controversial, the Act was marked by the prudence and circumspection characteristic of President Pompidou. In the ten years preceding the Act, despite pressures and incentives to encourage amalgamations, only 746 communes merged into 350 new municipalities; so

35

if the government's target of reducing the number of communes by ten thousand was left to purely voluntary action, it would take a very long time to achieve. The 1971 Act provided that in each department the prefect would make available to a commission, headed by the president of the departmental council and composed of departmental and municipal councillors, the work of a group of experts on the basis of which a new local authority map would be drawn up. The prefect would then decide whether to accept or amend the new boundaries suggested and would communicate his recommendation to each commune. If the communes concerned accepted the prefect's proposal, the merger would take place. However, in the likely event that his suggestion was opposed, it could still be acted upon provided the departmental council gave its approval or as a result of a local referendum. The initiative for calling such a referendum lies both with the prefect and the councils of either : half the communes affected, if they include at least two-thirds of the inhabitants; or two-thirds of the communes, if they include at least half the inhabitants. To secure approval at the referendum, the merger proposals would have to win the support of a two-thirds majority representing at least half the registered electorate. In such a referendum, which the minister of the interior called a 'perfectly democratic constraint', the voters in any particular commune could still avoid the loss of their identity if by a two-thirds majority they rejected the proposed merger. To soften the blow to parochial pride, the previously independent communes would retain a minor residual role; while as an incentive to merge, a 50 per cent increase in the central government capital grants-in-aid would be provided for the first five years after the merger. Carried against senate opposition, the 1971 Act gave each prefect a crucial role in this latest attempt to rationalize the basic units of French local government. He will need all his customary dexterity to induce compliance by the local notables. By comparison with the centralized brutality of the 1972 reform of British local government, the Pompidou approach is deconcentrated, piecemeal and gradualist.

The agricultural revolution of the 1950s and 1960s, leading to an accelerating rural exodus which transformed France into an increasingly industrial and urban society, has had an impact on the administrative partners of the commune. The field services of the ministry of public works and housing, which had dominated the old order, have had to reorganize to meet the challenge of towns which were able to deal with their own development programmes. Such a strategy meant that instead of spreading their staff throughout the countryside, the public works engineers should concentrate on the large towns where most development was taking place. As a result, they would no longer have the close relations with the mayor of each commune which had been customary. Their political influence might well decline as a result, the provision of technical services in the new context no longer being exchanged for political good will and lucrative fees which were such features of the integration of field services into the local political system. So, like the regional prefect in his allocation of regional investment, the field services along with the local notables have tended to slow down the process of modernization in local government. Not until a new regional political clientèle has emerged (which cannot occur unless the region becomes a new level of decision-making and implementation) will the field services of the central ministries enthusiastically embrace administrative reorganization.

The region as a focus of deconcentration and decentralization

The rationalization of authority was, for centuries, equated with the centralization of power in France. It has since been equated with political modernization, in conjunction with a hierarchical, disciplined and functionally differentiated power structure and mass participation mediated through groups. It is argued that in divided societies, particularly those in which change is being resisted, centralization is the rational response.[18] This undoubtedly helps explain the passionate anti-federalism of the Jacobins and the subsequent resistance to any 'dismemberment' of central control by most politicians and officials. Yet in contemporary France, which has undoubtedly been traversing a period of rapid change that has provoked bitter resistance, there has been a widespread reaction against centralization as the privileged instrument of political modernization. This movement in favour of administrative deconcentration and political decentralization long preceded the May 1968 challenge to authority. No less an embodiment of the authoritarian tradition than de Gaulle espoused it in a speech on 24 March 1968, two months before his first failure to grapple with the challenge and thirteen months before his second and self-destructive failure at the referendum of April 1969. He then said: 'The centuries-old centralizing effort required to achieve and sustain [France's] unity, is no longer necessary. On the contrary, it is its regional development that will provide the motive force of its future economic power.'

The department, at its creation in 1789, could be defended as a rational 'section of the state' for the administration of public services. In the twentieth century it was being displaced, thanks particularly to the rapid economic development of the 1950s and 1960s, by the region as the most rational administrative area for a wide range of major functions. Characteristic symptoms of the department's decline were the loss of functions to central government or to *ad hoc* bodies like the joint public-private enterprises that have taken over the tasks of urban redevelopment and major roads, or like the *Compagnie Nationale d'Aménagement du Bas-Rhône et du Languedoc*, a sort of French Tennessee Valley Authority. It was necessary to develop a new regional level of government to avoid either a disintegration into numerous, *ad hoc* agencies or a reinforcement of centralization. The department survives almost exclusively as an administrative unit for the implementation of decisions taken elsewhere and as a channel for the communication of grievances. The 'general competence' legally accorded to the department and the commune, as against the particular functions attributed to the local authorities in Britain, has in practice worked to their disadvantage. It has not prevented the erosion of their activities by central encroachment, whilst they have recourse to the expedients of conceding the provision of public services to private firms or of indirectly administering them through a municipal enterprise.

Regionalist initiatives came as a result of grass-roots pressure notably from regions such as Brittany, which were suffering the consequences of rural depopulation in an extreme form. Together with the planning commissariat's recognition of the need to give the National Plan a regional dimension, they led to the June 1955 decrees designating what were to become the twenty-one planning regions and to pioneering attempts at regional planning. These developments were bitterly opposed by authoritarians like Michel Debré who in 1947 had favoured reducing the number of departments to forty-seven rather than creating regional institutions. In

1956 he argued that in France centralization was indispensable because 'the permanent tendency to weaken power, due to political and social conflicts, makes the administration the discreet but tenacious guarantor of unity, particularly through uniformity'.[19] At that stage even the regionalist champions like J.-F. Gravier, whose *Paris et le désert francais* of 1947 had stimulated the reaction against centralism, did not wish to go beyond 'regional deconcentration' by 'adapting to our time a great French tradition: that of the *intendants*'.[20] The remedy was to be found in a transformation of French administration to enable it to cope with the demands being made upon government by the regional economic expansion committees and other pressure groups. Edgard Pisani, a prefect who became a senator and then a minister under the fifth republic, in an influential article (in the same issue of the journal that published the articles by Debré and Gravier) called for the creation, 'parallel to traditional administration . . . of a specialized, dynamic and creative administration' capable of undertaking the new planning tasks. After condemning the tradition of administrative centralization, he went on to champion the need for an enterprising *administration de mission* which would take the initiative. It would not seek to be neutral. It would be ready to act in a selective way, carrying out the government's strategy without constantly 'turning to Paris to obtain authorization, funds or a guilty acquiescence'.[21]

The emergence in the 1950s of regional pressure groups in the form of regional economic expansion committees deriving their support from both local authorities and local agricultural, industrial and even trade union organizations, forced the central government to react. Its prime concern was to combine the restoration of central authority with an attempt to canalize and neutralize these new regional movements. It sought to do this by standardizing and reinforcing an administrative regionalism placed under the aegis of the regional prefect. As a leading beneficiary of this new development, the regional prefect of Aquitaine wrote at the inception of the regional reform in March 1964:

When one is deeply conscious of the need to preserve French unity, any provincial creation must be prudent. . . . Can one imagine regional commissions, having deliberative power, rejecting the National Plan in five or ten French regions and thereby preventing its application? This would mean accepting a federal type of government. It is essential, in our republic which is still one and indivisible, that the government, the expression of the will of parliament, has the power to guarantee the primacy of the national over the regional. It is its function to distinguish, within the framework of the law, what serves the general interest from what can threaten it.[22]

The task of recentralizing regionalism was entrusted to just such exponents of traditional administrative orthodoxy. They subscribed to the Rousseauist conception that 'the only conceivable form of local or regional government would be a *delegation from the executive* – some members of the executive being selected as local administrators, and applying to a geographical fraction of the subjects the decisions of the general will ... it is a mere *subdelegation* of power....'[23]

The recognition of the need to deconcentrate sluggish, centralized decision-making, coupled with the decline of the department as the appropriate unit for such reorganized administration, led to the development of regional institutions. These had the further advantage of superimposing a more flexible instrument of public action on the existing institutions rather than trying to change them. Just as a major force for innovation at the centre was provided by the planning commissariat, which provoked or manipulated the ministries into a measure of modernization, in regional matters an equally small, but high powered and more overtly politicized 'parallel administration', the *Délégation à l'aménagement du territoire et à l'action régionale* (DATAR) or regional and spatial planning delegacy,* was the architect of reform from its creation in 1963. DATAR's success depended heavily upon its direct link with the prime minister (until a minister delegate for planning and regional development was interposed in 1967 and then abolished in 1972, when DATAR was attached to the ministry of public works and housing under Olivier Guichard) and also by the close political ties between its first head (Guichard) and President Pompidou. In conjunction with the ministry of administrative reform, DATAR played a leading part in the preparation of the March 1964 decrees that reasserted executive supremacy in the shape of the regional prefect. However, it was felt necessary to proclaim in the general instruction on the application of these decrees that the department remained 'the normal unit

* See below, p. 170.

of administrative management and would even extend this function through an increase in deconcentration, regional reform being confined to a strictly limited and particular sphere and not diminishing the role and vocation of the department'. The prefects were informed of their duties as follows: 'To impart a stricter unity and greater cohesion to administrative action, all the powers of the state in the department are concentrated in your hands. You will thus be able fully to exercise your vital role of stimulation, general direction and coordination of public services in the department.'

The regional prefect, who combined this function with being prefect of the department that contained the regional capital, was given the task of coordinating and directing the work of the departmental prefects in the field of regional development planning. This involves the preparation of the regional segment of the national plan, working through the regional administrative conference. The other prefects and the treasurer-paymaster general are represented on this body, the heads of the various ministerial field services attending when matters directly concerning them are discussed. The regional prefect is helped in this task by a small general staff of senior civil servants (called in Pisani fashion a *mission*) under a sub-prefect who is the regional prefect's main economic adviser and executant. Their task, within the framework of the central government's directives, is to work out and seek to impose a regional rationality upon what could and has all too easily degenerated into an allocation of public investment funds between departments on an unselective and piecemeal basis.

Finally, to curb the threat represented by regional pressure groups and the opposition parties, Guichard ensured administrative supremacy by refusing to set up either an elected regional council or an elected regional executive to counterbalance the power of the regional prefect. Instead, regional economic development commissions were created, composed of mayors and departmental councillors (25 per cent), interest group representatives (50 per cent), and prefectoral nominees (25 per cent), exercising only feeble consultative functions. Of the initial 924 REDC members, 72 were deputies, 53 senators, 202 departmental councillors and 286 mayors (bearing in mind, however, the overlap between these categories). Leading political figures, such as Chaban-

Delmas in Aquitaine, Pinay in Rhône-Alpes, Pleven in Brittany, Mitterrand in Burgundy, Edgard Faure in Franche-Comté, Maurice Faure in Midi-Pyrénées and Pflimlin in Alsace, were elected REDC presidents. They became impatient when they discovered how little influence they could exert. The result was rapid and widespread disenchantment with what had purported to be a major step in reorganizing central-local relations but which in practice consolidated the department and its traditional head, the prefect.[24]

Table 5 indicates the public's perception that power, whether political, economic or administrative, has remained in traditional hands, although the administrative field services and departmental councils fared badly. Both the unofficial expansion committees and the official REDCs failed to make much public impact. The same is true of the joint public-private enterprises, which play so important a part in local and regional development.

Table 5
The Relative Importance of Regional Policy-Makers *

| | Replies (*Oct.–Nov. 1965*) in order of importance | | | |
| Regional Policy Makers | | | | |
Category	*1st*	*2nd*	*3rd*	Total %
Deputies and senators	23	9	9	41
Prefects and sub-prefects	16	15	13	44
Mayors and municipal councils	15	16	17	48
Chambers of commerce, industry and agriculture	13	9	10	32
Regional economic development commissions	8	9	7	24
Occupational organizations	6	8	7	21
Departmental councils	6	14	11	31
Expansion committees	2	4	5	11
Administrative departments	2	5	9	16
Joint enterprises	1	2	2	5
No reply	8	9	10	—
Total	100	100	100	—

* Source: *Sondages,* 1966, nos. 3–4, p. 176.

It required a major upheaval to transform a situation in which the minister of the interior, addressing the members of the prefectoral corps in June 1964, could reassure them : 'The only possible hierarchy in our provinces is the prefectoral hierarchy and at its foundation, in the department, the prefect still remains in charge, the only person responsible.' The 1969 referendum proposal to elevate the region to a constitutionally recognized part of the governmental system was conceived by de Gaulle as an answer to the May crisis of 1968. It was profoundly ironic that in 1969 the French government should simultaneously prepare to celebrate the bicentenary of Napoleon's birth and to dismantle part of the centralized administrative system identified with him. However, this apparent contradiction quickly dissolved as it became clear that behind the rush of propagandist rhetoric about promoting 'popular participation', 'direct democracy', decentralization and autonomy, the prefects were not only to remain in charge; they were to be buttressed with powers deconcentrated from a megalocephalic administrative system that had proved in the crisis to have attained the pathological condition of paralysis at the centre and apoplexy at the periphery. The real aim of Gaullist neo-regionalism was to constitute a deconcentrated administrative system under the regional prefect that would be more capable of recognizing, resisting and reducing revolutionary discontents. Like Louis-Napoleon a century earlier, in his 1869 attempt to 'liberalize' an autocratic system, what purported to be decentralization was in fact a disguised reinforcement of central control. In the prophetic words of Odilon Barrot : 'It is the same hammer that strikes but the handle has been shortened.'

Nevertheless, the proposals that were defeated at the April 1969 referendum would undoubtedly have been approved had they not been linked with the unpopular amalgamation of the senate and the economic and social council. Opinion polls indicated that there were large majorities in favour of the proposed regional reform. Most of the public would have been content with a transfer of the power to take administrative decisions from Paris to give them to regional officials rather than changes that would involve any increase in mass political participation. The functions of the new regional authorities were to be restricted to prevent them, in the words of the minister mainly responsible, 'venturing along the dangerous path of federalism'. The local authority lobbies were assured that the powers acquired by the region would be exclusively at the expense of the central administration, being primarily an extension of their existing regional planning role

43

through a more resolute 'transfer of technocrats' than had hitherto been undertaken. This deconcentrationist view of regional reform was reflected in the financial arrangements which retained the traditional features of a reliance upon specific central grants, central approval of borrowing and a budget drawn up by the regional prefect, making it unlikely that regional councillors would abandon their 'public assistance' complex of dependence upon the central government and its nominees. The decision to retain the existing regional areas, except for minor adjustments, rather than reduce them to Paris and the eight 'counterbalancing' regional capitals mentioned earlier* was another conservative device, aimed *inter alia* at preserving the domination of Paris. The rejection of a directly elected regional council in favour of a tripartite composition of ex-officio deputies, representatives of local authorities and of the major organized interests, was also calculated to ensure that the representative element in regional politics remained under the tutelage of the administrative component.

The culmination of this administrative and centralist emphasis was the selection of the regional prefect as the undisputed executive authority. The most curt dismissal of the idea of an elected regional executive came in parliament from the ex-civil servant prime minister, Couve de Murville: 'The French nation was, through the centuries, shaped by the central government', monarchical and republican, culminating in the proclamation

by the 1793 constitution . . . of the one and indivisible republic. Napoleonic administration, still ours today, gave permanent practical application to this assertion of principle. None of this, which constitutes French political reality, has been to my knowledge challenged by anyone. The best proof is that few deny that in the new regional bodies, executive power can only be conferred on a prefect chosen by the central government because he alone is able to ensure not only effectiveness in action but also conformity with the general interest as against the private interest.[25]

That the spirit of Couve de Murville's claim is accepted by the bulk of French political and economic *notables* was made clear by the fact that in the preliminary consultation on regional reform, 80 per cent of them replied in favour of the regional prefect exercising the executive power, whilst only 11 per cent favoured

* See above, p. 32.

entrusting it to the president of the regional council. The traditionally diffident and dependent clientèle of the prefect continues to regard him as the manifestation of the 'one and indivisible', sovereign central authority which, in the French political culture, is considered solely capable of maintaining order, resolving disputes and taking decisions.

If one wishes to understand the rationale underlying the retrograde regional reform adopted by parliament in 1972, the admission made by Guichard in the December 1968 parliamentary debates already quoted is most revealing. It helps us to understand the new business philosophy that President Pompidou shares with the techno-bureaucratic élite. When they discuss decentralization they are concerned almost exclusively with managerial efficiency and not with democratic participation. Guichard recalled that having asked the managing directors of a number of large French businesses how they organized decision-making, he was told that they relied on maximum delegation. To ecstatic applause from the pro-government deputies, he asked : 'If the state is the largest French enterprise, should it not now be managed in the same way?'[26] In presenting the 1972 Bill, the prime minister described regional reform as above all an economic and administrative necessity and issued familiar warnings against the danger of political autonomy threatening both national unity and the departments. The regions were therefore not given the status of 'territorial authorities' like the communes and departments. They were to be mere 'public establishments' with specific functions primarily concerned with national planning. The twenty-two regional councils are composed of all the deputies and senators of the region and an equal number of local authority representatives chosen by the departmental council and by the commune councils. (The ex-officio inclusion of national politicians in the regional councils was in flagrant contradiction with the professed desire to avoid politics but it is a natural consequence of the close interrelationship of national and local politics in France and the UDR's desire to overcome its weakness outside parliament.) The regions' modest financial resources – not to exceed £2 per inhabitant – principally come from the driving licence revenue. Regional economic, social and cultural committees have replaced the REDCS. The regional prefect remains in managerial command of the new arrangements that were implemented in 1973. In the 1972

Messmer government, a new ministry of regional planning, public works, housing and tourism was created under Guichard and the ministry of administrative reform was wound up, its task of preparing the 1972 Act having been completed.

The failure to do more than tinker with traditional structures in the 1964, 1969 and 1972 attempts at regional reform, indicates that it is not enough to rationalize administration through deconcentration. Except in a purely managerial sense, innovation requires the redistribution of power through decentralization. Those who have examined the French experience most closely and imaginatively conclude that it will not be possible

much longer to evade the ineluctable choice between increased centralization, which can only guarantee the rationality of decision at the price of increased administrative authoritarianism and local irresponsibility whose social cost is incalculable, and a decentralization that involves important risks of irrationality in the present feeble state, in terms of men and skills, of local representative structures but which, in the long run, seems to be the precondition of an effective local contribution to economic development and regional planning.[27]

If provincial France is to be decolonized and Paris herself (now both a department and a commune) is to be entrusted with the right to run its affairs democratically rather than remain subject to the strict administrative tutelage of a score of prefects and sub-prefects, it will be necessary to shift not merely some of the political and administrative decision-making, but also many of the commercial, financial and research centres to the provinces.

It is after all the concentration of power in Paris that has persuaded the would-be revolutionaries, from the disciples of Blanqui to some contemporary elements on the French extreme left, that if you seize the capital you can take over the state. The attractions of centralization as a bulwark against disorder proved more apparent than real in 1968. Until disunity and the fear of disunity have been sufficiently conquered for Haussmann's dictum: 'The capital belongs to the government', no longer to be acceptable, modernizing centralism will evoke sullen, parochial protest rather than the mobilization of local energies in a concerted national effort. Provincial subordination to Paris and Parisian subordination to the central government will continue to increase.

The development of a civic culture which would fundamentally change the relationships between polity and society in France from a reciprocal blind and inflexible central authoritarianism and an irresponsible and intransigent local demagoguery will be indefinitely postponed.

3 The Representative Mediators

At the heart of French political culture there lies a tension between a passionate attachment to personal liberty, conceived as the absence of control by authority, and an intense feeling of dependence upon state power, source of protection and favours in a harshly competitive world. Although there are a great variety of voluntary associations in France, the civic culture remains feeble because liberty is conceived primarily in personal and negative terms. Freedom is fundamentally a matter of noncommitment, not the opportunity to promote common aims by joint endeavour. So, despite frequent exhortations to increased participation, most Frenchmen remain obstinately ambivalent in their attitude towards increased political involvement. As a perceptive analyst of French political psychology has observed :

On the one hand, people would like very much to participate in order to control their own environment. On the other hand, they fear that if and when they participate, their own behaviour will be controlled by their co-participants. It is far easier to preserve one's independence and integrity if one does not participate in decision-making. By refusing to be involved in policy determination, one remains much more free from outside pressures.[1]

The practical consequence is subordination to a remote and impersonal bureaucratic authority, resulting in the characteristic French combination of critical private thought and servile public conduct. Except for occasional spasms of revolt that shake French society to its foundations most Frenchmen are content to seek refuge in parochialism, securing a personal enclave of freedom in an over-regulated world.

This introverted individualism is, however, extended to embrace the family, traditionally reinforced by the importance of the family firm, farm and shop in the French economy. This fact has led some observers to make the sweeping claim that 'there are only two important social entities in the life of a Frenchman, the family cell and the state. Intermediary institutions, whether they be schools, clubs, trade unions or political parties, count for nothing. . . . Politics are perceived as essentially a question of private, individual conscience. . . . The Frenchman reserves his judgement and often voices his disagreement . . . but ends up by accepting and obeying the central authority.'[2] This assertion needs to be seriously qualified by reference to the political role of intermediate organizations, rooted notably in the occupational, educational and ideological sub-cultures, which exercise formative influences on the individual's political behaviour. Precisely because most Frenchmen 'want to be left alone so that they will not have to change' and believe that 'organization means power and power means the oppression of the individual',[3] they leave it to the skeletal trade unions and occupational associations to express their class-consciousness and wage the class conflict that is a datum of their daily experience. They rely on the Catholic Church and the communist party to express their rival value systems in well-organized mass movements, historically rooted in particular parts of the country. Education is an important link between the influences of social stratification and ideological indoctrination, the public/private school split being markedly correlated with cleavages in the political culture.* However, none of these movements attracts more than a minority of active members. The majority of the mass public refuse to be mobilized and express only a tepid interest in politics, with differences between sex, age, occupational, educational, partisan and income categories that are indicated in table 6. In large towns, especially Paris, there is an above average interest in politics.

There has been a shift away from the traditional centres of power, the deputies and senior officials who embody the central legitimacy concept of the French political culture, the one and indivisible republic. Some publicists have exaggerated this shift but it is reflected in the public's perception of the changing political process. When in May 1958, at the fall of the fourth republic, the monthly *France-Forum* published the results of a poll of its readers aged under thirty on the question 'Who runs French politics?' interest groups topped the list, ahead of the party leaders

* See below, chapter 7.

Table 6
The Adult's Interest in Politics, January 1969 (%) *

	Very	Fairly	Little	Not At All	No Reply	Total
All	6	14	38	41	1	100
Sex: Men	9	16	40	34	1	100
Women	4	12	36	47	1	100
Age: 20–34	8	14	42	36	—	100
35–49	5	16	41	38	—	100
50–64	5	11	37	46	1	100
65+	6	14	27	50	3	100
Occupation:						
Farmers	3	6	44	45	2	100
Workers	3	10	38	49	—	100
White collar employees	8	20	41	31	—	100
Industrial entre-preneurs and shop-keepers	6	22	41	31	—	100
Senior executive and professional	23	22	44	11	—	100
Retired	7	14	30	46	3	100
Education:						
Primary	2	9	36	51	2	100
Higher primary	7	23	34	36	—	100
Technical	7	17	45	30	1	100
Secondary	13	22	44	21	—	100
Higher	34	26	34	6	—	100
Party vote:						
Communist	17	18	39	26	—	100
Socialist	5	18	44	31	2	100
Centre	9	23	34	34	—	100
UDR	4	15	40	41	—	100
Independent republican	2	12	48	38	—	100
Not declared	3	7	27	60	3	100
Monthly Income:						
Under 500 fr.	5	10	32	52	1	100
500–799 fr.	2	9	35	50	4	100
800–1,249 fr.	5	11	40	43	1	100
1,250–1,749 fr.	7	12	40	41	—	100
1,750 fr. +	11	24	42	23	—	100
Not declared	4	14	32	48	2	100

* Source: *Sondages*, 1969, nos 1–2, pp. 13–14.

and well ahead of parliament, press and electorate. This denoted a new emphasis by young, relatively well-informed opinion, upon the middle levels of power at which the interest groups operate, rather than the 1930s emphasis upon an economic Establishment of 'two hundred families' or the parliamentary representatives of the unmobilized mass public. Such a recognition, albeit subjective, of the influence of interest groups, has been increasingly coupled in France, since the coming of the fifth republic, with concern about the growing importance of technocrats, public or private experts whose claim to a share in decision-making was based upon their command of some indispensable specialist skill. Between them, the spokesmen of special interests, with their claim collectively to represent the many publics that the citizen identifies with most intensely when it comes to dealing with down to earth, daily concerns, and the experts who have the knowledge required to implement public preferences, have invaded spheres of policy-making hitherto denied them. The consequent problems of representation and defence of the public interest can best be examined through the massive but unobtrusive proliferation of consultative bodies that have collected like barnacles around the bulk of official decision-making bodies with the extension of government intervention particularly into the economic and social problems of industrial society.

Bilateral consultation and direct action

Politics has been defined as 'the art of perceiving contradictions, either to elude or surmount them'.[4] The attraction of consultation to governments is that it offers the possibility of working out agreed solutions to problems instead of relying upon the controversial assertion of public power, even when decisions are legitimized by a parliamentary majority. Rather than appear to be imposing their will upon a minority, governments seek to obtain the consent of the interested parties. Because the liberal democratic ideology forbids formal representation of these interests in legislative assemblies, they are 'consulted' outside the parliamentary process. Parliament formally sanctions legislation but the compromises are generally worked out in advance between the minister's brains trust and the interested parties. However, to the extent that their 'advice' and 'consent' is valued and accepted –

and the attainment of unanimity is an important aim of such pivotal aspects of government activity as national and regional economic planning, in which parliament plays a minimal role – acts that are legally unilateral become ratifications of bilateral agreements. The environment of government is raised from the subject status of the 'administered' to that of fully fledged partner, and certain acts require the 'reciprocal consent' of the government and of the interested parties. Inability to obtain such consent explains the failure of incomes policy in France. The traditional distinction between advice and decision-making is not erased but it is blurred.

The main motives for creating consultative bodies are to improve communication within the administration and to avoid or smooth over conflicts with the administered, once they are well enough organized to conquer or to be groomed into the status of consultative partners of government. To undertake complex and rapidly changing functions, particularly in the economic sphere of planning development and provision of public services, the government's administrative officials need to acquire information and to correct their own departmentalism by coordination. The sources of information may be experts within the public service like the council of state or interested parties, or specialist 'sponsor' ministries, like industrial and scientific development or agriculture, which rely heavily on information (including statistics) from trade associations or farm organizations. In these latter cases, 'regular and organized advice from outside the bureaucracy is considered indispensable for a balanced relationship between power and knowledge'.[5] Within its own administrative system, 'horizontal' agencies like the planning commissariat or the DATAR were created to provide interdepartmental coordination in the preparation and implementation of public policies. They cut across existing hierarchies and establish negotiating and bargaining committees on which the various ministries' representatives can iron out their conflicts as they do with the administered. Particular ministries, like the government in general, have to recognize that they cannot simply issue edicts without consulting those affected. They must attempt to secure their agreement through persuasion, helped by offers of support (including financial support) and backed by the ultimate threat to impose a decision. The mutual concessions made in the confidential atmosphere of close and continuous relations between senior administrators and the officials of major, well organized interests, reduce the controversial character of many issues. Recourse to parliament is avoided except to register agreements made elsewhere.

It is extremely difficult to ascertain even approximately the number of consultative bodies that exist in France, and even more so of those that are in any real sense active. In the early 1960s there appear to have been about 4,700 consultative bodies at the national level: 500 councils, 1,200 committees and over 3,000 commissions, not counting the numerous sub-committees and working parties which they spawn. Furthermore, locally, the most conservative estimate is an average of about a hundred consultative bodies per department. So, not counting the regional bodies that have developed in the 1960s, there were then at least some fifteen thousand parent consultative bodies in France.[6] This suggests that consultation is more highly institutionalized in France than it is in other countries, although information on this subject is scanty. Most of these bodies are attached to a particular ministry, at the national level, or to the prefecture at the departmental level. Thus in 1957 the ministry of finance had over a hundred and thirty consultative bodies attached to it, of which eighty involved interest group representation. Mere numbers are not a very useful indicator because consultative bodies are seldom abolished even when they cease to function. A study of sixty-eight consultative bodies attached to the prefecture of the Drôme department in 1962 indicated that eight did not meet at all; thirty met only once, fourteen twice and sixteen three or more times (one meeting on twenty occasions). It is not possible to obtain a less crude measure than frequency of meeting of the number of really effective consultative bodies. In any case consultative bodies that are influential at one time may be short-circuited at another; somnolent committees may suddenly be resurrected to help deal with a crisis and subside into inactivity thereafter.

Given the traditional suspicion of any encroachment of private interests on public prerogatives, and the tendency of some civil servants to regard consultation as an extension of the historic duty of vassals to advise their feudal lord, a firm grip is generally maintained by the government and its officials over the consultative process. They seek to control the choice of members but since the practice was instituted in the case of the national economic council in 1925 (forerunner of the present economic and social council) of selecting after nomination by the 'most representative organizations', the interest groups have acquired effective control over their representatives. However, the government can alter the numbers from each organization and swamp the body with its own nominees. The dominant part usually played by civil servants (or ministers in the case of the more important committees) can be inferred from the fact that they usually occupy the key posts of chairman and *rapporteur* on behalf of the consultative body and are selected by the consulting authority. At the departmental level, the prefectoral staff monopolize the *rapporteur* function and supply the secretariat. The prefect is *ex officio* chairman of all administrative consultative bodies but he often delegates this task to his secretary-general who in turn may pass it on, in less important cases, to a division head.

At the national level, members of certain *grands corps* occupy most of the key posts : councillors of the court of accounts and inspectors of finance in economic matters, councillors of state and polytechnicians in other matters. (Councillors of state alone held over a tenth of all chairmanships in 1960.) University teachers and interest group representatives less frequently occupy the posts of chairman or *rapporteur*. For example, the important *ad hoc* Rueff-Armand committee on the obstacles to economic expansion, nominally presided over by the prime minister but in fact controlled by its two vice-presidents, had forty-three specialist rapporteurs, twenty-one of whom were officials from the ministry of finance (nine being inspectors of finance), eight court of accounts councillors, eight councillors of state, five senior officials from other ministries and one university teacher. So, consultative bodies depend mainly upon the administration to be created, to operate, to reach conclusions and to have them carried into effect. Depending on whether the consultative body is expressing a view on a project that has already been worked out in some detail following a decision, or is asked to make more or less detailed proposals in a matter on which the government has not yet made up its mind, it will be involved either in what is primarily a public relations exercise or in helping in the preparation, implementation or interment of policy.

However, over and above the institutionalized channels of communication provided by these consultative bodies, the leaders of the major interests meet members of the executive, sometimes the president of the republic and prime minister but more frequently members of the ministerial *cabinets* (i.e. personal staff) of their sponsor departments. Rather than the calm, concerted action which one would expect from an elaborate consultative system such as we have described, these meetings often occur as the result of a crisis in which some category of Frenchmen has decided to take the law into its own hands. The outburst of discontent usually takes almost everyone by surprise, although it is clear thereafter that a strong sense of grievance has been building up for some time and has been ignored by the authorities. They often try to shed the responsibility on to the shoulders of the organizations representing the group concerned. Even if one makes allowances for the fact that the channels of communication between interest group leaders and their rank and file (not to speak of the mass of the unorganized) are generally poor, part of the blame undoubtedly lies with the executive, which tends to deal with a problem only when it is vigorously and unavoidably pressed. By multiplying consultative committees whose powerlessness means that they are unlikely to resolve conflicts, the government encourages each sectional interest to respond to its unilateral decisions by uncompromising obstruction, which only confirms the government in its belief that change has to be imposed.

Under the fifth republic, the farmers of Brittany and the southeast have been celebrated for their recourse to direct action in defence of the *status quo*; resisting the impact of an agricultural revolution that drove 40 per cent of the French farm population from the land between 1954–68. All groups are prepared to resort to such blackmail against governments who, in the state idealist tradition, are forced to surrender when they cannot suppress the demands from organized interests, owing to a refusal to negotiate with them. In the trial of strength, the groups seek to extract concessions, not to overthrow the government. In its turn, once the crisis is over, the government seeks to make the groups revert to the status of subservient clients. Direct action by farmers took the form of obstructing roads with farm vehicles or unsaleable farm produce, coupled with violent confrontations with the police sent to deal with them. The main purpose was to discredit the government by forcing it into repressive actions that would win public sympathy for the farmers. These tactics paid dividends in the early 1960s. Shopkeepers and artisans have refused to pay taxes or social security contributions, attacking tax inspectors and tax offices. The Poujadist movement of the 1950s, which resorted to direct action against the forces of economic development which were 'rationalizing' the self-employed out of existence, was revitalized in the late 1960s by CID-UNATI (the defence committee of shopkeepers and artisans) led by Nicoud. After extracting numerous concessions from the government, the CID achieved the twin triumphs of an early release of its leader from prison and the creation of a new, small-business ministry of trade and crafts on 6 July 1972.

It is not only the self-employed lower middle class that has resorted to this type of direct action. Although the trade unions have called one-day general strikes as demonstrations to get the government to exert pressure on the employers to secure collective bargaining in the private sector, or better wages and conditions of work in the public sector, in 1936 and 1968 there have been extended general strikes, combined with occupation of the factories, which correspond to the strategy of blackmail referred to above. After years of fruitless attempts to influence educational policy, the students in May 1968 nearly precipitated the downfall of the régime when they adopted in their extreme forms the tactics of violent confrontation with the police and occupation of their place of work. Accustomed to an authority that seems congenitally incapable of negotiating a compromise, some groups feel that there is little alternative to forcing total surrender after suffering severe repression. Joseph Martray, former leader of the Breton regionalist pressure group CELIB, wrote in 1962, following the concessions won by the farmers' direct action: 'This state, which prides itself on its authority, has shown us that it is only moved by force.... The responsibility is entirely the government's which procrastinates, promises, cheats and defers as long as it is not faced by an irresistible pressure ... until it has no choice except between repression and capitulation.'[7] Thus, the behaviour of French pressure groups is explicable as the symmetrical response to the style and behaviour of executive authority in France, although the latter has itself been conditioned by past experience of group behaviour. However, times have changed since 1789 and 1871. The revolutionary tradition has been diluted into a propensity to direct action. Such action seems better suited to extracting short-term, piecemeal concessions than to securing the long-term welfare of categories of citizens who depend on sustained action within the framework of an overall strategy.

The role of the peak interest group organizations

Although it has been a long road from the status of outlaws to that of industrial statesmen, the major French economic interests have only achieved a rather limited degree of recruitment and cohesion. This fact is connected in part with belated industrial development as well as the tendency to split along ideological lines. The peak organizations are characterized first, by their tendency to press their own case directly rather than through the weak political parties. Even in the case of the communist-dominated CGT, where the major French trade union is in a symbiotic relationship with the communist party, its industrial activities have been more effective in challenging the capitalist régime and achieving benefits for the working class than have its strictly political activities. The interrelationship between the CP and the CGT is a complex compromise between the Leninist rule that the trade union must be controlled by the party and used to further its ends, and the 'syndicalist' apolitical tradition of the CGT enshrined in the Amiens Charter of 1906. Whilst no more than about 10 per cent of the CGT members are also members of the CP (a quarter of whose cells are based on the workplace) they are generally the most active union members and are elected to posts of responsibility at all levels of the. CGT, including its constituent federations. As well as providing the president and general secretary and most of the headquarters staff of the CGT, eight out of fifteen members of the executive committee are CP members (three being politbureau members). Even when they lack a formal majority, the CP members are able to exercise effective control thanks to the 'fellow-travelling' diffidence of others. The CGT can be relied upon to act as the CP desires but party tactics are in turn influenced by the union, as was evident at the time of the May-June 1968 general strike.

Secondly, in the absence of effective opposition parties to aggregate the demands being made on the political system, the various peak interest groups seek to fulfil this function and in the process take over part of the function of political opposition. However, this is a hazardous task because each major interest is itself so divided that it is very difficult for them to attain a common view-point. The CGT with nearly two million members represents over half the total trade union membership but has to face competition from three other general unions : in order of size, the left-wing socialist CFDT (with 680,000 members), the right-wing social-ist *Force Ouvrière*, and the residue of the Catholic CFTC, as well as the executive staff union, the CGC. Apart from the open split among the trade unions, almost all French peak organizations have great problems of internal cohesion. French business manages to preserve the semblance of a fragile 'confederal' unity through the *Conseil National du Patronat Français* but in fact medium and small business look to the vehement CGPME nationally and form the backbone of the chamber of commerce in most pro-vincial towns. A number of smaller organizations, such as the remnant of Pierre Poujade's UDCA and various shopkeeper and craft organizations, cater for the self-employed or the very small-scale employer. The CNPF has usually been paralysed by the pursuit of quasi-unanimity, evading controversial issues that might split the organization or formulating policies that it does not attempt to enforce on its members. The Grenelle Agreement of May 1968 that helped to end the general strike forced them to take a more authoritative line. It was negotiated between the leaders of the trade unions and the CNPF under the chairmanship of the prime minister, the CNPF leaders being compelled to make substantial concessions without authority from their member or-ganizations. This helped to bring about the 1969 reform in the CNPF, representing a step towards the centralization and concen-tration of power in the hands of peak organization leaders. Govern-ments in Britain and France have encouraged this redistribution of power within interest groups so that these leaders can acquire sufficient authority to enter into binding commitments that will subsequently be honoured. Given the highly decentralized and dispersed character of French interest groups, in which the rank and file retain much of the initiative and 'leadership from behind' is the rule, this process of shifting power to the top is a relatively slow process, not least in the business world. For the foreseeable future, autonomy will continue to take precedence over planned strategy and freedom of action over united action.

Thirdly, the executive is so powerful under the fifth republic that the peak organizations are more like pressured groups than pressure groups. While the government and administration seek to increase group prestige and status to use them as agents for their policies, they do not want them strengthened to the point where the interest groups can threaten the authority of the government. In France, successive governments have struggled with the problem of carrying through an agricultural revolution in which the protected, subsistence peasant farm would be mechanized and enlarged into a competitive, capitalist farm producing for the market. To achieve this, they had to overcome the opposition of the traditional farm organizations : the FNSEA (the main peak organization, of which about half French farmers are members, embracing thirty-six product organizations, notably the powerful cereals, meat, milk, wine, fruit and vegetables and sugarbeet associations) and the chambers of agriculture, elected on a departmental basis, whose presidents formed the APPCA. These organizations have the support of the influential *Amicale Parlementaire Agricole et Rurale*. However, the direct action tactics used in 1959–61 led the prime minister and notably the new minister of agriculture, Edgard Pisani, to use the 'young farmers' of the CNJA to carry out a policy of modernizing agriculture in close consultation with amenable farm leaders who 'got to know the Hôtel Matignon [the prime minister's headquarters] better than certain ephemeral fourth republic premiers'.[8]

With ups and downs, helped by the acquisition of the general secretaryship of the FNSEA in 1968 by Michel Debatisse, the previous leader (since 1958) of the CNJA, the policy of integrating a select few of the farm population into an industrialized agriculture was carried through. However, the cost in inflated prices for some farm products – especially cereals, because of the influence of the rich farmers of the Paris basin – to placate opposition and ease the process of transition was extremely high. (The burden on France would have been greater without the EEC common agricultural policy which enabled her to shed part of it.) The farm leaders have been accused of excessively close collaboration with the government and the unity of the FNSEA has been threatened. Meanwhile, a rival, communist-influenced organization, the MODEF, has emerged as the champion of the family farmers threatened by the prospect of absorption into the industrial proletariat and abandoned by the FNSEA to their fate.

The problem of what sort of stance an interest group should

assume vis à vis government or other groups has presented particularly severe problems to the trade unions. Their leaders seem to
adopt contrasting types of behaviour, depending upon whether
they are collaborating with government or business organizations
in consultative bodies discussing policy matters at the summit, or
are engaged in conflict with them at the office or factory level
when discussing the immediate issues of concern to their members :
wages and working conditions. The committee room is the sedate
context of consultation but until 1968 employer refusal to engage
in collective bargaining meant that strikes, demonstrations and
clashes in the streets and at factory gates were the staple of
industrial life. The union leader's activities on numerous national
consultative bodies are 'time consuming and burdensome for
organizations whose human resources are limited. Yet they seem
to take first priority, since the political and social status they give
union leaders permits them to be well informed and to exert a
certain amount of bargaining power. . . .' This apparent summit
'collusion' with government and business feeds the traditional
anarcho-syndicalist suspicions that the rank and file are being
betrayed. So 'workers distrust the militants; the militants distrust
the leaders and refuse to give them [the] means to build responsible
organizations. Weak unions try desperately to maintain the façade
that enables them to speak in the name of an active, aggressive
and unruly working class.'[9] The vicious circle of authoritarianism
and resistance to authority at all levels of French society can only
be broken if the mutual ignorance and the intense hostility
between and within organizations can be overcome.

Permanent multilateral consultation:
  the economic and social council

A major argument in favour of institutionalizing the government-
interest group dialogue in an economic council, such as has existed
in France since 1925, is that it offers the opportunity of substitu-
ting multilateral for bilateral bargaining, increasing the opportunity to work out comprehensive compromises. It provides the
context in which the interest groups can learn from each other
what they want; they discover from the government on what
terms they can obtain it; they may work together, where this
proves feasible, to secure it. It formalizes consultative procedures

which have developed haphazardly to meet specific situations, with consequent gaps and overlapping. It also enables the differential access of interest groups to the decision-making authorities to be corrected, hence the historical fact that the demand for interest group representation in this form originated with the CGT at the end of the first world war. Whereas other groups had their own informal and unobstrusive opportunities to influence policy, the trade unions had no such privileged access to government. The council has not fulfilled the hopes of early advocates of functional representation, who looked to such bodies to provide 'an element of sustained research, thought and formulation of policy . . . more public than a lonely thinker, more continuous, pressing and representative than a royal commission, more in touch with the vital elements of industry and society than political parties, less suspect than the creations of the "lobby", more sedate and objective in its deliberations and less given to sudden fears of partisanship than the political assembly.'[10] However, it has made the spokesmen of the peak organizations better informed about the broad economic and social issues and encouraged them to place their demands realistically in the context of the national capacity to fulfil them.

Seventy per cent of the economic and social council of the fifth republic are representatives of organized interests and 30 per cent are government nominees. The two hundred members are divided into fifteen groups whose strength in February 1970 is shown in table 7.

Table 7
Economic and Social Council's Composition

(a) Trade Unions		(b) Business		(c) Agriculture and Cooperatives	
1. CGT	14	6. Private business	27	9. Farmers	32
2. CFDT	16	7. Artisans	10	10. Cooperatives	10
3. FO	14	8. Nationalized industries	6		
4. CGC	4				
5. CFTC	3				

(d) Others	
11. UNAF (family associations)	8
12. Miscellaneous and middle classes	10
13. Qualified persons	16
14. Overseas and franc zone	21
15. Overseas territories and departments	8

There is thus a trade union bloc of fifty-one members, a business bloc of forty-three which is often joined by the forty-two representatives of agriculture and the cooperatives, while government nominees form the bulk of the last bloc, who also lean towards business rather than the trade unions.

The economic and social council reports and makes recommendations on matters referred to it by the government or takes up issues on its own initiative. It works primarily through seven sections, dealing respectively with planning and short-term economic policy; finance; social affairs and industrial relations; industry and trade; regional development and public works; agriculture; overseas economic expansion and cooperation. To each section are attached representatives of all the council groups together with ten nominated section specialists who serve for a maximum of two years and do not participate in the plenary sessions or vote in the full council meeting. Council members serve for five years and it is up to the organization selecting them to decide whether or not to renew their nomination for further terms. They receive two-thirds of the parliamentary salary, some paying back part of this to their organization. Nearly one-eighth of the CGT's income in 1965 was derived from this levy, just as the communist party used to derive an important part of its income from its parliamentary representatives when these were more numerous. One-seventh of the CFDT's income is received through a similar levy. Seats on the ESC thus provide a concealed subsidy to financially weak peak organizations.

The council's amalgamation with the senate into a new second chamber was part of the package of proposals that was defeated at the referendum of April 1969. The groups represented on the ESC were almost unanimously hostile towards this attempt to integrate them more fully into the decision-making process, although the new senate was to lose its legislative power and became a consultative body. Even though the title of senate was to be retained, Alain Poher, the senate president, could legitimately claim that it was not the ESC that was being abolished but the senate. With the coming of the Chaban-Delmas government, the prime minister made known during his address to the council in July 1969 that he regarded it as the centrepiece of his policy of 'permanent concerted action'. He would frequently consult it on the government's legislative programme as far as social and economic Bills were concerned. He would encourage ministers to attend its discussions and would pay the greatest attention to its suggestions and the positions adopted by the various groups. He consequently promised to respect the rule, only once fulfilled in July 1961, of publishing annually a report on what had been done about the council's recommendations and undertook to append them to each Bill submitted to the national assembly and the senate. Finally, he regarded close collaboration between the council and the government as indispensable and promised to maintain regular contact with its president and its bureau. Whilst these promises were only partially kept, the council has been brought more fully into the discussion of matters other than the National Plan, in which it has regularly played an important part.* Nevertheless, the third chamber is likely to remain – partly because of the private character of its proceedings – one of the less well known of France's political institutions, as shown in table 8.

Table 8
How Many French People Considered Themselves Well-Informed in 1969 About the Following Institutions (%)*

President of the republic	71	Chamber of commerce	30
Municipal council	70	Economic and social council	28
National assembly	60	Council of state	21
Government	56	Court of accounts	14
Senate	40	Regional economic development	
Departmental council	40	commission	11

An imaginary 'democratic council' received 8 per cent.

* Based on SOFRES poll published in *Le Figaro*, 10 November 1969, p. 6.

Polarized pluralism: class and 'catch-all' parties

The highly abstract character of most French political commitments, based on divisive ideologies as well as a rarefied consensus expressed in loyalty to the republican state, encourages a divorce between the individual's behaviour as the member of an interest category or group and his partisan or electoral behaviour. He frequently votes for a candidate who supports the government,

* Although the council does not avail itself of the right to send its *rapporteurs* to speak in the two chambers, they frequently testify before parliamentary standing committees.

against which he will violently demonstrate, and then meekly votes for the same candidate at the next election. This has made it more difficult for French political parties to channel interest group demands. Despite attempts to keep the interest groups free of direct partisan entanglements in France, the distinction between political parties and interest groups is only clearcut in countries with disciplined two-party systems where each is likely to gain office. In a multipolarized party system such as has existed in France since the early days of the third republic, those parties, for example the communists, who are permanently excluded from office are reduced to the *de facto* status of pressure groups; while pressure groups – peasants or shopkeepers – can become the backbone of a political party, as occurred with the conservative CNIP and the Poujadist UFF under the fourth republic.

Moreover, parties and interests tend to be more closely connected in a multipolarized party system. First, the narrower electoral appeal of each party encourages closer ties with a specialized clientèle and greater identification with a particular cause. It also allows more scope for interest group manoeuvre, especially where two or more parties compete for the same voters. Thus the Catholic school lobby can rely on the UDR, RI and centre parties to compete for its backing, whilst the secularist school lobby has the communists, socialists and radicals competing for its support. Finally, the would-be all-embracing UDR is wide open to pressure group influence in a similar way to the undisciplined 'catch-all' parties of the United States. However, it is more resistant to group pressure than were the weakly disciplined and non-ideological fourth republic parties of the centre and right who formed most of the coalition governments from 1947–58.

The traditional French multipolarized party system tended either towards immobility or disorderly change, maximizing demands on the political system but providing unreliable support for the government of the day. The unified political superstructure superimposed by a centralized state authority upon a society with deep and complex divisions led to a 'mixture of deference and distrust' towards authority, while a retarded industrial development led to political claims outstripping socioeconomic changes, which, when they did come in the form of class-based mass movements, were not properly integrated into the established institutional and political structures.[11] Despite the emergence of the UDR as a majority party in parliament, which has had a stable majority since 1962 with its coalition allies and has attained an unprecedented consolidation of the traditionally fragmented right, it is premature to claim that this achievement represents 'a real change in the French political system'.[12] Without going to the opposite extreme of assuming that the heterogeneous coalition that makes up the UDR will prove as ephemeral as the successive titles that the Gaullist party has adopted since 1958, France is still a long way from Malraux's polemical claim that the political scene was made up of the Gaullists, the communists and nothing. Apart from the UDR's own problems of cohesion, there are rival claimants for the votes of the right-centre, notably the independent republicans and the weaker CDP (*Centre Démocratie et Progrès*); whilst on the left, we have the spectacle of disintegration, following the collapse of the socialist-radical federation in 1968 and the fragile alliance between socialists and communists. For the present, the UDR successfully combines the third republic radical style of an open-ended, all-embracing party of government, concerned primarily with winning a majority of supporters in the assembly, with the centralization, discipline and nationwide organization in depth of the class-based communist party. Until 1972, the absence of a comparable polarization on the left meant that there was no plausible alternative government or opposition, so political change had to come from within the right-centre coalition of which the UDR is the nucleus and which embraces all possible majorities. The effective head of the government, the president of the republic, perpetuating the pretence that the president is above party, does not accustom the French people to party government.

Table 9 presents a somewhat simplified perspective on how the major French parties have fared since the second world war. It shows that the communists continue to secure a fifth or more of the popular vote, which since the fifth republic has not been reflected in seats won owing to the electoral system and the variable effectiveness of second ballot alliances of the left. A force to be reckoned with (some 300,000 members, 37,000 section and cell activists, 3,600 full-time party officials, 20,000 municipal councillors, 1,400 mayors and 186 departmental councillors) they have, by their calculated ambiguity towards liberal democracy at home and loyalty to the Soviet Union in foreign policy, paralysed both

Table 9
National Assembly Elections in France, 1946–73
(i) % *of Votes Cast*

	Commun- ists	Social- ists	Centre Radicals	Centre MRP	Indepen- dents		Gaullists
June 1946	26·2	21·1	11·5	28·1	12·8		—
Nov. 1946	28·6	17·9	12·4	26·3	12·9		1·8
June 1951	26·4	14·8	13·0	13·1	12·5		20·9
Jan. 1956	25·5	15·5	12·8	11·3	13·9		4·3
Nov. 1958							
1st ballot	18·9	15·5	11·5	11·6	19·9		17·6
2nd ballot	20·7	13·7	7·7	7·5	23·6		26·4
Nov. 1962							
1st ballot	21·7	12·6	7·5	8·9	9·6	4·4	31·9
2nd ballot	21·3	15·2	7	5·3	7·8	1·6	40·5
March 1967							
1st ballot	22·5	18·8			17·9		37·8
2nd ballot	21·4	24·1			10·8		42·6
June 1968							
1st ballot	20·0	16·5			10·3*		43·7
2nd ballot	20·1	21·3			7·8*		46·4
March 1973							
1st ballot	21·5	21·2			13·1‡		36·4
2nd ballot	20·6	25·1			6·1‡		46·2

(ii) *Seats in the National Assembly*

	Commun- ists	Social- ists	Centre Radicals	Centre MRP	Indepen- dents		Gaullists
June 1946	153	129	53	169	67		—
Nov. 1946	183	105	70	167	71		6
June 1951	101	107	95	96	98		120
Jan. 1956	150	99	94	84	97		22
Nov. 1958	10	47	40	56	129		206
Nov. 1962	41	66	43	55	37†		233
Mar. 1967	73	121		41	44†		201
June 1968	34	44	13		31*	64†	296
March 1973	73	102		34‡	30	55	183

* Centre parliamentary group called *Progrès et Démocratie Moderne* (PDM).
† Independent republican group led by V. Giscard d'Estaing.
‡ Reformers, made up of the democratic centre in alliance with some radicals.

the parliamentary and extra-parliamentary left. They have therefore helped to maintain the system to whose destruction they are dedicated. The socialists had been in decline since the second world war until their resurgence at the 1973 election and, unlike the communists, are nonexistent as an organization at the local level over most of the country. It had increasingly become a parliamentary-centred and local council-centred cadre party, relying on the ageing faithful to preserve what was possible of the party's heritage rather than accepting, as a reformist party should, the need to modernize itself. The radicals have preceded the socialists along this path, the periodic attempts to rejuvenate it having hitherto failed dismally because its remaining strength lies in the declining areas of south-west France. There are too few radicals to form a separate assembly group (minimum of thirty members), so in 1972 most of them were 'attached' to the socialists.

The right and right-centre parties of the fourth republic have also largely dwindled into hangers-on of the powerful UDR. The CDP and the independent republicans, with UDR support, win the bulk of the assembly seats, whilst the reformers and the CNI, who remain beyond the fringes of the 'majority', hold on to most of the seats in the senate and local councils where the UDR is weak (except in the Paris region). The UDR has been the party which, following the fourth republic collapse of its RPF predecessor, has since 1958 regularly increased its strength up to the election of 1968, when it won, in alliance with the independent republicans, 44 per cent of the first ballot vote and secured *on its own* fifty more seats than it required for an absolute assembly majority. It owed this dominant position to the voters' post-May 1968 panic and it lost as expected many of these seats at the 1973 general election. It would therefore be unwise to project from the special circumstances of the 1968 election, although the UDR's steady accretion of electoral strength since 1958 cannot be denied.

To understand the behaviour of the political parties, it is helpful to have a sex, age and occupational profile of their voters, such as is provided in tables 10 and 11. From the former, we can ascertain that all parties other than the UDR and independent republicans have a marked male predominance. The communists, with a somewhat younger electorate, receive almost half their support from manual workers; the socialist and radical voters are an accurate cross-section of the nation; whilst the right and right-

Table 10
*The Constituent Elements of Party Support, June 1968 (%)**

	Adult French Population	Communist Party	Socialists and Radicals	Democratic Centre/ PDM	UDR and Independent Republicans
(i) Sex					
Men	48	60	55	54	46
Women	52	40	45	46	54
(ii) Age					
20–49	56	61	57	57	55
50+	44	39	43	43	45
(iii) Occupation					
Farmers	17	8	18	16	18
Industry and trade (proprietors)	10	5	9	15	14
Professional and managerial	5	2	3	10	6
Employees	15	18	16	19	18
Workers	31	49	34	22	25
No occupation	22	18	20	18	19

* Source: *Sondages*, 1968, no. 2, p. 101.

Table 11
*The French Public's Voting Intentions, June 1968 (%)**

	Communist Party	Socialists and Radicals	Democratic Centre/ PDM	UDR and Independent Republicans	Other
(i) Sex					
Men	25	18	12	35	10
Women	18	16	11	46	9
(ii) Age					
20–49	23	17	11	38	11
50+	20	17	12	43	8
(iii) Occupation					
Farmers	12	20	12	48	8
Industry and trade (proprietors)	10	13	15	53	9
Professional and managerial	10	9	23	48	10
Employees	21	15	12	40	12
Workers	33	18	8	31	10
No occupation	21	19	11	42	7

* Source: *Sondages*, 1968, no. 2, p. 102.

centre predictably attract a disproportionate number of business-men. From table 11 we see that the UDR and independent repub-licans won, in June 1968, 46 per cent of the women's vote, 48 per cent of the farmer, professional and managerial vote, and 53 per cent of the industrial and trading proprietors' vote. The centre did best among the professional and managerial voters, the social-ists and radicals held on best to the farm vote. The communists secured 21 per cent of the white collar vote and 33 per cent of the manual worker vote, in contrast to the UDR and independ-ent republicans who collected 40 per cent of the white collar vote and 31 per cent of the manual worker vote. It is its managerial and white collar voters that have abandoned the UDR as it becomes more clearly a conservative party following de Gaulle's departure.

Parliament and the legislative process

Two of the greatest mid-nineteenth-century observers of the British parliament's apotheosis (Walter Bagehot) and the French parliament's abasement (Alexis de Tocqueville) had this to say about their respective country's legislatures. 'A Parliament,' wrote Bagehot, 'is nothing less than a big meeting of more or less idle people. In proportion as you give it power, it will inquire into everything, settle everything, meddle in everything.'[13] While Bagehot lived to see the French parliament develop into just such a body, Tocqueville, writing during the second empire, declared : 'A nation that is weary of internecine conflict is quite ready to be duped provided it is given peace, and history tells us that at such times all that is needed to satisfy public opinion is to gather together from all parts of the country a number of obscure or pliable men and make them play the part of a national assembly at a fixed salary.'[14] Even though the 1968 crisis and the sweeping UDR electoral victory of June 1968 do have analogies with the events of 1848, it is not necessarily true that 'under the new régime, the parliament of France, once among the most power-ful in the world, became one of the weakest', 'somewhat weaker than the British House of Commons'.[15] Despite the emergence of a stable majority in the national assembly, supporting a stable government, there are a number of qualifications that must be made to sweeping judgements on the decline of the French parlia-ment. First, the assembly majority and the government are coalitions made up of three parties, whose contours are rather blurred and whose mutual trust is not great. Secondly, the weaker discipline and cohesion of the parties in power, exacerbated by the absence of an effective opposition-cum-alternative government, challenges any argument from the secure hold on power of the executive. Thirdly, both chambers of the French parliament still secure substantial amendments to government legislation, and although severely curtailed in effectiveness the standing specialist parliamentary committees play an important role in the legislative process without encroaching on executive authority. The abdication of its sovereignty by parliament in favour of de Gaulle in 1958 was followed in 1969 by de Gaulle's abdication after the failure of an attempt to bypass parliament by referendum. The new president proclaimed his intention to work in conjunction with parliament rather than to steam-roller it. However, the hopes this raised have so far not been satisfied.

Table 12
Composition of the French Parliament, April 1973

Party	National Assembly	Senate
Communist	73	18
PSU	1	—
Socialist		49
Radicals*	102	38
Reformers	34	—
Centre Union	30	46
Republican independents for social action	—	16
Independent republicans	55	59
UDR	183	38
Non-party	12	19
Total	490	283

* The left radicals are attached to the socialist parliamentary group in the assembly, while the rump of the radical party forms part of the reformers movement.

Table 12 indicates the contrasting strength of the various parties in the two chambers in 1973. The parties of the centre and right-centre are heavily over-represented in the indirectly elected senate, reflecting their entrenched position in the local politics of the rural and small town communes. On the other hand, the socialists do equally well in both chambers, while the UDR and communists are notably under-represented in the senate although they have both made strenuous efforts to establish themselves more firmly on local councils. In the traditional French conception, a deputy is primarily a local representative, the spokesman for local grievances and the source of local patronage. Whilst local connections are vital for candidates of the old-style centre parties, which give them *ex-post facto* party endorsement, they are less significant for the centralized and well-organized communist and UDR parties whose 'parachuted' candidates subsequently attempt to acquire a local identity. The reversion to single member constituencies in 1958 has encouraged the constituency-orientation of the deputies. In contrast with the clear British demarcation between local and national politics, the two are intimately related in France. Both local and national office must be held concurrently if the politician is to play his role as privileged mediator between the mass public and the political or administrative executive. In the 1971 municipal elections, 379 out of 487 deputies and 191 out of 283 senators were candidates. (Thirty-six out of forty-one ministers, including the prime minister, also stood as candidates in 1971 to retain or acquire a grip on a constituency so that they had a comfortable *point de chute* when they left ministerial office. Twenty-eight were elected and their constituents could confidently expect that their dealings with central government would be facilitated as a result.) Mayors who are also members of parliament spend a large part of their time in their constituencies. Even when in Paris, deputies and senators are busy contacting ministries on behalf of their councils and constituents, so that absenteeism has been a major problem, both on the floor of the house and in the committee work of both chambers.

Under the fourth republic, the French suffered from 'government by assembly'. Fleeting ministries were overthrown by shifting majorities. Symbolizing the fifth republic's attainment of stable government based upon a loyal majority, the UDR since 1962 occupies seats in the assembly extending from extreme right to extreme left (see figure 1). The price has been acceptance of a series of draconian curbs on the assembly's powers over legislation, finance (dealt with in chapter 6), the executive and constitutional amendment. The constitutional limitations on parliament's legislative power are numerous. Article 34 specifies the subjects on which parliament may legislate. On some matters, parliament is entitled to 'make rules' and in others it can fix the

Figure 1 : The French National Assembly, 1972

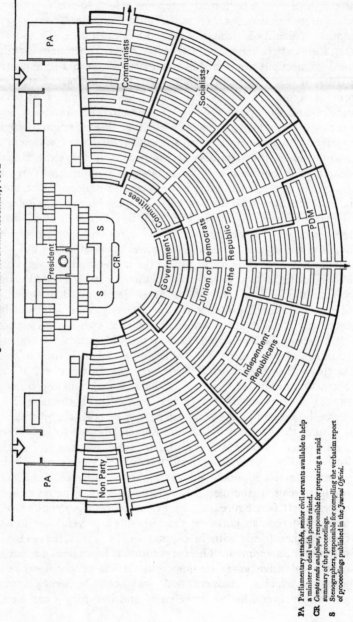

PA Parliamentary attaché, senior civil servants available to help
    a minister to deal with points raised.
CR *Compte rendu analytique*, responsible for preparing a rapid
    summary of the proceedings.
S   Stenographers, responsible for compiling the verbatim report
    of proceedings published in the *Journal Officiel*.

'fundamental principles'; but Article 37 states that all matters not enumerated in Article 34 are part of the government's regulatory power and need not be submitted for parliamentary approval. The executive's decrees and orders are now on a separate but equal footing with the laws enacted by the legislature.* Furthermore, Article 38 provides that parliament may delegate its legislative power to the government which makes ordinances. This occurred in 1967 when the government had a slender parliamentary majority and wanted to carry through unpopular social and economic reforms.

To prevent parliament from 'meddling excessively' in government, Article 28 restricts the length of parliamentary sessions to less than six months annually. The assembly held about one hundred and forty sittings a year just before the second world war. This increased to over two hundred under the fourth republic but has fallen back to about one hundred and forty sittings under the fifth republic. An example of the rushed legislation that results is provided by a comparison between the Acts reducing conscription to one year in 1928 and 1970. The third republic Bill was presented in August 1926. After being examined by the standing committee, it was discussed in the chamber of deputies eight times between June 1927 and January 1928. The fifth republic Bill was decided upon by the government on 3 June 1970, examined by the assembly's defence committee from 4 June, by the assembly itself on 9–10 June 1970, and by the senate on 25 June, becoming law after a conference committee on 29 June. At its autumn 1969 session, parliament devoted about half its time to a discussion of the 1970 budget. It adopted in all fifty-three Acts, forty-four government Bills out of the sixty-nine presented and nine out of the 167 private member's Bills presented. The government (under Article 48) controls the parliamentary agenda and uses it to give priority to its own Bills. There has been a consequential fall from nearly 30 per cent in the fourth republic to about 10 per cent in the fifth republic of the private member's Bills share of all legislation adopted. There is no equivalent of opposition 'supply days' which allow the government's opponents in the House of Commons time to debate a subject of their choice. In France they must put down a censure motion.

* Regulatory *decrees* emanate from the president of the republic and prime minister. Regulatory *orders* are issued by lesser executive authorities.

Other changes in procedure and organization were devised to incorporate features of the British parliamentary system which strengthen the executive. Government Bills are discussed in the form presented by government, not, as was the practice (and still is in the United States) as amended by the relevant parliamentary standing committee. In major debates the minister speaks first but on other occasions the traditional practice is adopted of the committee's *rapporteur* opening the debate, being followed by the minister who explains whether he accepts or rejects the committee's proposed amendments. They generally speak from their specially reserved seats at the front of the assembly (as shown in figure 1). Through Article 44 of the constitution, government legislation can escape the 'death by a thousand cuts' which the assembly used to inflict on executive-sponsored Bills under the fourth republic by insisting that its legislation be voted *en bloc* and unamended. This device has frequently been used to restrain the government's own supporters from voting for electorally popular amendments at the instance of pressure groups.

Before the establishment of the fifth republic, governments tended to follow the lead of parliament and this meant primarily the chairman and *rapporteurs* of the twenty or so specialist standing committees, approximately one for each government department. The fourth republic situation has been described as follows : 'The standing committees were the central feature of French parliamentary procedure. All Bills, before the House debated them, went to the committees, which killed the majority and redrafted the remainder. . . . It was through its committees above all that parliament asserted legislative and encroached on executive power.'[16] Ministers and officials did and do appear before them (though ministers require the prime minister's permission to testify) but they do not hold elaborate public hearings on the American model, nor do they have a comparable investigatory staff. The number of standing committees in both chambers was reduced to six by Article 43 of the constitution but they remain more specialized, on the American as contrasted with the British pattern. They are, in the assembly : (i) finance and economic affairs, the most powerful committee and the one which attracts the best-calibre parliamentarians; (ii) foreign affairs; (iii) defence; (iv) constitutional, legal and administrative affairs. These four committees have some sixty members each, but (v) produc-

tion and trade, covering all industrial, labour, transport and housing matters; and (vi) cultural, family and social affairs, including
education, health and the social services, have over one hundred
and twenty members each. Thanks to selective absenteeism an
element of unofficial specialization has crept in. In the senate the
smallest standing committees are those on finance and legislative
affairs because, paradoxically, they have the most work to do!
While the Gaullists, on the 'winner takes all' principle, control
the chairmanships of all six assembly standing committees, they
held only one of the six senate chairmanships in 1969, the
independents occupying two and the centre, the radicals and the
socialists one each. However, standing committee chairmen do not
have the power to control the flow of legislation enjoyed by their
American equivalents.

The constitutional council is charged by Article 41 with the
task of acting as the executive's watch dog against any attempt by
parliament to recover its old power to harass the government, and
it has assiduously done so. Nevertheless, usage has undermined a
number of the new rules of parliamentary procedure, notably in
the failure to restrict either the reading of speeches or their length,
or to check on attendance and make salary deductions for absenteeism. Because of electronic voting, when a 'public vote' is taken
instead of a show of hands (intended to circumvent the severe
restrictions on proxy voting) deputies are 'now required to leap
up and down the benches switching keys for their absent
friends instead of merely putting ballot papers into a box'.[17] The
attempt was made to replace the traditional practice of 'interpella-
tion' – a question that is debated and concludes with a vote of
confidence – by the innocuous House of Commons' device of the
private member's motion and by oral questions. This has proved a
failure, questions being dealt with on Fridays when most members
are travelling to their constituencies. Despite the 1970 speeding up
of answers to questions that were of current interest, 'question time'
is not taken seriously by either ministers or deputies. Only those
who have put questions bother to attend and embarrassing questions are often left unanswered. Written questions, directed most
frequently at the minister of finance, were in use before the establishment of the fifth republic and have increased in importance as
a source of information, especially when parliament is not in
session. In the autumn 1969 session, ministers replied in the

assembly to twenty-seven private member's motions, fifty-three oral questions without debate, and 1,162 written questions.

Finally, in the matter of restraints on parliament's legislative power, by Article 45 of the constitution the government has secured the means to break a deadlock between the assembly and the senate by supporting the assembly version or by using the senate to block the wishes of the assembly when these conflict with the government's will. Under the fourth republic, the assembly insisted on the last word only in 1 per cent of Bills between 1954 and 1958. Despite the fact that the senate has been controlled by the government's opponents, from 1958–68 the two chambers were able to agree on 96 per cent of the 829 Acts of parliament passed. Of the seventy-eight Bills (9 per cent) that went to a conference committee of the two chambers (seven members from each) in that period, agreement was reached in forty-five cases, leaving only thirty-three disputed Bills in which the government imposed the assembly version. Of these, twenty-one Bills only met with senate opposition because the government refused to accept *some* of the senate amendments (for example the Agriculture Guidelines Act of 1960, the Finance Acts of 1962 and 1966, the 1964 Broadcasting Act) or had insisted on an *en bloc*, unamended approval. This left twelve Bills (notably three on the atomic programme in 1960, 1962 and 1964, the 1963 creation of a state security court, the 1967 Act authorizing the government to reform the social security system by ordinance, and the 1968 Act ratifying these ordinances) on which the senate felt it had to express its total disapproval. The senate has always acted expeditiously in considering Bills from the assembly and delays that have occurred in implementing the Acts, often passed in a few days, are due to the slowness with which the necessary detailed decrees are issued. The July 1966 Act on the health insurance of the self-employed, voted in twenty days, took two and a half years to be implemented by decree and was then the cause of a violent series of demonstrations by those affected, necessitating a new Act in 1969.

The constitutional rules (Article 49) enforcing government accountability to parliament are based upon the presumption*

---

* An exception arises when the prime minister, usually on assuming office, seeks approval of the government's programme or of a general declaration of policy, when a simple plurality is necessary.

that the assembly majority will be precarious and needs to be bolstered up by procedural devices. The main one is the provision that the government is deemed to have retained the assembly's confidence unless a censure motion is carried by an absolute majority. The same is true, paradoxically, when the government makes the adoption of a Bill an issue of confidence. This device was frequently used (thirty-four times by the fifteen-month Mollet government of 1956–7 and twenty-three times in forty days by the ephemeral forty-day Edgar Faure government of 1952) to secure a debate, reject hostile amendments and carry a Bill under the fourth republic. Under the fifth republic only opponents vote on censure and confidence motions. From its parliamentary supporters, the government does not seek explicit, positive confidence but implicit, negative acquiescence. This helped the government, which in 1967–8 had only a tiny majority in the assembly, to survive thanks to a procedural device that counted all non-hostile votes as tacit votes of support. This draconian safeguard has been superfluous throughout most of the fifth republic because stable governments have been supported by a loyal majority in the assembly. There has been a polarization of the inconsistent government supporters (which amounted to over half the deputies until the 1962 dissolution of the assembly following the defeat of the Pompidou government by a vote of censure) into the rival blocks of a majority of consistent supporters and a minority of consistent opponents. The 1968 assembly elections and the 1969 presidential election have increased this polarization by shifting most of the centre's inconsistent supporters of government into the ranks of the majority. Faced by a UDR-dominated majority who consistently support the government, the parties out of office have become defeatist, concentrating on the next electoral opportunity to remove the government rather than on attempting to hold it to account.

Parliament's role in amending the constitution (under Article 89) has been curtailed by requiring that the proposed amendment must either be passed by both the assembly and the senate before being approved by a referendum (the most difficult procedure and not used) or by both chambers meeting jointly and carrying it by a three-fifths majority. (Characteristically, the latter procedure applies only to constitutional amendments proposed by the government.) However, anticipation of senatorial opposition led de Gaulle twice to adopt a third, unconstitutional, method of amendment by referendum alone, invoking Article 11 concerned with 'the organization of the public authorities'. After his success in 1962 on the issue of the popular election of the president of the republic, de Gaulle sought to repeat his feat in April 1969. It resulted in defeat and resignation. This result makes recourse to Article 11, bypassing parliament, unlikely as a method of constitutional amendment in future. Furthermore, it restored the prestige of the senate, opinion polls showing that, in February 1969, 38 per cent wanted a more important role for the senate, 27 per cent a retention of the *status quo*, and only 7 per cent a reduced role, with 28 per cent not replying. The Chaban-Delmas government fully reintegrated the senate into the legislative process after a prolonged period of ministerial boycott in the 1960s. While the composition of the senate may be made more representative of urban areas, its basic features and functions are likely to remain unchanged.

Parliament, which did not enjoy much public esteem under the fourth republic, has recovered favour now that it has been reduced to a more modest role. An opinion poll at the end of 1969 (table 13) shows that despite the fact that a third of the population do not express an opinion, an absolute majority consider parliament to be useful in the fifth republic, and we shall see in the next chapter that they would like parliament to take a larger part in deciding major issues, especially in the sphere of social policy. When they were asked which of the following parliamentary functions they regarded as important (table 14) it is noteworthy that the accountability of government only came fifth, whilst

Table 13
Public Assessment of Parliament's Role
under the Fourth and Fifth Republics (%)*

	Fourth Republic	Fifth Republic
Very useful	5 } 36	8 } 52
Rather useful	31	44
Rather harmful	23 } 27	11 } 15
Very harmful	4	4
No reply	37	33

* Based on a SOFRES poll in *Le Figaro*, 10 November 1969, p. 6.

Table 14
The Importance of Selected Parliamentary Functions to the Public (%)*

Protect liberty	83	Make government accountable	65
Vote budget	81	Represent all political shades of opinion	62
Vote laws	78	Represent constituency interests in Paris	57
All opinions to be freely expressed	70	Provide a majority to form a government	47

* Based on a SOFRES poll in *Le Figaro*, 10 November 1969, p. 6.

providing a majority for the government was rated the least important.

Domestic policy-making in France was, until the fifth republic, closely linked with legislation. However, the decline of laws or Acts of parliament in favour of executive decisions, associated with the subordination of law-making itself to the government, has made it unrealistic to expect parliament to recover, after de Gaulle's departure, more than a fraction of its old power and prestige. We have seen that there has been an increasing tendency for the government to negotiate directly with the interest groups, the subsequent settlement being sanctioned by the prime minister or president. Because 'both the integration of interests and the legitimization of policy decisions now take place outside parliament',[18] the interest groups have partially displaced the political parties as the representative mediators between the people and the government, which has successfully acquired a quasi-monopoly of formal policy-making. However, the May 1968 crisis demonstrated that to avoid the accumulation and explosion of public grievances, parliamentary representatives may provide the 'feedback' that is indispensable to long-term political stability. It indicated the dangers of provoking extra-parliamentary opposition when proper opportunities are denied for the parliamentary expression of opposition. However, the same crisis shattered the previous fragile left-wing alliance, though it was patched up in 1972 for electoral reasons. This leaves the political and techno-bureaucratic executives to manage as best as they can with the inadequate mediation of the interest group élite.

4 Making and Implementing Government Policy

The political executive

Before Pompidou succeeded de Gaulle as president of the republic, anyone who had predicted that the new president would not merely maintain but accentuate the subordination of the prime minister to him would have been regarded as indulging in eccentric humour. Between 1944 and 1946, before the fourth republic was established, de Gaulle was both president and prime minister, so there was no problem of ensuring that the two leaders of the political executive worked in harmony. Thereafter, until his return to power in 1958, it was the premier, responsible to parliament and not the head of state who was in control of government. Clemenceau expressed the traditional Jacobin standpoint when he declared : 'There are two things in the world for which I have never seen any use : the prostate gland and the president of the republic'; but the extreme left-wing champions of the view that the president of the republic should be reduced to a figurehead did not get their way under the fourth republic. Vincent Auriol (president from 1947 to 1954) used his constitutional position to the full. Through his selection of the prime minister, his chairmanship of the council of ministers and his intervention particularly in foreign, defence, colonial and judicial matters, he preserved the régime from the communists and Gaullists, provoking the latter into criticizing him for exceeding his powers. Auriol's successor, Coty, legalized the transition from the fourth to the fifth republic by inviting de Gaulle to form a government in May 1958 and threatening parliament with his resignation if it did not approve of his nominee for the premiership. De Gaulle himself frequently used the threat of resignation to get his way, until April 1969 when it led to his downfall.

At the outset of the fifth republic, the allocation of responsibilities within the bicephalous executive was declared by Chaban-Delmas to be between the president's exclusive policy sectors of foreign, defence and post-colonial affairs, deriving from his supreme responsibility as protector of national integrity and independence on the one hand and the mass of mundane, domestic political concerns on the other. The latter were the subordinate responsibility of the prime minister who, in conjunction with the other ministers, prepared, coordinated and implemented policy decisions. The president intervened only when a matter impinged on his own sphere (for example the cost of defence) or had assumed crisis proportions (his refusal to devalue the currency in 1968). This distinction corresponded to the 'ontological one between the interests of France and the concerns of Frenchmen'.[1] It was reflected in the long tenure of office by Couve de Murville (foreign affairs), Messmer (defence) and Foccart (in charge of the general secretariat for African and Malagasy affairs) and the fact that matters within this exclusive presidential sector were not discussed in cabinet, which merely heard statements from those responsible for carrying out the president's orders.

However, although de Gaulle was content to reign rather than rule over large areas of public policy, he had made it clear that he did not accept any such limitation as was implied by the notion of an exclusive presidential sector. At his press conference of 31 January 1964 he asserted that 'the indivisible authority of the state is completely delegated to the president by the people who elected him' and in his *Memoirs of Hope* he contrasted 'the supreme office of head of state, responsible for the fate of the nation ... and the secondary role of the prime minister, whose function it is to run the executive, to direct current policy and to deal with day-to-day contingencies'. His claim to supreme and uncircumscribed power was defended by Prime Minister Pompidou in an assembly debate in April 1964 at which this interpretation of the constitution was challenged. Pompidou admitted that there had been an 'evolution' since 1958 in the role of the president (notably since the 1962 constitutional amendment providing for the direct election of the president by the people) but reminded the assembly that as early as 1946 de Gaulle had proclaimed at Bayeux that 'executive power should emanate from the head of state'. He presented the relationship of president and prime minister as one based upon 'a close identity of views', policy being decided jointly between them and then discussed with the ministers concerned and finally with the whole government.[2] When he succeeded to the presidency some five years later, Pompidou proceeded to assert in his own right the presidential pre-eminence he had attributed to de Gaulle. He preserved all the president's prerogatives. The relationship with the prime minister established by his predecessor, which as premier he had formulated as 'to the president of the republic the major policy decisions, to the prime minister the price of milk', is becoming accepted as normal.

After six months in which the new president, with characteristic caution, took a grip on the situation, Pompidou bluntly reasserted the primacy of presidential power : 'I have conducted the affairs of France with the help of the prime minister and government I appointed. My first decision was to devalue.' He went on to declare that he had 'accepted' a liberalization of ORTF, the national television and broadcasting corporation, implying that this was principally the responsibility of the prime minister. Thus, there are some matters in which the prime minister is given his head and can be made a scapegoat if, as in the case of ORTF reform, they lead to hostility from the UDR parliamentary party. From 1969–72 Chaban-Delmas accepted the Pompidou interpretation of their relationship, denying that his 1959 conception of a presidential sector was intended to be more than a provisional assessment of a situation that was bound to change. In January 1970 he put it thus :

Our constitution has an Achilles heel. This weakness can be summarized as the requirement of close, almost intimate relations between the president of the republic and the prime minister, between whom mutual trust must be complete. . . . [The latter's] subordination should not be rigorous or rigid. . . . They must work together, it being understood that the final decision lies with the head of state. . . .

The conservative parliamentary majority being mainly concerned with the preservation of the *status quo*, the policy embodied by President Pompidou, was hostile to the 'new society' programme of Chaban-Delmas, a title conflated from Kennedy's 'new frontier' and Johnson's 'great society'. Orthodox UDR suspicion of proposals derived from left-wing ex-collaborators and sympathizers of Mendès-France (whose minister Chaban-Delmas had been) forced the premier to shelter increasingly under the president's protection with a consequent increase in subservience. Speaking to the UDR national council on 27 June 1970, Chaban-Delmas acknowledged that it was the programme put forward by the successful presidential candidate, legitimized by popular vote, that authorized the president to 'give directives to the government, which was responsible for carrying them out'. On the same day, speaking at Strasbourg, President Pompidou lauded the fact that France was 'a strong state, where the authority of the president of the republic, elected by universal suffrage, guarantees the stability of governments and the unity of leadership'.

The extent to which the French public have tended increasingly to identify the president and the prime minister is shown by a study of the convergence in their popularity in the period 1959–71.[3] In a first phase (1959–63) the president's overwhelming superiority in public esteem was indicated by an average gap of 29 per cent between his standing and that of the prime minister. This was the period when de Gaulle was moving towards an Algerian settlement, followed by his triumph over parliamentary opposition to the direct election of the president. Once the spotlight shifted from ending military entanglements and institutional reform to domestic, social and economic policy, President de Gaulle's popularity declined. The spring 1963 sharp fall in presidential popularity followed the failure of de Gaulle's personal 'requisition order' to force striking miners to return to work. As the president rather than the prime minister was personally blamed for the unsuccessful and authoritarian conflict with the coal miners, the gap between their respective popularities fell from 32 per cent in autumn 1962 to 17 per cent in spring 1963. This second phase lasted from 1963 until spring 1967, via the 'desacralization' of de Gaulle at the December 1965 presidential election when he was forced to a second ballot. Over this period, the average gap in popularity between president and prime minister fell from 29 per cent to 16 per cent. The third phase does not begin, as one might expect, with the May 1968 events. The further decline in the president's popularity started in the latter half of 1967, the gap falling to 13·5 per cent. The very narrow victory in the March 1967 general election, the rise in unemployment and unpopular social security reforms were factors that foreshadowed the May 1968 events via a decline in the president's popularity. From autumn 1967 to spring 1969, when he resigned, de Gaulle's popularity remained at 55–6 per cent but the gap with the prime minister narrowed to 9·5 per cent in the year before his departure, owing to an improvement in the premier's standing. When former prime minister Pompidou became president in 1969, the gap at first narrowed further in 1970 to 3 per cent, the responsibility for the acts of the political executive being attributed almost equally to president and premier, but in 1972 the gap reopened following Prime Minister Chaban-Delmas' fall from public favour when it was revealed that he had managed to avoid paying income tax for a number of years. This reopening of the gap heralded the prime minister's dismissal in July 1972 and his replacement by Pierre Messmer.

The seal on the relationship between executive and executant, in which the prime minister is not the 'first among equals' but the first among the president's subordinates, was set by Chaban-Delmas at the start of his September 1970 campaign for re-election as deputy for Bordeaux. He recognized that since 1962 the prime minister was 'not on the same level as the president of the republic, simply because he has not been chosen by the people but designated by the head of state. As a result, he directs the government along the lines laid down by the president. . . . The head of state lays down the general lines of policy in all matters without exception.' President Pompidou was the captain, the prime minister being his first mate. 'There can be no real conflict between the president of the republic and the prime minister, for the solution would inevitably be a change of prime minister.' Such self-abasement is exaggerated, except where the prime minister is not in effective command of the parliamentary majority, which looks for leadership instead to the president. For France does not have an outright presidential form of government but a 'semi-presidential' system. This system requires three types of agreement to work successfully. First, there is the agreement between president and prime minister, on which we have dwelt. Secondly, there must be agreement between the assembly majority and the government, based upon the principle of government accountability to the assembly. The Pompidou government, having been censured in 1962, remained in office thanks to the prime minister's retention of the president's confidence and to the results of the general election of November 1962 in which a Gaullist majority was returned. The need for a president either to sacrifice his premier or to dissolve the assembly, with the danger that electoral defeat would result in his resignation, necessitates a third type of agreement, which has existed since 1962, between the president and the assembly majority. It was threatened by the narrow Gaullist electoral victory in March 1967, buttressed by the massive victory of June 1968.

There is a danger of overemphasizing the 'presidential' character of the fifth republic, just as there is a danger of exaggerating a trend towards party government, associated with the emergence of a majority party or stable majority coalition of parties in the assembly. A dominant president and a dominant party, respectively controlling the executive and the legislature, with the latter loyal to the former, are essential to the smooth working of a hybrid type of political régime like the fifth republic. The prime minister has a key role in maintaining agreement between the president, government and party coalition in the assembly. Pompidou dramatically reasserted presidential primacy in July 1972, dismissing Chaban-Delmas as prime minister only six weeks after he had received a massive vote of confidence (368 votes to 96) in the assembly. He was replaced by Messmer just after the end of the parliamentary session, Pompidou putting the legislature even more firmly in its subordinate place vis à vis the executive.

The president of the republic

The president's dominant position, from a constitutional standpoint, has been based upon eight traditional presidential powers (most of which have been transformed from formal into real powers) and seven prerogative powers, not requiring ministerial countersignature and made on his own nonaccountability (barring an unlikely impeachment for high treason). His prerogative powers are :

(1) The appointment and dismissal of the prime minister, dismissal not being stipulated in Article 8 but assumed by de Gaulle when he secured the resignation of both Debré in 1962 and Pompidou in 1968 when neither had been defeated in the assembly, and when he retained Pompidou in 1962 despite his

defeat. As president, Pompidou dismissed an undefeated Chaban-Delmas in 1972.

(2) The right to send messages to parliament, which was used in October 1962 to announce the referendum on the election of the president by universal suffrage.

(3) The right to call a referendum on nonconstitutional modifications of the organization of government or for the ratification of treaties, nominally at the 'request' of government or parliament. Article 11 was invoked illegally in 1962 and 1969 because the constitutional procedure (Article 89) gave either parliamentary chamber veto power.

(4) The right, with certain restrictions, to dissolve the assembly (Article 12) which was decisively used in 1962.

(5) The right to nominate one-third (including the president) of the constitutional council and to refer matters to it (which he has left to the prime minister). Pompidou served as one of de Gaulle's nominees to this judicial office from 1959–62, between his period as director of de Gaulle's personal staff (1958–9) and as prime minister (1962–8).

(6) He assumes emergency powers under Article 16 of the constitution when he considers that there is a serious and immediate threat to political institutions *or* national independence *or* territorial integrity *or* the implementation of the country's international commitments *and* the normal working of constitutional government and administration is upset. The president takes 'whatever measures are required by the circumstances' for as long as required to meet the crisis. Foreign or civil war are the circumstances envisaged and Article 16 was invoked during the April 1961 Algerian 'generals' insurrection'. The revolt collapsed within a week but de Gaulle retained emergency powers for over five months.

(7) On the basis of Article 15 designating the president head of the armed forces, a 1964 decree gave him the sole and awesome right to decide on the use of France's strategic nuclear force.

The traditional powers of the presidency, which de Gaulle and Pompidou have extended to the point of universal oversight of policy, are :

(1) The appointment and dismissal of ministers, nominally at the prime minister's request.

(2) The president is chairman of the council of ministers,

which is now the effective cabinet. Its decisions are prepared by three types of inter-ministerial meetings, the most important of which – interministerial councils – meet at the Elysée under Pompidou's chairmanship.

(3) He is commander-in-chief of the armed forces and presides over the national defence committee. Owing to the appointment of the assertive Debré as minister of defence, there was some shift of power away from the president in defence matters from 1969 until 1973 when Debré left office.

(4) The president promulgates statutes, signs all ordinances and some decrees and can refuse or delay signing provided the government is willing to accept responsibility for his actions.

(5) Under Article 52, the president is empowered to negotiate and ratify treaties and has directly controlled foreign policy and diplomatic dealings, notably in breaking off EEC negotiations with Britain in 1966, agreeing to resume them in 1970 and bringing them to a successful conclusion in 1971.

(6) The president appoints to a wide range of senior judicial, administrative and military posts, including councillors of state and judges, ambassadors and senior officers, prefects and rectors (who control the field services of the ministry of education), the divisional heads of ministries and the heads of certain nationalized industries. In some instances the appointments will be only formally by the president but in others his selection is personal.

(7) The president is 'protector of the independence of the judicial authority' (Article 64), appoints and presides over the higher council of the judiciary and exercises the right of reprieve. (The higher council advises the president on his use of the power to reprieve and on senior judicial appointments.) Pompidou as prime minister persuaded de Gaulle to reprieve General Jouhaud, sentenced to death for his part in the 1961 'generals' insurrection', by threatening to resign. As president, Pompidou reprieved all those sentenced to death until his November 1972 decision to send two men to the guillotine.

(8) The president can initiate an amendment to the constitution at the 'request' and with the countersignature of the prime minister. If he chooses, he can submit such an amendment, after it has been carried in both chambers, to a joint session of parliament where a three-fifths majority renders a referendum unnecessary. Constitutional amendments of parliamentary origin

must go to referendum, a procedure unpopular with parliamentarians and therefore unlikely to be used, leaving the initiative in the hands of the president.

To help the president discharge these wide-ranging responsibilities, there is a small president's office which has come to be regarded (with some measure of truth) as the real government. The official ministers are in charge of day-to-day administration and the preparation of proposals whose fate will ultimately be settled by the president, who relies on the privy counsel of his own personal collaborators. This has inspired the savage dictum that France, like Britain, has a 'shadow cabinet' but in her case it is in office. The president is assisted by a general secretariat and a personal military staff (the general secretariat for African and Malagasy affairs* having in 1969 been transferred to the ministry of overseas departments and territories, attached to the prime minister). The general secretariat (which has absorbed the president's personal staff) is the main instrument of presidential supervision and intervention in the ministries. Its members report directly to the president on their dealings with the personal staff of ministers or the ministers themselves. Through their silent presence at all interministerial meetings, at which the preparatory work for the cabinet is done, they collect and assess the information on which the president will make up his mind.

In 1969, President Pompidou's secretariat was headed by three long-standing collaborators, whom he saw daily; notably the secretary-general, Michel Jobert, who headed his personal staff from 1963–8 and Pierre Juillet, who has played a decisive role in sensitive political matters such as the selection of ministers and parliamentary candidates. They were seconded by a 'kitchen cabinet' of nine concerned with specific policy matters: two each for foreign affairs, finance and economic affairs, and for information services; one each for agriculture and housing, industry and equipment, and education. (In 1970 the president's press and information staff expanded to four, its head being concerned with general policy and broadcasting, whilst the others specialize in foreign policy, military policy and economic and social policy.) Briefed by them, President Pompidou maintained especially close contact with six key ministers: he received the prime minister

* See below, p. 251.

three times a week and set aside at least one hour a week for the ministers of finance, foreign affairs, defence, interior and education. Decisions are taken at these informal meetings or at working lunches and are subsequently ratified in the cabinet. The president's personal staff, who control access to him, are in a position to exercise great occult influence in a 'court politics' environment.

To ridicule the accusation that he had exercised presidential power in a 'personal' and 'solitary' fashion, de Gaulle, at his September 1965 press conference, reviewing his first seven-year term and preparing his re-election, gave a statistical summary of his numerous political contacts in the libidinous tone of Leporello's catalogue song in *Don Giovanni*. He had convened the cabinet 302 times and inter-ministerial councils 420 times. He had received the prime minister 505 times and other ministers two thousand times. He had seen the presidents of both chambers of parliament 78 times, the chairmen or *rapporteurs* of parliamentary committees or party groups over a hundred times and senior civil servants and interest group leaders some 1,500 times! Pompidou would certainly be able to give an even more impressive catalogue if his native discretion did not preclude it. He is unlikely, however, to emulate de Gaulle's record of securing nearly a hundred convictions for 'insulting the president of the republic' between 1959–66, whereas previous presidents seldom had so exaggerated a sense of their dignity that they took citizens to court to preserve it.*

The prime minister

Although after 1820 the premiership was occasionally separated from other governmental posts, it is only since 1934, when the nucleus of a prime minister's office was established at the Hôtel Matignon, that it has become customary for the premier to hold no other office. The transition lasted throughout the fourth republic, when four premiers were also foreign minister, three finance minister, two minister of defence and two minister of the interior. It is only since the inauguration of the fifth republic that the

---

* However in 1971 the French government suppressed the sale and circulation of a book by a former Congolese minister and instituted legal proceedings against the author and publisher for insulting a *foreign* head of state.

prime minister has clearly emerged as the minister who, under the president and as long as he retains his confidence, is in undisputed control of the government. However, he still has to reckon with the finance minister, who has two instruments which he can use to challenge the prime minister's control and overall coordination of government policy. The minister of finance must signify his approval of all laws and decrees involving public expenditure. Apart from outright objections, he can slow down the process of decision-making by taking plenty of time to examine each matter. Furthermore, he has a financial controller in each ministry who is responsible for supervising all acts involving public expenditure and for authorizing disbursements. If this official receives instructions from his parent ministry to slow down authorizations to spend, policy approved by the cabinet can be successfully modified. In 1952, Pinay refused Edgar Faure's offer of the finance portfolio on the grounds that the office should be held jointly with the premiership. When he became premier forty days later, he combined the two offices. His conflicts, as minister of finance in 1959, with the president and prime minister led to a paralysing period of 'work to rule' and to his replacement in January 1960. In 1962 the prime minister was strengthened by the transfer of the planning commissariat from the minister of finance. To reduce conflicts, it would also be necessary to transfer the key budget division from the finance ministry to the prime minister but this might be regarded as making him too powerful for the president's comfort.

The energetic Chaban-Delmas exerted himself to increase the power of the premiership which had suffered an eclipse under Couve de Murville, a passive and impassive tool of the presidential will. The main instruments of the prime minister's resolute effort from 1969 to 1972 to mobilize the government for the fulfilment of his 'new society' programme were the two parts of the prime minister's office : the general secretariat of the government and his personal staff. The former, inspired by the British cabinet office, has the vital task of coordinating the heterogeneous and proliferating responsibilities accumulated by the prime minister under successive republics. Its staff of about thirty prepares and circulates the agenda of the cabinet and the various inter-ministerial committees, together with relevant documents, for example draft Bills or decrees, preparing notes for the prime minister alone, informing him about the matters that are to be discussed. The secretary-general attends cabinet meetings and keeps its minutes, notifying all concerned of the decisions taken. Those who have to carry them out are required to send him copies of all their instructions so that his staff can follow up the implementation of cabinet decisions for the prime minister. All draft legislation and decrees must be sent to the secretariat who check that all concerned have been consulted. The secretary-general consults the council of state (and occasionally of the economic and social council) before sending the proposals to all ministers prior to the cabinet meeting which will examine them. The secretariat makes the necessary arrangements with parliament each week for discussion of the government's legislative programme and receives the Bills passed so that they can be signed by the president. It also arranges for written and oral parliamentary questions to be answered. Finally, it collects and publishes a large amount of information, a task fulfilled by the central office of information in Britain.

Under Chaban-Delmas, the prime minister acquired an unusually large and important personal staff, officially thirty-five in number, but President Pompidou 'joked' that with all its unofficial members it amounted to 150. (Debré had had a personal staff of up to thirty, whilst Pompidou when prime minister had been content with twenty-two.) As well as looking after his Bordeaux power base, such a staff was necessary to galvanize an immobilized France and bring about the great changes necessary 'to construct a new society' and 'a flexible, decentralized and desacralized state'. Chaban-Delmas announced these aims in his speech of 16 September 1969, presenting his government's general policy declaration which won him the substantial vote of confidence of 369 to 85 in the assembly. The size of the task was indicated by the fact that in January 1970 the prime minister declared that the attainment of the new society would be 'the work of a generation' and that to study fifty-two 'mutation points' he intended to create 'a hundred working parties embracing all the public and private, individual and collective activities that make up the nation's existence'. Unfortunately, the 1968 assembly had been elected to preserve order rather than to attack the immobilisms that had provoked disorder and President Pompidou, backed by the bulk of the UDR, successfully restrained the impetuous but imprecise reforming zeal of the prime minister. By July 1972 when he was dismissed, Chaban-Delmas' 'new society' programme had lost most of its credibility.

The prime minister's team of collaborators is headed by a brains trust of four. The director of his personal staff has general duties, notably liaison with the president's office, with which there is plenty of scope for conflict but with which close cooperation is essential. There are meetings each Wednesday afternoon (following the cabinet meeting) between him and the secretary-general of the presidency.

To ease the burden on the prime minister, whilst allowing him to retain an oversight of certain especially sensitive or residual areas of responsibility, he delegates a number of his functions to four junior and two senior ministers attached to him. The latter are the minister delegate for relations with parliament and the minister delegate for nature and the environment (created in January 1971). Among the junior ministers, the most important is the civil service minister who supervises the embryo civil service department created in 1945 to unify and manage the public service. In July 1972 he acquired the supervision of 'information services' which had been the direct responsibility of the prime minister following the abolition of the separate ministry of information as promised by Pompidou in the 1969 presidential election campaign. (When, in 1947, the ministry of information had previously been abolished, the premier had assumed responsibility for his functions through a junior minister.) The other three junior ministerial posts attached to the premier in the 1972 Messmer cabinet were the government spokesman, whose main task is to read the communiqué summarizing the cabinet discussions and decisions each Wednesday; the junior minister for overseas departments and territories; and the junior minister for youth and sport.

From time to time, functions are hived off. Thus in 1969 the new ministry of industrial and scientific development took over the prime minister's responsibility for the atomic energy commissariat and the delegacies for scientific and technical research (DGRST) and computers. The premier retains numerous other responsibilities, acquired thanks to innovating initiatives at particular times. These include the high committee for the defence and extension of the French language! Taken in conjunction with the prime minister's role as chairman of numerous interministerial committees, his need periodically to defend his government in parliament, to keep his party and coalition partners content, to placate irate interests and ensure conformity of his actions with the president's will, he is fully extended.

The government

When Chaban-Delmas was chosen as M. Pompidou's first prime minister in June 1969, he was asked 'to present proposals with a view to forming a government' which implies that the president intended to have the final word. The minister of finance, Giscard d'Estaing, confirmed at the time: 'It is the president of the republic who chooses the ministers and defines policy.' Although all thirty members of the Messmer government of July 1972 (twenty senior ministers and ten junior ministers) formed the cabinet, the Chaban-Delmas cabinet had excluded all but two of the junior ministers (whom it would be misleading to trans-literate as secretaries of state). The two privileged junior ministers were the government spokesman and the minister of state for the budget, who needed to be present throughout because of the financial implications of most matters discussed. The increased size of the 1973 Messmer government (twenty-two senior and sixteen junior ministers) has not denied junior ministers the prestige of attending cabinet meetings, although most of the real business is transacted elsewhere.

How does one become a minister and achieve preferment under the fifth republic? Traditionally, it was parliament that provided the source of recruitment but in the name of the separation of powers, a principle characteristic of American presidentialism, Article 23 of the constitution renders 'incompatible' simultaneous membership of the executive and the legislature, although ministers remain responsible to the assembly in accordance with British parliamentarism. The intention was to reduce the incentive to government instability attributed to deputies out of office seeking to become ministers so that they could attain the prized life long status of ex-minister. This explanation of government instability under the fourth republic has been seriously undermined but it was a popular view when the constitution was drafted. However, insofar as government instability was due to the resignation of ministers in the cabinet, the current arrangements were intended also to make it more difficult for ministers to remain active in politics after resignation because they could not retire to the backbenches unless they did so within a month of being appointed to office. Initially it seemed that parliamentarians would be replaced by 'non-political' super-bureaucrats and it is certainly the case that many key posts have been held by career officials. However, there was a steady increase in the number of ministers sitting in parliament at the time they acquired office; 60 per cent in the Debré government (1959–62); increasing from 64 per cent to 83 per cent in the four Pompidou governments (1962–8); reaching 97 per cent in the Couve de Murville government (1968–9)[4] and 100 per cent in the Chaban-Delmas and Messmer governments.* However, in cases like those of Couve de Murville and Ortoli, it was as officials that they established their claim to office. They only acquired a parliamentary seat as a gesture to the traditional electoral basis of ministerial legitimacy.

Although constitutionally compelled to resign their parliamentary seats in favour of their substitutes, ministers have successfully circumvented the spirit of the incompatibility rule. They seek re-election at every opportunity, even when it is clear that they will not themselves occupy the seat because they will be ministers. They maintain close contact with their constituencies, openly boasting of the advantages they can procure for their constituents thanks to membership of the government. Their replacement generally resigns to enable them to be re-elected to parliament immediately should they lose office, as in the cases of Edgar Faure and Pierre Messmer, but not in the case of Couve de Murville in 1969. Finally, when a substitute has died, the minister has stood at the by-election and then handed the seat over to his new replacement, as in the cases of Roger Frey in 1965 and Chaban-Delmas in 1970. The link between legislature and executive has proved too difficult to sever and the fifth republic practice has marked a reversion to a more parliamentary type of relationship based upon the interpenetration of government and parliament. However, ministers seldom attend parliamentary debates except to preserve their Bills and their share of the budget more or less unscathed. It is recognized that the real threat to

* Three members of the 1973 Messmer government were non-parliamentarians.

the government comes, in France as in Britain, not from parliament but from the people at the next general election.

Apart from the distinction between senior and junior ministers, there is undoubtedly a 'pecking order' distinguishing the major ministries: finance, foreign affairs, defence, interior and justice from the minor ministries: health, transport, cultural affairs, postal services, ex-servicemen and even labour, which tend to be regarded as 'stop-gaps' when making cabinet appointments. In between are the major spending ministries: education, agriculture, industrial and scientific development, regional planning, public works and housing, together with the minister for relations with parliament. The personal political weight of each office-holder is important, particularly because it is a tripartite coalition government. (The parties represented correspond to the coalition which Pompidou attempted when he first became prime minister in 1962. It only survived for a month owing to the resignation of the centrist ministers following de Gaulle's attack on European federalism.) Table 15 shows the changing party complexion and increase in the size of the government through a growth in the number of junior ministers in the first four governments following the May 1968 crisis and a decline in the 1972 Messmer government. From a two-party Pompidou coalition in 1968, in which nearly a quarter of the ministers had not been elected to parliament, the enlarged Couve de Murville government eliminated all non-parliamentarians except Malraux, the UDR claiming twenty-six out of thirty-one posts. The Chaban-Delmas government of 1969 marked the elimination of the non-parliamentarian element, the inclusion of three CDP ministers in cabinet posts, and the expansion of the government thanks to a

Table 15
The Political Structure of French Governments, 1968–72

Party	Pompidou 31 May 1968 Minister	Junior Minister	Couve de Murville 12 July 1968 Minister	Junior Minister	Chaban-Delmas 22 June 1969 Minister	Junior Minister	Chaban-Delmas 7 January 1971 Minister	Junior Minister	Messmer 7 July 1972 Minister	Junior Minister
UDR	15	4	15	11	12	17	14	17	14	8
Independent republican	3	—	3	1	4	3	4	3	3	2
CDP	—	—	—	—	3	—	3	—	3	—
Non-parliamentarians	5	2	1	—	—	—	—	—	—	—
Total	23	6	19	12	19	20	21	20	20	10

substantial increase in junior posts allocated to the UDR. The January 1971 reshuffle involved a strengthening of UDR representation at the cabinet level, while the July 1972 Messmer government halved the number of junior posts while preserving the party balance within the coalition. It should be noted in passing how much smaller French governments are than British governments.

Most of the important offices were held in 1972 by more or less prominent fourth republic politicians: Maurice Schumann (foreign minister), Edgar Faure (social affairs), René Pleven (justice), Raymond Marcellin (interior). However, they adapted themselves to the style of the fifth republic and in the cabinet only ex-prime minister Debré intervened on almost all matters. Most of the other ministers confined themselves to matters concerning their department. If they wished to have a say on other issues, they tended to speak privately to the president of the republic who is recognized as the supreme arbiter. Although a minister's advancement will be influenced by his standing with his colleagues, with his senior civil servants, with deputies and senators, even with the press, he will receive his crucial first appointment and be promoted primarily on the strength of his standing with the president. Whilst ministers are collectively responsible to parliament, they are personally responsible to the president. The stability of government has been combined with frequent changes of minister (and policy) in certain sensitive departments like education. The fundamental ambiguity of the fifth republic executive pervades all: the president decides but ministers are held responsible.

Attempts to assess the mass public's perception and attitude towards the distribution of policy-making power are confused by the attempt to distinguish the presidency from the government, when, as we have seen, there is not duality but unity of authority within the executive. Nevertheless, table 16 indicates a public desire for a shift of power within the executive from the president to the government and from both to parliament. While the government is placed first in all policy fields, it is only in foreign and economic policy that it is decisively ahead of parliament. This indicates that there is still public support for a more traditional, parliamentary-style allocation of roles between the executive and the legislature.

Table 16
Public Opinion on the Distribution of Policy-Making Power in France(%)*

(i) At present, who mainly decides and who should decide major policy issues?

	Does	*Should*
Government	40	36
President of the republic	38	24
Parliament	13	33
No reply	9	7

(ii) Who should take the decisions in the following fields?

	Economic Problems	*Justice*	*Foreign Policy*	*Industrial and Social Problems*
President	15	23	25	9
Government	49	35	51	43
Parliament	30	33	17	43
No reply	6	9	7	5

* Based on a SOFRES poll published in *Le Figaro*, 10 November 1969, p. 6.

Interministerial coordination

The complexities of modern government require coordination between the divisions of ministries, between ministries and with the non-governmental 'partners' of the administration, before a matter is ready to be dealt with by the cabinet. The administrative 'in-fighting', the patience, cunning and determination necessary to secure a minimum of cooperation and agreement even within ministries that tend to be agglomerations of introverted specialist divisions, each jealously protecting its own assigned area of responsibility, results in such extreme compartmentalization that it is vital to bring all concerned round a table to achieve a reconciliation of rivalries that threaten to paralyse action. The logic of an administrative system based on the watertight separation of sub-systems, pursuing their own particular policies up to the point where they need the sanction of a higher authority, requires the preparatory work to be done as secretively as possible. To be in a strong bargaining position when the time comes for interministerial negotiations, the scheme should be presented in a fully worked-out form. At this highly politicized level, decisions will not necessarily be made on the merits of the case but in relation to the political weight, expertise and support that the protagonists can muster.

After the second world war France attempted to imitate the British system of semi-permanent cabinet committees to fulfil the function of coordinating policy preparation prior to consideration by the government as a whole and by the council of ministers. However, with the exception of the national defence committee, this arrangement did not survive under the unstable coalition governments of the fourth republic. Although there are three permanent committees with a determinate membership and a permanent secretariat (regional planning and development, scientific and technical research and occupational training) a more flexible system of *ad hoc* interministerial meetings quickly developed. They are basically of three types. First, there are *interdepartmental committees* composed of senior civil servants, held at the prime minister's residence at Matignon, with a member of the prime minister's personal staff as chairman. These inter-departmental meetings are organized and staffed by the general secretariat of the government which receives the proposals to be discussed from the sponsor-ministry's interministerial relations section. It circulates them to the ministries concerned. Before the meeting, each ministry prepares its case carefully. It will be represented by a member of the minister's personal staff, accompanied perhaps by senior officials and experts. The representatives of the minister of finance (though the budget and treasury division spokesmen are not necessarily in agreement) have great influence, with power to brake but not veto proposals. The meeting is concluded by the prime minister's representative summarizing the discussion and if agreement cannot be reached, transmitting the proposals for decision at the *interministerial committee* level.

Here it is the prime minister himself who is usually in the chair. Although senior civil servants may attend, they speak only when invited to do so by ministers who will have received an account of the discussions in the interdepartmental committee. The interventionist Michel Debré took a leading part in developing the interministerial committee as the premier's main instrument for resolving disputes and working out proposals that substituted a governmental for a departmental viewpoint on any given problem. One or two members of the president's staff are present to report to him on the proceedings. If agreement is not reached or if the president so decides, an *interministerial council* is summoned. This is the most exclusive of coordinating bodies, usually consisting of a few senior ministers who meet at the Elysée under the chairmanship of the president, although very senior officials such as the planning commissioner are sometimes in attendance. President Pompidou has particularly developed this method of centralizing decision-making power in his own hands. Under de Gaulle, the cabinet functioned as his privy council; under Pompidou, most issues have been settled before the cabinet meets. The ministers and their personal staff spend a great deal of time at such interministerial meetings. In an important department it may amount to more than a day each week attending and the same amount of time preparing for such meetings. Such is the cost of trying to secure that the large and cumbersome governmental apparatus works with a minimum of cohesion.

The techno-bureaucratic executive

At the peak of the interministerial coordination pyramid is located the small informal nucleus of power at the highest levels of the French state. However, this nucleus of decision-makers needs the support and assistance of an outer circle of senior officials and specialists whose minimal function is to prepare the data on the basis of which the fundamental choices are made. They devise ways of carrying policy choices out and may actually decide many issues – not necessarily unimportant ones – which the overburdened political executive explicitly or by omission delegates to them. There is a peculiarly close connection in France between the suffrage-made political leaders and the school-made techno-bureaucrats, who by their training and experience are indispensable collaborators in administering things and governing men. Both the political and techno-bureaucratic executives have increased their power under the fifth republic at the expense of the assembly but it is not always clear where the influence of the one ends and that of the other begins.

The concept of techno-bureaucracy represents a conflation of the traditional notion of a body of officials characterized by hierarchy, permanence, professionalism and *esprit de corps* within a disciplined and centralized organization, and a more recent emphasis upon the specialist skill of the expert who has acquired knowledge necessary to making and carrying out political decisions. Both the bureaucrat and the technocrat claim to exercise power in a rational way; but whereas the bureaucrat is primarily a routine administrator, relying upon conventional wisdom to 'muddle through' by adjusting conflicting interests and enforcing rules in an impersonal manner, the technocrat seeks systematic innovation calculated to increase efficiency, based on assessments of the future rather than loyalty to the past. The technocrat purports to reduce partisan political conflicts to the serene scientific dimensions of a series of equations. Presented in this caricature form, it is difficult to see how two such contrasting 'ideal types' can be combined. Although the French administrative élite does not represent a complete fusion between bureaucrat and technocrat, the prestige acquired along with specialist knowledge in training, following on the close ties born of a common social and educational background, culminating in an organization into exclusive corps, has created a distinctive type of public official who commands both specialist skills and a general, all-purpose competence. Far from being content to apply rules rigidly, as is the custom of the mass of civil servants, the techno-bureaucrats offer informed advice and leadership without which the political executive would be unable to induce the file-bound officials to undertake new tasks using new methods. Some ministers have rejected both the bureaucratic and technocratic approach as equally statist and preached reliance upon the economic rationality of the market. However, this goes so much against tradition that despite the revival of economic liberalism in France, attempts to end what a former minister has dubbed 'administrative totalitarianism' have so far proved ineffective.

Bureaucrats tend to stress a political rationality based upon the attainment of consensus through a piecemeal and incremental process of mutual adjustment. Short-term improvisation rather than medium and long-range planning predominate. By contrast with this prosaic approach, there is a 'heroic model of policy-making'. Aims are explicitly stated and the means to implement them are systematically tested by the criterion of efficiency. The assumption is that the best solution can be identified by technical calculations rather than through political argument.[5] Alongside the transition from a legislature-centred fourth republic to an executive-centred fifth republic, there has been a shift in emphasis within the higher administration from the consensus norms of political rationality to the efficiency norms of economic rationality. However, owing to the difficulty of reorganizing the traditional administration, the new technocratic norms have found expression in entrepreneurial, *ad hoc*, 'parallel' or 'missionary' agencies which seek to circumvent obstruction by the ministries. Though prototypes of such bodies were created under the fourth republic, notably the planning commissariat and the atomic energy commissariat,* they became much more common under the fifth republic. Their piecemeal character, separate agencies being created to deal with each new problem, led to profoundly irrational results because it was not possible to compare the costs and benefits of such intervention with alternatives. Thus, the interministerial mission for the development of tourism in Languedoc-Roussillon, launched in 1963 as part of the Gaullist strategy for shaking the left-wing hold over the area and placed under the aegis of Debré's closest collaborator and director of the national school of administration, Pierre Racine, monopolized the public funds available to the neglect of other parts of France. Helped by the regional planning delegacy to overcome the finance ministry's reluctance to forgo the usual budgetary and accounting constraints, an on-the-spot team of five senior officials was able to coordinate a variety of operations with the flexibility essential to a commercial operation, demonstrating that challenging new governmental responsibilities need not be abandoned to joint public-private enterprises. We have already referred to the regional application of this conception of 'missionary' rather than 'managerial' administration as advocated by an official turned politician, Pisani.† He frankly accepted that the pretence of administrative neutrality would have to be sacrificed to the overt 'direct dependence upon the government from whom derive the necessary means and authority to act outside the limits of common law'.[6]

The tendency of the techno-bureaucrat partially to supersede the politician and the civil servant is reflected in each minister's personal staff (usually from ten to twenty in size), who provide the crucial link between the political and administrative executive, playing a part corresponding to that of both junior ministers

* Discussed in chapters 6 and 8 respectively.
† See above, p. 39.

and permanent secretaries in Britain. The absence of permanent secretaries from most French ministries means that the task of coordinating and directing the work of the various divisions has to be undertaken by the minister's *cabinet*. Under the third republic, the minister's personal staff consisted of young, ambitious amateurs who were concerned primarily with public relations and with seeing that the civil servants were faithfully carrying out ministerial policy. During the fourth republic a few technically qualified people upon whose political support the minister could rely were added. They enabled the minister to acquire the knowledge to be on equal terms with his civil servants.

Under the fifth republic, the fact that decision-making has become a more exclusively executive matter has meant that the key members of the minister's staff are not the parliamentary attachés but the specialist aides borrowed from the civil service who are concerned with preparing, coordinating and supervising the implementation of policy. Consequently, they work closely with the offices of the president and the prime minister and other ministerial staffs.* The impetus to reform has frequently been secretively originated by the minister's personal staff. They are then faced with the problem of securing the support or acquiescence of other parts of the executive, of the official and unofficial representative bodies and of the mass public. It is at this point, where the products of competitive examination and competitive election may come into conflict, that the senior officials' conviction that their rationality is equated with the public interest is exposed to the most searching test.

Public servants or corporate masters?

After a 1930s preoccupation with domination by finance capitalism in the shape of the 'two hundred families' who elected the court of the Bank of France and a 1950s concern with rule from the 'house without windows' or government by assembly, the 1960s were characterized by a dual concern with personal rule by the president and by an interlocking directorate of senior civil servants. Behind the impressive figure of de Gaulle, the heirs to a secular tradition of administrative power were deemed to have

* On ministers' personal staffs, see below, p. 110-13.

resurrected their dominance of a century earlier in the administrative empire of Louis Napoleon. Whilst the president as head of the political executive personified the state, it was the military, administrative and judicial agents of the executive rather than the people's representatives, the deputies, who were most closely identified with the state. This is reflected in a 1970 opinion poll, which sets out (in order of preference) the extent to which various institutions are conceived as forming part of the French state (see table 17).

Table 17
What Are the Constituent Elements of the French State? (%)*

Institution	Yes, Without Reservation	Sub- stantially	A Little	Not At All	Don't Know
President of the republic	80	15	3	1	1
Government	74	18	5	1	2
Army	67	21	9	2	1
Ministries	65	19	12	1	3
Prefects	59	26	11	2	2
Judiciary	52	25	17	4	2
Deputies	48	26	19	4	3

* Source: adapted from SOFRES poll published in *Les Français et l'Etat*, spring 1970, p. 8.

The some five thousand senior civil servants who occupy the most important administrative posts are not at odds with the general public when they consider themselves the most permanent manifestation of public power and the best protectors of the public interest. However, because the legitimacy of authority is conferred by universal suffrage, the senior civil service can only maintain the routine working of the political system in the absence of political direction. They can preserve continuity but they cannot implement change. This was clear from the paralysis, as far as important innovations were concerned, during the periods of governmental crisis under the fourth republic. It also partially explains the enthusiasm of many senior civil servants for the fifth republic. It has enabled them to act within a more secure political framework.

However, if the national assembly is castigated as a 'house without windows' the administration has also been criticized as an impersonal, Paris-centred élite, superimposed upon field services that are in direct contact with the problems but are denied the discretion to adapt the rules. This self-reinforcing bureaucratic system is based upon a vicious circle in which poor communication between the administration and the administered does not lead to corrective action because of the lack of an efficient feedback process. The field services, who have the necessary information, cannot decide. Their hierarchical superiors in Paris could decide but lack the necessary information, control over which enables the field services to preserve a measure of autonomy. The result is a dysfunctional recourse to centralization to protect the administration from its clientèle, coupled with comprehensive regulation. Bureaucratic power is exerted by making general standardized rules and having the discretion to ignore or adapt them in particular cases, such discretion being generally reserved to the senior officials at the centre. French administration is characterized by being rule-bound in principle but swamped by exceptions in practice. This is because rule enforcement becomes a bargaining counter when applied in particular cases. Four-fifths of the French public feel both that they are treated by civil servants as anonymous cases, without personal consideration and that everyone is not treated equally. Some are singled out for favouritism. Taxation provides an excellent example of the accuracy of this public sense of official unfairness. The Rueff Committee asserted in 1958 that 'French finance is honeycombed with special exceptions and exemptions. The burgeoning of exemptions results from the surrender of public authorities to pressures from private interests, always in the guise of the public interest.'[7] More recently, the general legal prohibition of sea pollution is qualified by numerous prefectoral exemptions in particular instances. To secure conformity by those of the administered who can resist the rules, officials may be prepared to make an exception because the prime aim of a bureaucratic system is the avoidance of conflict.

When the equilibrium is disturbed and conflicts generate irresistible pressures to change, decisions are transferred up the hierarchy to those who alone have the necessary authority to make the adjustments in an excessively rigid system. However, such changes generally come as a result of a crisis. When made, they must apply everywhere because of the centralized nature of the bureaucratic system. The crisis brings into play the agents of change who are the indispensable mediators between the administered and the administrators in a situation where the old rules are no longer effective. The agents of change *par excellence* are those senior civil servants who belong to the mobile, meritocratic élites known as the *grands corps*. Their 'old boy network' re-establishes face-to-face dealings, at the highest level, as a corrective to the compartmentalized character of French administration. (For example, as many as nineteen separate sub-divisions within five divisions of the finance ministry dealt with agriculture in 1972.) It is at this level that the indispensable interdepartmental coordination takes place. Disturbing the sluggishness verging on paralysis into which a highly bureaucratized system all too easily subsides is the special task of these mandarins. They are expected to restore internal communications so that the various parts of the administration can be united and the public service given impetus as well as cohesion. Their *esprit de corps* is dedicated to the attainment of what they conceive to be the public interest. Imparting substance to this protean concept is regarded as their particular if not their exclusive prerogative; a propensity that the fifth republic's transfer of power from legislature to executive and from law to regulation has exacerbated.

The French civil service, divided into four general or 'horizontal' classes, labelled A, B, C and D, might at first sight seem to correspond to the now superseded British distinction between administrative, executive, clerical and messengerial classes. It is similarly related to educational differences and corresponds to distinctions of social class. The most significant divergence is that the A grade, which constitutes 25 per cent of the total civil service, covers not merely the policy work undertaken by the old British administrative class but also the managerial work of the higher executive posts and university and secondary school *professeurs*. The French equivalent of the administrative class consists of the *grands corps* and the corps of civil administrators. The latter was modelled on its British counterpart after the second world war but in practice was subordinate to the entrenched, peculiarly French *grands corps*.

Table 18 shows the relative size of the staffs of the major French ministries in 1970 alongside the situation in 1914 to provide some historical perspective on their growth in the twentieth century.

Table 18
The Staffing of French Central Government Departments, 1970

Department	Class A	Class B	Class C and D	Total 1970	Total 1914
Agriculture	10,525	4,424	3,982	18,931	8,400
Cultural affairs	1,159	683	3,552	5,394	—
Defence*	1,427	10,013	24,442	35,882	—
Economic affairs and finance	30,555	30,566	71,689	132,810	73,100
Education	216,079¶	354,289	93,939	664,307	150,100
Ex-servicemen	405	1,021	5,839	7,265	—
Foreign affairs	1,607	533	790	2,930	1,100
Industry	1,242	493	1,347	3,082	900
Interior†	5,590	4,984	13,601	24,175	1,800
Justice‡	6,159	4,977	5,531	16,667	14,900
Labour and health	3,712	5,842	9,299	18,853	1,500
Postal service	28,693	61,455	202,453	292,601	122,800
Prime minister	12,428	7,446	2,300	22,174	—
Public works and housing	7,231	7,509	45,830	60,570	21,400
Transport	3,484	5,031	2,987	11,502	—
Miscellaneous	318	157	295	770	1,300
All departments §	330,614	499,423	487,876	1,317,913	468,500

* Not including 312,136 civil and military defence personnel.
† Not including 92,359 Paris police attached to the ministry of the interior.
‡ Not including 8,196 prison officers attached to the ministry of justice.
§ Also excluded are 181,000 temporary and trainee staff.
¶ Includes secondary school *professeurs* as well as university teachers.

What emerges very clearly is the dominant place occupied by the ministry of education and the postal service, which between them accounted for 58·3 per cent of the total in 1914 and 72·6 per cent of the total in 1970. The large number of teachers (who in Britain are not employed by the central government) inflates the proportion of the French civil service in the A and B classes and renders comparisons with Britain misleading. On the other hand the exclusion of non-administrative defence personnel, Paris police, prison officers and all temporary and trainee staff should be noted. Bearing all this in mind, the size of the ministry of economic affairs and finance (with its substantial staff concerned with taxation) is particularly impressive. On the other hand, an important ministry like foreign affairs can remain extremely small, although over half its staff is in the A class. The size of the ministry of agriculture is a reflection of the economic and political importance of rural France and of the services provided for the farmers. It can be contrasted with the ex-ministry of industry, which is a small and inadequate reflection of France's industrial ambitions. However, the prestigious corps of mining engineers is associated with the renamed ministry of industrial and scientific development, and through its ramifications it helps to give this ministry such influence as it has in the administrative system.

Much more important than the classification into four general grades is the 'vertical' division into some 1,200 corps, which usually correspond to functions within particular ministries rather than the acquisition of specialist qualifications. At the summit of this vertical hierarchy and superimposed on the horizontal classes are the *grands corps*. Their main channels of recruitment are by competitive examination. The *Ecole Nationale d'Administration* (ENA) has a legal, diplomatic and economic emphasis. The engineers are trained at the *Ecole Polytechnique* (known familiarly as 'X') and its two principal extensions, the *Ecole Nationale des Mines* and the *Ecole Nationale des Ponts et Chaussées*. Established as recently as 1945, the ENA was consciously modelled on the eighteenth-century, specialist élite school tradition of the mining and road engineers schools (established in 1747) and *Polytechnique* (established after the revolution in 1794, although Napoleon subsequently put its students into uniform, like his own creation the prefects). It represented a triumph for those who wanted to extend to the whole senior civil service the prestige and independence of the *grands corps* by making the ENA an élite school excluded from the relatively egalitarian university system. Warnings against the establishment of a techno-bureaucratic caste – 'a corps of senior civil servants who would decide public business in an almost sovereign fashion, sheltered from initiatives by the people'[8] – were discounted.

France has for centuries been convinced that the state should train its own specialists outside the ordinary university system, regarded as too theoretical in its educational emphasis. Governments have preferred to rely on specialist post-entry training, stressing practical experience applied to the tasks of the public service, provided under their own control. This unique tradition of technocratic training was extended from the engineering schools to the recruitment and training of the other *grands corps* through the ENA. Together, the ENA and the engineering schools are the source of administrative leaders, the graduates of the former being infused with some of the technocratic characteristics of the latter. Both provide a general as well as a specialist training, although there is a more 'generalist' economic and legal emphasis at the ENA. This valuable combination of administrative and technical expertise, in conjunction with highly selective post-entry training, increases *esprit de corps*, a source both of cohesion and of rivalry. The ENA has an annual output of approximately one hundred, *Ponts et Chaussées* of about sixty. The close ties developed in the years at these élite institutions prove invaluable, not merely in advancing the career of the individual senior civil servant but in overcoming the rigid compartmentalism of French administration. Neither the American partisan colonization of the top echelons of the civil service through the nineteenth-century 'spoils system' and the twentieth-century transplants from business (republicans) and universities (democrats), nor the British reliance upon unassertive and non-partisan amateurs selected from among the academically successful, would appear to have proved a match for their French counterparts. However, the distrust of the school-made technocrat has been fostered by the fact that expertise provides no immunity from error. Rather, it may increase both the self-assurance of the decision-maker and the magnitude of the miscalculations. Each period has its equivalent of the French Panama Canal fiasco and associated political scandals, which may have prompted the remark of a famous banker: 'There are three ways to ruin: gambling, women and engineers. The first two are more agreeable, but the last is more certain.'

The nursery from which the ENA recruits the overwhelming majority of the future administrative élite is the Paris *Institut d'Etudes Politiques* (known familiarly as *'Sciences Po'* after its forerunner). The founder of the *Ecole libre des Sciences Politiques* wrote in 1871 that it was vital to reinforce the bureaucratic bulwark against the pressures of democracy which he foresaw: '. . . democracy cannot be halted. The higher classes . . . can only maintain their political dominance by invoking the right of the most capable.'[9] A century later we can see that the validity of Boutmy's warning that the old élite of birth and wealth should be bolstered by merit has been recognized and implemented. Although recruitment has extended to the lower-middle class, the successful ENA candidates (like those of the other *grandes écoles*) come predominantly from children of the upper-middle class, notably the senior civil servants, senior private sector executives and the liberal professions. The élitist link between *grandes écoles* and *grands corps* is only an extreme case of France's unequal educational opportunity being reflected in the Parisian upper-class origins of the senior civil service. Despite the rhetoric about 'democratizing' recruitment, little progress has been made. This is perhaps because it was never seriously intended by the privileged 'caste' who are the beneficiaries of the system, content to co-opt to a self-perpetuating meritocracy. Such co-option is facilitated by the large part played in ENA training by senior civil servants.

Another aim of the 1945 reform establishing the ENA was to unify recruitment to the senior civil service and increase mobility within it. Not merely was the ENA to replace the separate recruitment to the non-engineering *grands corps* but a new interdepartmental corps of civil administrators, attached to the prime minister's office, was intended to contain the pretensions of the traditional *grands corps* to occupy the top posts throughout the civil service. However, in allowing the successful ENA candidates to choose which corps they would join according to their examination rank, the custom developed that the fourteen best candidates went to the high-prestige *grands corps*, thereby fortifying the traditional divisions within the civil service and preventing the emergence of a unified administrative class. A 'pecking order' prevails, the attractive corps being those of the inspectorate of finance,* linked with the ministry of finance, the administrative lawyers of the *Conseil d'Etat*, the public accountants of the *Cour des Comptes*, the diplomatic corps associated with the ministry of foreign affairs and the prefectoral corps attached to the ministry of the interior. The civil administrators corps (which absorbs two-thirds of the ENA output as well as most recruits from within the civil service) is the source from which are first filled senior posts in the high prestige ministries (finance, foreign affairs, interior) with those at the bottom of the examination list going to the 'less eligible' ministries such as labour and health. They also staff the less elevated posts in the more attractive ministries, attraction being measured partly by the disparity in earnings between similar posts in different ministries. Out of an optimum total of 1,048 civil

---

* See below, p. 159.

administrators, the target allocation between ministries gives the lion's share to the ministry of economic affairs and finance (450), with the ministries of the interior and industry being the only others entitled to over a hundred civil administrators. Because certain ministries were notoriously 'under-administered', in the sense that they had been shunned by the best ENA graduates, the prime minister announced in September 1969 that from 1970 all the *grands corps* ENA graduates would have to spend their first year at either the ministries of education, health or labour. (It is particularly important that the education ministry, which is the largest spender of public money, should have an injection of talent.) However, the spectacular Chaban-Delmas decision, at best a palliative, was abandoned after only a year's trial, testimony to the civil service capacity to resist unpalatable change. However, two-thirds of the 1972 graduates voluntarily chose to shun the *grands corps*. If this gesture is repeated in subsequent years, an important step will have been taken towards a united higher civil service. Since 1972 ENA graduates are required to spend their first four years in the ministry to which they are initially appointed.

Civil administrators generally remain immobilized for most of their career in a single ministry. Members of the *grands corps* prior to moving out of the civil service into senior managerial posts in a public or private corporation through the practice known as *pantouflage*, or directly into politics, occupy many of the top posts in the key central departments, notably in the prime minister's office and the ministry of finance. The dominance of Paris and of the ministry of finance is reflected in the fact that in 1968, out of some 1,500 ENA graduates in the public service, 1,300 were Paris-based and 700 were attached to the ministry of finance, an administrative bastion of the one and indivisible republic, together with the ministry of the interior. A staging post for a finance inspector or councillor of state to a top post in a ministry will be membership of a *cabinet ministériel,* the personal staff attached to each minister. This staff, situated at the point where administration and politics are at their most inextricable, provides a vital link between the political and administrative executive.

French ministries are compartmentalized aggregations of divisions which are themselves confederations of autonomous *bureaux.* The lack of coordination between and within the various divisions is due to the jealous regard for their independence both of each senior civil servant, and of the minister. The interposition of a secretary-general, an official head of each ministry on the pattern of the British permanent secretary, has therefore been avoided (except at the ministry of foreign affairs), ministers preferring the head of each division to be directly responsible to them. The minister can thereby more effectively retain political control over the choice of priorities, the director of his *cabinet* becoming the *de facto* source of administrative coordination within the ministry. Usually, there are weekly meetings between the heads of all the ministry's divisions and the minister, either accompanied by all his staff or simply by the director. The director is at the focal point of the ministerial communications system. He receives all documents to be signed by his minister, selecting those he will refer to the minister because of their political importance and dealing with the remainder himself. Instructions to officials from the director are deemed to come from the minister himself. As well as coordination within the ministry, the director of the minister's personal staff is also responsible for preparatory coordination between ministries at the highest level. When the minister cannot attend an interministerial meeting, he is usually replaced by the director of his *cabinet*. On each Tuesday, preceding the cabinet meeting on Wednesday, the directors of the personal staffs of all ministers meet at Matignon to prepare the ground.

The overwhelming majority (90 per cent) of the 383 official members* of ministers' personal staffs in 1971 were recruited from the senior civil service. This is indicative of the fact that they are more a parallel hierarchy to the heads of the ministry's divisions than substitutes for the parliamentary secretaries and parliamentary private secretaries which abound in the British system. It no doubt reflects an acknowledgement of the greater need in France to ensure bureaucratic accountability to ministers than ministerial accountability to parliament. Another advantage of recruiting civil servants is that they can continue to draw their pay although on leave from their previous posts. However, this salary will be supplemented, perhaps out of secret 'special funds' provided by the prime minister. About three-quarters of the most important posts of director and specialist adviser are recruited from among the *grands corps*, notably the administrative lawyers

* This figure is exclusive of the numberless 'unofficial' and 'clandestine' members.

of the council of state and the economic experts of the finance inspectorate. Members of the prefectoral corps generally occupy half the posts of *chefs de cabinet* (not to be confused with the *directeurs de cabinet*), who are primarily responsible for supervising relations between the minister and his ex (and future) constituents, parliament and the press, political work in which they are well experienced. Parliamentary attachés (whom we have already encountered*) keep the minister informed about the state of parliamentary business and when his presence is required. They also keep an eye on the activities of relevant standing committees and during the parliamentary recesses they share in the task of answering the voluminous correspondence from deputies and senators.

The bulk of the personal staff consist of specialist advisers and *chargés de mission* who have been given responsibility for special areas of the ministry's work. They discharge four main functions. First, they prepare memoranda for the minister on matters to be considered in cabinet, their role ranging from almost pure research to actual decision-making as far as the ministry's policy is concerned. Second, they coordinate the work of the ministry in their field and conduct its relations with other ministries, involving numerous meetings with the members of other ministers' staffs. They deal with the interest groups who seek to influence the ministry or whose support the ministry wishes to mobilize on behalf of its policy. They also play an important part in dealing with the hundreds of thousands of requests, from those of ministerial colleagues down to those of local notables seeking special favours, which often amount to no more than speeding up a decision. Third, they draft outlines of the minister's speeches and interviews. Fourth, they supervise the implementation of the ministry's policies, necessitating close and frequent contact with the senior officials who are their opposite numbers in the ministry. The role of the minister's personal staff varies between ministries, tending to be especially great in those that are either relatively new (public works and housing) or excessively routine-bound (agriculture) and so badly need the administrative leadership that a *cabinet* can provide. It tends to be relatively more circumscribed in its role in the ministry of foreign affairs, which possesses a

* See above, figure 1, p. 72.

secretary-general supported by powerful divisions capable of resisting any propensity to invade their spheres of action.

Although they are drawn mainly from the ministries themselves,
these specialist staff members are often in role conflict with their
'line' colleagues who run the ministry's divisions and who have
frequently themselves been ministerial staff members, often in the
same ministry. Their respective roles, with different political and
administrative priorities meeting at the crucial point at which
they must be either reconciled or subordinated one to another,
bring the bureaucratic desire for autonomy into conflict with the
need for change. It is as members of the minister's personal staff,
rather than as heads of the ministry's 'line' hierarchy, that senior
civil servants are most effective as agents of change. It is in this
role that they can win, at an early age, accelerated promotion to
the hierarchical posts within the minister's discretion (although
heads of divisions are appointed by the cabinet and the president or
prime minister may have his say). In their 'line' posts, they will
become more concerned to administer according to the rules
rather than to make exceptions for reasons of political expediency
or imaginative innovation. However, the system enables the
appointment of the staff member who prepared a reform to the
'line' post in which he can ensure that it is faithfully implemented.
The government can also make discretionary appointments to the
grands corps (notably as prefects and councillors of state) of those
who have given it loyal political-cum-administrative service, so
the link between these corps and service on a ministerial staff is
further strengthened by appointment to the corps afterwards.
Usually, only prefects are *removed* from office on political
grounds. Should differences develop between a minister and the
head of a division within the ministry, this will normally be
settled by promotion or at least transfer to an equivalent post
elsewhere.

Much has been made of the contrast between administrative
stability and political instability in France, at least until the advent
of the fifth republic. While this is valid, its significance should not
be exaggerated, because members of ministerial staffs, like
ministers, often survived cabinet crises under the fourth republic.
On the other hand, the tenure of office by the heads of divisions
may be under three years, as was the case with the ministry of
foreign affairs during the fourth republic (average of 2·7 years)

compared with ministers of foreign affairs who served an average of 1·6 years. Overall, however, while ministers averaged 1·1 years in office under the fourth republic, division heads held their posts for an average of 4·1 years. The gap narrowed under the fifth republic to an average tenure of 2·9 years for ministers and 3·4 years for division heads between 1958–66. Significantly, in the light of the subsequent May 1968 crisis, the most unstable ministry was that of education, whose ministers held office for an average of 1·2 years and whose division heads survived for 2·3 years.*[10]

As well as leaving the civil service to occupy a top post in a public or private corporation, senior officials have in recent years been increasingly tempted by political careers, particularly in the UDR party. It is noteworthy that the first four prime ministers of the fifth republic were members of a *grand corps*: the council of state in the case of Debré and Pompidou (although the latter graduated from the *Ecole Normale Supérieure* and was appointed to the council in 1946 for his services to de Gaulle, who had just resigned) and the finance inspectorate in the instances of Couve de Murville and Chaban-Delmas. Messmer was merely a graduate of the *Ecole Coloniale*. Compared to the fourth republic, when civil servants (excluding school and university teachers) provided only 11·8 per cent of ministers, in the first decade of the fifth republic they more than doubled their representation, rising to 25·3 per cent. This also explains in part the increase in the 'Parisian' background of ministers as between the fourth and fifth republics.[11]

Let us finally consider civil servant candidatures to the national assembly, which are once again becoming a prerequisite of ministerial office. However, it is now only necessary to have been legitimized at a recent election rather than to have served an extended parliamentary apprenticeship. Table 19 shows how the composition of non-educational civil service candidatures has changed between the fourth and fifth republics. Whereas *grands corps* candidates were only a third of the total in 1956, they had risen to nearly 40 per cent in 1958 and to 60 per cent in 1967. Among those elected, the *grands corps* already formed half the total in 1956 and have steadily increased their proportion of a total that had nearly doubled by 1967. Senior civil servants have

* See table 32, p. 200.

also become increasingly involved in local politics. Whereas they traditionally took office in relatively apolitical rural communes, where their ability to deal on equal terms with the prefect and to facilitate negotiations with the Paris ministries was appreciated, in recent years they have headed lists associated especially with parties forming the government coalition.[12] Thus the evidence accumulates of a civil service élite extending its grip within and beyond its bureaucratic confines, to the point where one can talk of a *République des hauts fonctionnaires,* corresponding to the economically interventionist fifth republic, by contrast with the *République des professeurs,* Thibaudet's description of the anticlerical third republic.

Table 19
Civil Servants and Election to the National Assembly, 1956–67 *

Non-Educational Civil Servants		Election			
		1956	1958	1962	1967
(a) *Candidates:*	Grands Corps	48	68	94	109
	Other civil servants	109	114	68	72
	Total	157	182	162	181
(b) *Elected:*	Grands Corps	16	31	40	53
	Other civil servants	16	12	11	8
	Total	32	43	51	61

* Source: adapted from C. Debbasch, *L'administration au pouvoir,* p. 58.

5 Public Order and Civil Liberties

Public power and public service: the tradition of French legalism

As we saw in chapter 1, state sovereignty was a sixteenth-century revival of a Roman Law conception of the ruler's unlimited power. The government used its police power for the maintenance of public order and security. The leading French seventeenth-century jurists who formulated the 'apology' for absolute monarchy on the Louis XIV model used the elastic concept of the public interest to justify what Domat called 'the universal policing of society'. Together with Le Bret, whose *Traité de la Souveraineté du Roi* was 'inspired' by Richelieu, Domat developed a theory of comprehensive police power which reflected the post-medieval state's aspiration to unlimited hegemony and expressed the unbounded capacity for state intervention that has been such a feature of French political and administrative life. The ruler alone could judge what was in the supreme interest of the state and *raison d'état* substituted the authority of the ruler for the justification of any government action through judicial process.

This traditional state idealist French public philosophy, which survived the transition from the royalist 'police state' to the republican 'legal state', was recalled by President Pompidou in an April 1970 speech to his ex-colleagues of the *Conseil d'Etat*: 'All our law stemmed from the conception of a strong state, stronger perhaps for limiting its intervention to the most characteristic functions of public power: justice, defence, order. In these spheres, the state alone expressed the general interest and alone took the decisions to ensure that it prevailed.' (Pompidou's emphasis upon the limited range of state intervention was a revealing combination of his anachronistic views about the past and his personal preferences for the future.) He went on to justify this monopoly of coercive decision-making : 'Only the state ... can have a complete and disinterested vision of the general interest. ... For more than a thousand years, France has owed its existence to the state, a state to bring it together, organize it, extend it and defend it not only against foreign threats but equally against group egotisms and rivalries.' This paternalistic conception of a state prerogative police power, conceived as the general regulation of French society for the public good, is indivisibly concerned with domestic and foreign threats to national security, with ominous implications for civil liberties.

Until the end of the second empire, the traditional principle that the sovereign state was not responsible for its actions reigned unchallenged, except by liberal advocates like Tocqueville of the rule of law on the Common Law pattern. The isolation rather than separation of powers, achieved by the revolution and reinforced by Napoleon, strengthened the autonomy of executive power, the instrument of popular sovereignty, which was made independent of the ordinary courts in 1790. However, although the thrust of the French tradition has been to subordinate the judiciary to the administration, there was a liberal counter-attack, especially under the third republic, against the autonomous administration being a judge in its own cause. The council of state, initially the most elevated of Napoleon's authoritarian instruments of executive domination, reintroduced an element of liberalism. It counter-balanced the requirements of administrative action by the protection of the rights of the administered, establishing that the responsibility of the executive and its agents was the rule and immunity was exceptional. The dangers involved in making the executive independent of the judiciary were partially corrected by the council's emergence from the 1870s as an independent administrative legal authority through the functional separation of those parts of the government machine concerned with legal work from those doing administrative work. The council demonstrated its independence by drastically curtailing the *raison d'état* principle that any governmental act was immune from judicial review if it was politically inspired. The only overt survivals of the doctrine of state prerogative power are strictly enumerated (including notably the use of emergency powers under Article 16, the conduct of diplomacy and of war). However, we shall see that the legacy from regal, revolutionary and imperial absolutism is much more pervasive than this would suggest.

The early years of the third republic were also marked by an attempt to replace 'public power' as the basis of administrative law by 'public service', corresponding to a shift from an authoritarian to a liberal democratic polity. Although the public service criterion was adumbrated in 1873, it was only in the first decade of the twentieth century that its implications were fully worked out. Public service was loosely defined in terms of the satisfaction of a public need as conceived by the state's agents, guided by the general interest norm. The main advocate of the new view, the constitutional lawyer Léon Duguit, emphasized the changing character of state activity, shifting from the sovereign assertions of power in the fields of police and war to the provision of economic and social services. Wishful thinking supplementing observation, he went so far as to claim that 'in place of the regal, Jacobin and Napoleonic conception of the state as power is substituted a fundamentally economic conception of the state, which becomes the cooperation between public services functioning under the control of the government.'[1] This reassuring view so appropriate to a replacement of the warfare state by the welfare state, which seemed plausible just prior to the first world war, never held the field unchallenged. Duguit's main rival among French jurists, Maurice Hauriou, argued that public service had not replaced public power as the synthetic norm underlying administrative law; they were its dual supports and of the two, public power was the more important, qualitatively if not quantitatively.[2] The public service norm has since been partially abandoned as imprecise in definition and inoperative as a criterion of the sphere of administrative law (public services such as social security and public corporations being the responsibility of the ordinary courts). However, the commitment to the principles of equal access to public services, equality of treatment of the administered, and neutrality, are of immense value in an administrative system addicted to the discretionary adaptation of the rules to suit the political convenience of governments. The survival of the public service criterion in competition with the norm of public power reflects a reluctance to subordinate the purpose of executive action to those in control of the executive, the service of the public to the public's 'servants'.

The citizen's rights in principle and in practice

Whilst the French revolution bears part of the responsibility for strengthening the executive as against the judiciary, it sought to protect the citizens from government by proclaiming in the Declaration of the Rights of Man (Article 2) that the fundamental purpose of political organization was to preserve man's natural rights, including the right to resist oppression. Freedom of the person from arbitrary detention, freedom of thought and expression, freedom to own property, were the rights that seemed most important in 1789, together with the presumption of innocence until guilt was established and the accountability of government to the people. However, Article 3 confers sovereignty on the nation and declares that 'law is the expression of the general will'. Consequently, although these and other rights were later enshrined in preambles to successive constitutions, there was no provision for judicial appeal against violation of these rights, the citizen being left at the mercy of a sovereign legislature which represented popular sovereignty. The third republic did nevertheless extend public liberties substantially; notably by guaranteeing the right of assembly and press freedom in 1881, the right to form trade unions in 1884, the right to association without prior government approval in 1901, and religious freedom in 1905. This period also witnessed the birth of the League of Human Rights (during the trial of Emile Zola in 1898, arising out of the Dreyfus Affair) which has given institutional expression to the defence of civil liberties in France, although each 'affair' has stimulated an *ad hoc* response, particularly by intellectuals. In 1946, the Preamble to the constitution of the fourth republic added equal rights for women, the right to employment, to collective bargaining and to strike, protection of the sick and the aged, equality of access to education and culture. However, many of these are patently aspirations rather than enforceable rights, although the reaffirmation of the Declaration of 1789 and of the 1946 Preamble in the 1958 constitution became the basis in 1971 for an important decision of the constitutional council concerning the right of association, to which we shall return.

There is general agreement that, especially since the second world war, there has been an erosion of civil liberties in France. The country which likes to think of itself as the home of Voltaire and human rights has refused to ratify the 1950 European Human Rights Convention. Colonial wars in Vietnam and Algeria had made nonsense of the Preamble to the constitution of the fourth republic which proclaimed that France 'will never employ its forces against the liberty of any people'. The Algerian struggle in particular led to numerous infringements of all the basic freedoms in France, which had still not recovered from the gangrene of 1954–62 when the May 1968 crisis led to another bout of repression. The 1958 constitution's Article 66 assertion : 'No one may be arbitrarily detained' does not provide a French equivalent of *habeas corpus* because no steps have been taken to implement it. Telephone tapping and interference with correspondence by the police (in the latter case with the cooperation of the *concierges,* the caretakers of blocks of flats, who together with pimps are the main source of police information in France) are only two of the ways in which the privacy of the citizen is invaded.

Censorship was officially abolished in 1789 but it was quickly reborn. Although censorship in the theatre ended in 1906, the cinema suffered until recently from a stringent 'pre-censorship' (that is, before the film is actually made) as well as ordinary censorship which was, in about 15 per cent of the cases, used to eliminate films which were adjudged politically undesirable. Films on the Algerian war and on the May 'events' have suffered particularly from such political censorship. However, there is appreciable public support for censorship. When asked in 1970 whether the government should censor films and magazines, 49 per cent were in favour whereas 44 per cent thought individuals should be left to decide for themselves. As one moves from the young to the old and from left to right of the political spectrum, support for censorship increases. Among occupational groups, farmers are most inclined and workers least inclined to favour censorship. The ambivalence of Frenchmen, who simultaneously look to the state to protect them from disorder yet resent its tendency to infringe their freedom, emerges clearly from the same opinion poll. It nevertheless shows that those of right-wing views emphasize the threat of disorder while the left-inclined stress the interference with personal liberty.[3]

Frequent infringements of civil liberty, coupled with the fact that they attach more importance to freedom of the press and judicial independence than to parliament or political parties,[4] lead the French public to adopt a rather more critical attitude toward the effectiveness with which their rights are protected compared with the protection of existing society (see table 20). Slightly more Frenchmen think their liberty is badly protected than believe it is well protected, whilst relatively more are inclined to think existing society is well protected than the reverse. What is more, the French public attach more importance to the protection of personal liberty (50 per cent) rather than existing society (30 per cent, with 20 per cent abstaining). This preference is particularly great among the young, well-educated city dwellers and left-wing voters, while the old, farmers, women and UDR voters attach relatively more importance to 'defending the republic' which is often given by governments as the motive for restricting liberty.

Table 20
How Well Does the French Judicial System Protect
(a) *Personal Liberty*, (b) *Existing Society?*(%)*

Reply	Personal Liberty	Existing Society
Very well	2	4
Rather well	35	38
Rather badly	33	27
Very badly	6	3
No reply	24	28

* Source: IFOP in *L'Express*, 26 April 1971, p. 68, and *Sondages*, 1971, nos 1–2, p. 91.

The role of the judiciary

The establishment of a constitutional council in 1958 was part of the attempt by the authors of the new constitution, notably Debré, to preserve its innovations from subsequent counter-attack. The champions of the traditional doctrine that the legislature was the repository of national sovereignty had to be prevented from eroding the constitutional constraints imposed on parliament. This involved another departure from traditional French practice, the constitutional council being entrusted with the power to decide that laws passed by parliament were unconstitutional. The behaviour of the executive was not subject to judicial review by the constitutional council, being the preserve of the council of state. The constitutional council's main function and early activities marked it down as a watchdog on behalf of executive supremacy. Although the presidents of the two chambers of the French parliament choose six out of the nine members, the remaining three – including the president – are chosen by the president of the republic. However, because the presidents of the republic and assembly have so far shared the same political views, there has been a majority of six to three in favour of the Gaullist interpretation of the constitution. Furthermore, there has been a tendency to appoint men who have been active politicians – five of the present nine members are ex-ministers – and there have been cases of movement from the council into active politics, notably by Pompidou.* While the examples of supreme constitutional courts in the United States, Federal Germany and Italy indicate that political influence over the membership of a body called upon to decide politically controversial matters has been unavoidable, the degree of politicization attained in France is particularly great.

The existence of a constitutional council to which the three men who appoint its members – the presidents of the republic, assembly and senate – together with the prime minister are alone capable of referring issues of constitutionality, has not merely restricted the powers of the legislature vis à vis the executive. It has made the citizen's constitutional rights, as set out in the 1789 Declaration of Human Rights and in the Preambles to the 1946 and 1958 constitutions, judicially enforceable as they have not been hitherto. In 1950 the council of state had already invoked the Preamble as embodying 'the fundamental principles that should inspire legislative action as well as that of government and administration'. However, because civil liberties had never been precisely defined and because of the difficulty in getting an issue raised before the constitutional council, it was not until 1971 that the council moved from regulatory to normative action.[5] Faced by mounting unrest amongst its own parliamentary and extra-parliamentary supporters at the violent challenge to authority and order from the extreme left, the government and especially the minister of the interior, Marcellin, decided in the words of St Just to deny freedom to the enemies of freedom. The minister instructed the prefect of police in June 1970 to refuse the 'Friends

* He will become an ex-officio member of the council when he ceases to be president of the republic.

of the *Cause du Peuple'* – a periodical whose editors were sent to jail until Jean-Paul Sartre assumed the editorial role – registration under the 1901 Act, essential if it was to have a legal existence. However, the Paris administrative tribunal quashed the refusal to register the association, which it declared should be automatic. Even if the government regarded an association as subversive (the *Cause du Peuple* had been the organ of the *Gauche Prolétarienne*, dissolved in May 1970) it could not be outlawed in advance. Dismayed at this judgement, the minister of the interior had a Bill prepared and adopted by the cabinet at a meeting on 9 June 1971, amending the 1901 Act guaranteeing freedom of association.

The main purpose of this Bill was to give prefects the power to refuse registration to any association which they thought would engage in illicit activities, subject to a subsequent decision of the courts. The government would thus be in a position to decide in advance whether an association should be presumed to be illicit and even in the event of a contrary decision by the courts, delay the association acquiring legal personality meanwhile.* Having initially intended to proceed by decree, the minister of the interior accepted the council of state's advice that a Bill would be necessary and secured parliamentary permission to discuss his Bill as a matter of urgency. It was rushed through the assembly between 2 am and 4.30 am on 24 June 1971, at a period when the parliamentary timetable was particularly congested. It was carried against left-wing opposition by 373 votes to 97. On 28 June 1971, however, the senate rejected the Bill as unconstitutional (by 129 votes to 104) and Poher, its president, Pompidou's former opponent at the 1969 presidential election, was pressed to refer the Bill to the constitutional council should the assembly persist.

The two chambers having failed to reach agreement (the assembly confirming its support for the Bill by 357 votes to 100) the president of the senate referred the Bill to the council, which gave its verdict two weeks later. It transpired, despite the secrecy of the vote, that a majority of six to three of the council ruled

---

* Because of the backlog of work in the courts, instead of an association enjoying the benefits of the delay, the government would be the beneficiary. The existing procedure would not permit the minister to have recourse to the repressive state security court (see below, p. 127).

that by virtue of the Preamble to the constitution, the right to form an association 'cannot be subject to advance authorization by either the administrative or even the judicial authorities'. The council, by this decision, emerged as a guardian of civil liberty capable of imposing respect for constitutional rights even on the president and his ministers. Paradoxically, the Bill contained a provision requiring the prefect to register an association within five days if he did not decide to refer it to the courts, so the promulgation of the remainder of the amendment to the 1901 Act in fact restricted the discretionary power of the prefect rather than increased it. It remains to be seen whether this modest but promising decision marks a new departure in French judicial audacity, which past experience has not led us to expect except from the council of state.

The constitutional council and the council of state have more in common than their proximity in the Palais Royal. They use similar judicial procedures, related to the fact that the constitutional council's early membership, including its first president and first two secretaries-general, were members of the council of state. The latter's direct influence as a source of personnel for those parts of executive decision-making where politics and administration are most intermingled, as well as its expanded advisory function owing to the extension in the executive's activities, have somewhat overshadowed its traditional judicial function of protecting the administered. Nevertheless, the council of state deliberately sought to increase judicial control commensurately with the extension of executive power, in contrast with its policy under earlier republics of strengthening a weak executive.

This intention emerged most clearly in its use of the general principles of law contained in the Preamble to the constitution to restrain claims by the executive power that the necessities of government or *raison d'état* should prevail over judicial scruples. A military court of justice having been set up to deal with rebel officers and OAS terrorists in 1962, the council of state in the *Canal* judgement of the same year invalidated the ordinance creating the court. This was done at a time when assassination attempts were still being made on the life of the president of the republic who was locked in a decisive struggle with the assembly which had censured the government. The then minister of justice, a member of the council, declared that the prime, albeit unpopular, duty of judges was to defend the state. In an extra-ordinary outburst, in which his ministerial functions dominated his loyalties as a jurist, Chenot asserted in Napoleonic manner :

The council of state was created to weight unequally private rights and the prerogatives of the public service but many of its members have wished to make it a temple of private interests asserted against the state. . . . The administration has become their Aunt Sally; quashing its decisions, once rare, has become a vocation for them.

De Gaulle complained that the council's 'meetings, in the absence of those of its members who had been seconded to me or the government, were noisily dominated by notorious and avowed partisans, former ministers or members of parliament and future political candidates', his complaint not being against the council's political bias but against the fact that it favoured his opponents.[6] However, not content with replacing the military court of justice by a state security court which was free of the former's blemishes (purely military composition, no right of appeal), de Gaulle threatened drastic reprisals against the council of state but he was prevailed upon to establish a committee (whose membership included Chenot) under the chairmanship of the Gaullist president of the constitutional council and former councillor of state, to advise on reform. By the time action was taken, the temperature had fallen and the most objectionable proposals were dropped. The 1963 decree's main aim was to reduce the separation between the advisory work of the council's administrative sections and its judicial work, to make the latter more sensitive to the *raison d'état* propensities of the former. There is no evidence that this attempt to reverse the council's liberalizing trend over the last century has been successful, despite Chenot's appointment to head the council.

While individual citizens cannot have recourse to the constitutional council, no such restriction applies in the case of the council of state. Although the plaintiff has to prove his case against a minister or official, the inquisitorial nature of the French judge in this instance works in the citizen's favour as the council will require the production of relevant official files and the justification for the regulation or decision made. This procedure ensures the enforcement of the personal accountability for administrative acts that in Britain is evaded through the fiction of ministerial responsibility. The council's main achievements as a champion of individual rights through the enforcement of administrative law have been through annulment of acts by which the administration has exceeded its powers on five grounds. The narrowest and earliest ground is *ultra vires*, action beyond the powers attributed to the administrative authority. Secondly, the formal or procedural irregularity of an administrative act may lead the council to quash a decision or regulation. Thirdly, the abuse or misuse of power for a purpose other than that for which it was granted involves the administrative judge in an examination of the intentions of the public agent. On this ground an administrative act may be quashed because discretionary power has been used improperly, being inspired, for example, by personal enmity, corruption or political favouritism. Fourthly, there may be no legal justification for the action or the alleged motives do not exist. Finally, the purpose of the act may be illegal.

Nevertheless, the constraints upon the judicial control exercised by the council of state are important. First, the council has refused on grounds of political discretion to interfere in certain matters, treated as unchallengeable acts of government, as we have seen above. Secondly, governments have frequently resorted to *ex post facto* legislative validation of acts of dubious legality, thereby removing them from the council's jurisdiction either before or whilst the council is examining them. One of its most distinguished members complained in 1960:

Recently, the intervention of the legislative power in the working of administrative justice has tended to increase. . . . Such action is acceptable and even desirable in certain exceptional circumstances when the implementation of judicial decisions would lead to serious difficulties . . . but it is tending, for certain branches of the administration, to become a permanent temptation. If such practices spread and become a habit, the very principle of administrative litigation will gradually be threatened.[7]

The 1963 Act creating the state security court retrospectively validated the military court of justice (which the council of state had earlier ruled to be unconstitutional); reaffirming de Gaulle's view that his legitimacy took priority over mere legality. Thirdly, since 1959 parliament has annually given *ex post facto* validation in the Finance Act to regulations and individual decisions quashed by the council. Fourthly, the executive has frequently refused to implement the council's judgements, varying in degree from procrastination to inertia and even manifest bad faith, combined occasionally with explicit criticism of the verdict. Such non-implementation may be partial or total or the delay may be such as to render the judgement ineffective. It has been estimated that about *a third of the council's decisions are so nullified in practice,* with the ministry of finance being particularly adept at circumventing the council's judgements in taxation matters. French administrative justice is both extremely inexpensive and extremely slow. Because of its backlog of work, the council is itself to blame for rendering many of its decisions ineffective. Despite priority having been given to 'excess of power' actions, the council in first and final instance dealt in 1965–6 with 19 per cent of such cases in a year or less; 48 per cent in two years or less; 68 per cent in three years or less. On appeal from administrative tribunals, the council dealt with 16 per cent of cases in one year or less; 56 per cent in two years or less; 77 per cent of cases in three years or less.[8] Thus the 'law's delay' fortifies 'the insolence of office' and in October 1972 Messmer announced his intention to adapt the Scandinavian institution of the Ombudsman to secure rapid redress of grievances through the creation of a 'Mediator'.

The state security court, offspring of the early 1960s terrorism and subversion from the extreme right seeking to defend the indivisibility of Algeria and France, has been used since 1968 primarily against the extreme left and autonomists from the overseas departments. Established in 1963, its five carefully selected members – of whom two are army officers – are appointed by the government for two-year terms. They can be removed at will and know that they will receive very rapid promotion during 'good behaviour'. The minister of justice can remove a case from any other court on the grounds that a *political crime* has been committed and confide it to the reliable hands of the state security court. However, a number of its judgements have been quashed on appeal, the existence of which is due to the council of state's 1962 invalidation of the military court of justice. Shorn of the most offensive features of its predecessor, to assert that 'the state security court is military justice in peacetime for everyone'[9] is an overstatement. However, minister of interior Marcellin regarded it as the best judicial auxiliary available to his police in their repression of what he claimed to be an international revolutionary conspiracy threatening France.

The state security court has been kept busy despite attempts by the senate in 1963 to prevent its establishment and again in 1970 to secure its abolition, and despite the repeated attacks by Mitterrand against this manifestation of the fifth republic's 'permanent *coup d'état*'. Only in the length of time that suspects can be held incommunicado, reduced in 1970 from ten to six days (twelve during a state of emergency) has liberalization occurred. Between May 1966 and May 1970, 257 people were held incommunicado, 88 of them for more than six days. This right to detain a suspect in a police station without bringing him before a magistrate or allowing him to consult his lawyer, originally fixed at twenty-four hours to give rural gendarmes the time to convey a suspect to the nearest town, has been utilized by the police to carry out a preliminary interrogation aimed at extracting a confession at all costs.

The ordinary judicial hierarchy, headed by the minister of justice, bears the indelible mark of Napoleonic authoritarianism with its requirement that the judiciary should be a docile extension of executive power. The public prosecutors, who represent the government and form a quarter of all judges, are most directly under government control but the osmosis between the judges who sit on the bench and the prosecutors enables the government, through its control over promotion, to favour the pliable members of the judiciary. So, though the non-prosecutors are irremovable, they are in practice no less dependent upon government, in contrast with members of the council of state where promotion is by seniority rather than at ministerial discretion. The virtual subordination of the bench to the prosecutors in turn leads to the dominance of the police, whose minister of the interior is much more powerful than the minister of justice. Forced to remain content with less than 1 per cent of the national budget, the ministry of justice devotes its energies to the organization of the courts, codes, prisons, probation and pardons. The crisis in recruitment to the judiciary is in part a consequence of the decline of 'judicial power' in France both as a function and as an institution. The French public's perception in February 1971 of the lack of judicial independence is indicated in table 21.

Table 21
Judicial Independence in France (%) *

Reply	Judicial Independence From		
	Capitalists	*Government*	*Police*
Wholly independent	12	12	14
Relatively independent	27	38	34
Totally subservient	30	25	22
No reply	31	25	30

* Source: IFOP in *Sondages*, 1971, no. 1–2, p. 92.

The feeling that the judiciary is at the beck and call of the government received startling confirmation during the May 1968 'events' when Prime Minister Pompidou announced a number of measures calculated to placate the students, notably that a court would almost immediately hear appeals against sentence, with the implication that the accused would be let off. This proved to be the case, yet the subordination of the judiciary to the political convenience of the government did not earn them the gratitude of the hard-line elements in the UDR ranks. Once the crisis was over, it was the police who needed to be placated and the fear which the UDR had felt was projected on to the judiciary. An incident in the police repression of a leftist demonstration brought matters to a head. A schoolboy bystander, Gilles Guiot, had on police testimony been summarily sentenced to six months imprisonment, then rapidly released on ·appeal when a public campaign of massive proportions had been launched to press the case for his innocence. At a press conference on 16 February 1971, the then general secretary of the UDR, René Tomasini,* denounced the judiciary which had 'acquired the habit of being prudent during the Occupation'. Defending the police, he asserted : 'If acts contrary to law have been repressed in regrettable manner, the fault lies not with those whose duty is such repression but – I weigh my words carefully – with the cowardice of the judiciary.' Although a chorus of protests, led by the minister of justice and necessarily backed by President Pompidou as

* Tomasini was one of the few politicians compelled to resign his post following Gabriel Aranda's September 1972 revelations in the *Canard Enchaîné* (see below, p. 143) of numerous attempts to obtain lucrative political favours by prominent UDR personalities.

constitutional protector of the independence of the judiciary, forced Tomasini to retract, it is ironically the case that all he was doing was letting the cat out of the bag. He abandoned the myth of judicial independence from political pressure and called for a docile devotion by the judges to the unflinching repression of all threats to the established order. The judges were to become the auxiliaries of the police and repress without regard to the rights of the accused, Guiot having in the first instance been summarily sentenced without any serious preliminary investigation and without the help of a lawyer. Despite the fact that he had no previous convictions, he was denied bail pending his appeal.

The public standing of the courts in France is low, as is evident from table 22. Following a partial recovery in public esteem in the mid-1960s, due to the end of the Algerian war, there has been a further slump to a 2 : 1 attitude of hostility and suspicion since the crisis of May 1968. Despite the ups and downs of the last decade, it should be noted that the number of those who consider that the judicial system works badly has consistently exceeded by a wide margin those who believe that it works well. The judicial system for its part gives the representatives of the public, the jury, a rather modest role in the assize criminal courts. Since 1941 (a legacy of the Vichy régime) the nine jurymen and three judges decide their verdict together, which – despite the requirement of a majority of eight votes – allows the president of the court to exercise a decisive influence on the verdict.

Table 22
The Public's General Assessment of the
Working of the French Judicial System (%)*

Reply	September 1962	March 1966	March 1969	February 1971
Works very well	3	3	2	1
Works rather well	19	32	28	29
Works rather badly	43	39	38	44
Works very badly	17	9	14	15
No reply	18	17	18	11

* Source: IFOP in *L'Express*, 26 April 1971, p. 68.

The judge as an instrument for the investigation of crime on behalf of public power was introduced by Napoleon in the shape of the examining magistrate. Together with the provision for remand in custody for twenty-four hours (increased to forty-eight with the semi-automatic approval of the public prosecutor), this has effectively neutralized Article 9 of the Declaration of the Rights of Man which asserted the presumption of innocence until guilt is proved. When a trial begins, defence and prosecution are formally on an equal footing but it is preceded by a protracted phase during which a *prima facie* case is prepared by the police and the examining magistrate. French procedure is directed at securing a confession of guilt. Generally, the examining magistrate is not concerned at how the confession has been obtained by the police, even though the person brought before him shows obvious signs of having been beaten up. The police know that the examining magistrate will not inquire into their actions because he is in practice subordinate to the ministry of justice's public prosecutors, who will not allow the minister of interior's police to be censured by the judiciary. Such police immunity, coupled with the examining magistrate's dependence on the police for his information and the knowledge that his promotion prospects depend on his pliability, converts him in practice into the auxiliary of the police commissioner. The examining magistrate may himself be under police surveillance if his loyalty to the government is in doubt. In cases which are politically sensitive he may receive very explicit threats of the career consequences of independent action.[10] This means that when the police – and counter-espionage services – are themselves implicated in a political crime, as allegedly in the murder of the Moroccan exile Ben Barka, the minister of justice can prevent proceedings leading in dangerous directions. The indivisibility of the judiciary from the police is a day-to-day demonstration of the unitary nature of the one and indivisible state in 'the classic land of political scandal'.[11]

The public prosecutors are the main link between the ministry of justice, the judiciary and the police, so it was naturally to them that the minister of justice sent a circular in April 1971 when he sought to place the repression of threats to public order at the forefront of their activities. The judicial authorities 'can only carry out their task to the extent that they remain regularly in close touch with the prefectoral authority and the various police authorities ... involving genuine coordination in action between the prosecutors and prefectoral and police authorities, without which rapid, firm and consistent repression of infringements of public order cannot be guaranteed.' Pleven went on to 'emphasize the need to give priority to inquiries and cases concerning public disorder' and also that 'examining magistrates be as far as possible freed from other commitments' so as to expedite such cases. This circular from the minister of justice to his field services emphasizes the priority, despite the fact that ordinary crime rates are rising sharply, which he and the minister of the interior accord to the more political side of their function of preserving law and order, as well as the close collaboration required of the 'forces of law' and the 'forces of order' exemplified in the notion of 'judicial police'.

The police

'A judge without a policeman is nothing. A policeman without a judge is everything.'[12] Whilst the first part of this assertion by a group of French judges is generally true, the second part is misleading in its exaggeration. Still, it is a salutary corrective to the formalistic treatment which this subject often receives in France. Its truth derives from the fact that France has not – in this as in other spheres – broken the grip of that statesman-policeman, Napoleon. Ironically, he is remembered for his legal codes, which were really a legacy from the revolution, rather than the surreptitious police state which he built with the help of a master policeman-statesman, Fouché, like him brought to power by Sieyès as part of the 1799 Brumaire *coup d'état*. A ministry of police had been established in 1795 by the counter-revolutionary Directory in the hope that all plots would in future be foreseen and forestalled. Fouché's achievement, as Napoleon's instrument, was to put the police above the law. The requirements of public order, whose guardians were the police, had priority over the protection of the citizens' freedom. The refusal to recognize a legitimate opposition loyal to the régime has meant that the police must be entrusted with the elimination of all opposition and the surveillance and repression of all domestic enemies. In such a situation, 'every branch of the administration has a part which subordinates it to the police.'[13] The French failure to institutionalize opposition has resulted in a semi-permanent cold civil war, which led contemporary police statesmen like minister of the interior

Marcellin to continue to see in the *gauchistes* and communists the threat to state security which they had been in 1968.

Because of the extensive prerogative police power that exists in France and the latitude accorded to the police forces in exercising these powers, of all the liberal democratic countries the French police system would most effortlessly fit into a totalitarian form of government which the fear of revolution and civil war might bring about. The ministry of the interior, which absorbed the ministry of police in 1818, having lost in the nineteenth century the wide range of welfare functions that it used to discharge, relies largely upon the prefects and the police to impose its conception of public order. The prefects are controlled through a political affairs division, for which they provide a political intelligence service on behalf of the government, which is useful for electoral as well as police purposes. This division is also responsible for dissolving local councils and removing mayors – who have police powers in communes with a population of under ten thousand people – although there is a local authorities division which deals with most of their activities.

The ministry's four police divisions come under a secretary-general of police but he does not control the whole of France's police forces, of which there are several, pluralism being regarded as a safeguard against excessive police power. The ministry of the interior controls nearly 100,000 police. The 33,500 ordinary urban provincial police or *Sûreté Nationale* operated in the 1,643 communes with a population of more than ten thousand in 1970. In 1966 this force was nominally amalgamated with the twenty-six thousand Paris police. The 1966 Act remained a dead letter as far as the attempt to end the Paris prefecture of police's status as privileged enclave was concerned until the 1971 reorganization by the minister of the interior; although cutting the prefect of police down to size will never be complete until Paris acquires a mayor who can become the authority responsible for public order alongside the Paris prefect. Finally, the CRS is a mobile reserve force of fifteen thousand men who combine military discipline and organization with civilian control and functions. In addition, the ministry of defence controls the 66,300 strong *gendarmerie*, recruited from among servicemen, who act as military police to the three armed services but are also the police in the communes with less than ten thousand inhabitants. This is the role of the 'white' departmental *gendarmerie* (36,000). The 128 squadrons of 'red' mobile *gendarmerie* (16,700) are organized on a regional base and equipped with tanks and helicopters. They are reserved for use in times of crisis. Finally, there are a number of specialist units of the *gendarmerie*, such as the republican guard (3,000) which is controlled by the prefect of police for use in Paris, notably on ceremonial occasions. However, there are unofficial police forces, some being paid out of the ministry of the interior's secret funds to spy on their official colleagues.

This brings us to the two most mysterious police divisions; the general intelligence service and counter-espionage. The former constitutes the French political police. About 3,500 policemen are involved in this work. The task of its field services, who are controlled by the departmental and regional prefects, is to collect information about all parties, trade unions or movements whose activities might have political significance. On the basis of this information reports are presented to the president of the republic, the minister of the interior and the secretary-general of police, with confidential bulletins receiving wider distribution. In 1970, the headquarters of the general intelligence service received 167,000 detailed reports and 1,900,000 succinct reports, its main targets for investigation being the leftist organizations and agitation amongst peasants and shopkeepers. As well as paying informers with the help of secret funds, generous use is made of telephone tapping. There are about a thousand staff engaged in telephone tapping who work for the *Groupement des écoutes téléphoniques* (GET) under the prime minister, the specialist personnel coming from the ministries, notably interior, defence and foreign affairs, while the technical staff are seconded from the post office. Telephone tapping requires the authorization of the prime minister (in fact of a member of his personal staff) and is coordinated by an interministerial control group which allocates its resources – 1,500 telephones in Paris and 2,500 in the provinces can be tapped simultaneously – between the general intelligence service (800) and the other intelligence and counter-espionage agencies.[14]

There is an overlap between the *Direction des Renseignements Généraux* and counter-espionage or *Direction de la Surveillance du Territoire* (known as DST) the activities of whose 1,200 agents include spying on communists, who are regarded as foreign agents.

Whilst the general intelligence service was born in the struggle against Boulangism in the late 1880s, counter-espionage was brought under the ministry of the interior as a result of the Dreyfus Affair, and the distrust of the war ministry's *Deuxième Bureau* which it aroused. There is also a substantial overlap with the work of the SDECE, the euphemistically entitled external documentation and counter-espionage section, nominally responsible only for activities outside France threatening national security. It was directly under the prime minister until 1966 when, following the Ben Barka affair, it was transferred to the ministry of defence so that discipline could be restored. Its staff of 2,000–2,500, financed partly out of secret funds, includes some fifty 'analysis service' agents engaged in telephone tapping within the GET. Since 1970, the appointment of a civilian rather than a general to run the SDECE (more particularly one who is reputed to have close contacts with the president of the republic), coupled with a reorientation of its work towards industrial and scientific espionage, is part of an attempt to reduce the traditional inter-service rivalry with the DST. Some twenty top SDECE staff were purged in the year following the appointment of the new head and a policy of closer collaboration with NATO countries and the surveillance of communist countries was reinstituted.

The brutality of French police methods is notorious and is related to the fact that police efficiency is judged by the number of arrests and convictions achieved. The habitual use of force to extract confessions has sometimes led to the death of the detainee. Any act of self-defence against the police is treated as 'rebellion' and as we have seen the judiciary almost invariably sides with the police. Far from being punished, those responsible have frequently been promoted and apart from isolated protests, notably from the League of Human Rights, which helps police victims with legal advice, the French public seems to accept such police behaviour fatalistically. Although at times of crisis, such as June 1968, the majority of French vote for 'order', they detest the police who are responsible for enforcing it. During the period of police persecution of the *gauchistes* that followed, under the aegis of the minister of the interior Marcellin, far from the public considering that the police were acting with undue severity, it is clear from table 23 that there was public support for greater rigour. Such support was weakest among young men, the better educated, those living in Paris, and those of left-wing political views. In such a context, some policemen are likely not merely to use force but even their firearms indiscriminately and with impunity. Many a minor criminal, who would not have merited the guillotine – the death penalty still exists in France – is shot 'whilst attempting to flee'.[15]

Table 23
The Public's Attitude Towards Police Methods, 1970 (%) *

Description of police methods	In General	Towards Leftists
Too severe	9	12
Just right	32	28
Not sufficiently severe	44	33
No reply	15	37

* Source: IFOP in *Le Nouvel Observateur*, 9 November 1970, p. 21, and *Sondages*, 1971, nos 1–2, p. 97.

Until 1971 the minister of the interior refused to publish the figures of disciplinary action taken against policemen. He then disclosed that in 1970 fifty-one were punished by disciplinary bodies, twenty being sentenced to dismissal, suspension or demotion; whilst 282 were punished without appearing before a disciplinary body, involving four dismissals, suspensions of less than four days, reprimands and less serious sanctions. Reluctance to take disciplinary action is due to the feeling of dependence that French governments have upon the police, as well as the conviction that 'spying, brutality, arbitrary use of power and pre-paredness to take the law into their own hands is an integral part of the nature of any police system'.[16] A police strike in 1958 helped undermine the fourth republic and an attempt by Pompidou to placate rampaging students by implying that the police were to blame came close, in mid-May 1968, to provoking a police strike which might have destroyed the fifth republic. Only generous wage concessions enabled the police unions to prevent a spontaneous strike and since then the minister of the interior has deliberately assumed the role of the '*premier des flics*', delivering frequent eulogies of the police, guardians of the state and the government. Nevertheless, police morale has remained low because they feel that they are not being sufficiently rewarded for doing the government's dirty work.

The domestic role of the military*

As the French police are also armed, it would be a misnomer to refer to the military, as one does in Britain, as the 'armed forces'. The *gendarmes* are a permanent link between the police and the military. Furthermore, the military have – notably during the Algerian war – waged 'police actions', for which they are not trained, in which the temptation to torture is not resisted and its utilization by the ordinary police is encouraged. The services have their own parallel political police, military security (1,500 strong), which inquires into the political opinions of every young conscript and to which the ordinary police are required to furnish information.[17] This is because the army does not see its role simply as that of protecting the country's territorial integrity against foreign enemies. The regular army is associated through a joint military-prefectoral staff with the CRS and *gendarmerie* in the *Défense opérationelle du territoire* which, according to a 1962 decree, seeks to 'deal with enemy forces over the whole country, whether they are "implanted", parachuted, landed or infiltrated', in the context of nuclear or subversive war. Thus the military also protects the régime against revolution by internal enemies but in 1958 the army itself played a major part in overthrowing the fourth republic in a forlorn attempt to preserve the indivisible union of Algeria with France. However, in retrospect, the period between the defeats of 1940 and 1962, in which de Gaulle at the start set an example of military indiscipline and then at the end quelled his would-be imitators, was an interlude in the traditional military obedience to civil authority.

Despite the fact that contemporary public opinion places the army second only to the political executive in its conception of what constitutes the French state (see table 17, chapter 4), the post-revolutionary French solution to the problem of military-civil government relations was to give the army autonomy, allowing the military to regulate itself within a closed and united apolitical community. The third republic went so far as to deprive military personnel of the right to vote and stand at elections or belong to political parties. In return, the post of minister of war was usually held by a general on active service until the anti-militarist reaction following the Dreyfus Affair.[18] One of the most

---

* Defence policy will be discussed in chapter 8.

important achievements of the fifth republic, after an era of delegations of civil power to the military, has been to curtail military autonomy drastically. Debré, as minister of defence from 1969, carried on the work inaugurated by de Gaulle, whom he helped the military bring to power in 1958. However, the May 1968 crisis showed that the fragility of French political régimes may at any moment involve the army in politics, President de Gaulle finding it expedient to reassure himself about the loyalty of the troops before bringing the crisis to an end by reasserting his authority.

Regular army officers have their own professional grievances which may become sources of disaffection. The twentieth-century decline in the social and meritocratic élitism of the pre-first world war army was reflected in its 'proletarianization' by promotion from the ranks, whilst fewer and fewer direct-entry aristocrats and graduates of the *grandes écoles* choose a military career. A good example of this is the waning attraction of the military academy of St Cyr (founded by Napoleon) and the refusal of most graduates of the *Ecole Polytechnique* (which Napoleon militarized) to pursue a military career. The nuclear deterrent forces now absorb an increasing share of the budget, while the bulk of the army seem demoralized, having lost any function with the end of colonial wars. As Alfred de Vigny wrote of the *Servitude et grandeur militaires* after the heroic Napoleonic era : 'Today, as the conquering spirit withers, the only greatness which a noble character can bring into the military profession appears to me to be less in the glory of fighting than in the honour of suffering in silence and of accomplishing with steadfastness duties which are often odious.'[19] As a corollary, ex-servicemen's organizations are far less influential than they were under the fourth republic and the ministry of ex-servicemen has dwindled into insignificance. Political capital made out of the decline in the military's share in the national budget further contributes to the decline in military morale, as it is regarded as an indicator of a fall in public esteem.

Under the fifth republic there has been a marked evolution in the revolutionary legacy of compulsory military service, conscription having been broadened into national service in 1959 to include non-military defence service. Because the numbers available exceeded military requirements once the Algerian war was over, exemptions were generous (one-quarter of the total eligible in 1969) until a 1970 Act reduced military service to one year. In the interim, a 1965 Act had provided a third type of national service through technical assistance in French overseas departments and territories or technical cooperation with foreign countries, particularly ex-French colonies in Africa. The reduction in the size of the French services meant that by 1970, out of 500,000 servicemen and servicewomen, only 52·6 per cent were conscripts. They formed 64 per cent of the army but only 36 per cent of the air force and 23 per cent of the navy. Despite this trend, French public opinion in 1970 did not agree with the view that technical progress had made defence a specialist matter and that conscription should be abolished. By 61 per cent to 30 per cent they rejected this view, with farmers and UDR supporters being keenest to preserve conscription and those in the middle-class occupations and non-communist left being the keenest abolitionists. Though young men, those most directly affected, were less enthusiastic than the average, a large majority even of them favoured the retention of conscription.[20]

The enduring mystique of compulsory universal military service is reflected in the difficulty and belatedness with which provision for conscientious objection was made in France and the extent to which it is still not accepted by public opinion. Between 1952 and 1961, 470 conscripts were imprisoned because, on conscientious grounds, they 'refused to obey' orders to join the services, many of them being Jehovah's Witnesses. In 1962 the end of the Algerian war and an ardent one-man campaign by a veteran anarchist Louis Lecoin, culminating in a twenty-two day hunger strike, led de Gaulle to press a reluctant government and parliament to enact legislation, which they did in 1963 only after tortuous manoeuvres.[21] The Act grants conscientious objectors a hearing before a board consisting of a judge, three officers, and three government nominees, with an appeal to the council of state. If their objection is sustained, they discharge double the length of the normal period of national service in a noncombatant branch of the forces or in civilian work. However, a 1970 public opinion poll shows that 64 per cent still do not accept the right to conscientious objection, rising to 73 per cent in the case of the over-65s, 77 per cent among UDR voters and 81 per cent among farmers. While 30 per cent accept a civilian substitute for conscription, this rises to 47 per cent among voters of the communist and non-communist left and 51 per cent in business and the professions.[22] Nevertheless, in the wake of the May 1968 crisis, objectors increased beyond the hundred or so from each call-up between 1964–8, although propaganda encouraging conscientious objection – illegal under 1963 and 1971 Acts – is severely punished as 'undermining the morale of the army'.

The mass media and political control over information

The major contrast between the mass media channels of communication is that whereas the government has a monopoly of television and a semi-monopoly of radio, the press is not owned by the state. This does not mean that it is free from government control but it is more difficult to exercise this control without openly challenging the freedom of the press. To prevent the source from which newspapers draw much of their information being poisoned, the fourth republic in 1957 effectively secured the independence of *Agence France Presse* from government control. Unlike Reuters, which is jointly owned by its British, Australian and New Zealand newspaper-customers, or *Tass* which is owned by the Soviet state, the French press agency is controlled by a board, on which a majority of the fifteen members (eight) are chosen by the daily newspaper associations. There are, in addition, two representatives of the *Agence France Presse* (AFP) staff, two representatives of the state radio-television service (ORTF) and three ministerial nominees (of the prime minister, finance minister and foreign minister). The director-general is chosen by the board and can only be removed by a council whose function is to safeguard the AFP's objectivity.[23] The government keeps a distant surveillance of AFP through the general secretariat of the government's technical and legal service for information. The government does not wish to restore Napoleon's total subordination of the press to state control as an adjunct of the police state, with official papers exclusively disseminating official information. However, its more authoritarian members bitterly resent press criticism of the institutions 'that make for the strength and solidity of our country; the police, the army and the authorities'.[24]

It is at times of stress that the freedom of the press comes under governmental pressure, even in liberal democratic régimes; authority regarding freedom of the press as being sacrosanct in principle but expendable in crisis. In France the gap between principle and practice has varied between republics. The third republic was amazingly tolerant towards the extreme right-wing press, which did not merely advocate the overthrow of the régime in the most violent language but incited its readers to assassinate political opponents. This is in contrast with the fifth republic's treatment of the extreme left press. As was the case during the Algerian war, selected fringe newspapers are repeatedly seized (not merely the statutory four copies to provide evidence for a subsequent indictment but the whole issue) without any intention of bringing the matter to court but simply to drive them out of existence. Prefects, acting on the instructions of the minister of the interior, know that they have little to fear from appeals to the council of state, owing to its slow and *a posteriori* judgements. In the Paris region the prefect of police has power to control the distribution of all publications and he has used this to harass the street-sellers of leftist papers. In the four months between 22 November 1969–22 March 1970, 890 people were detained by the police in the Paris region for selling leftist newspapers and distributing tracts. They are taken away for 'verification of their identity' and any resistance leads to indictment for 'rebellion and violence against a policeman'. Few are in fact subsequently charged although some are fined for 'obstructing traffic'. To dissuade readers, the police sometimes also detain not merely the sellers but the buyers of leftist newspapers and if they are so ill-advised as to protest, they are beaten up. So, even if a paper is not seized, its sale can be seriously threatened. The main target of this police persecution was *La Cause du Peuple*, organ of the Maoist proletarian left group, whose first two editors were jailed for incitement to murder. To forestall further arrests and to establish the discriminatory nature of the prosecutions or to force a show trial, Jean-Paul Sartre took over nominal editorship of the journal in 1970. Nevertheless, *La Cause du Peuple* continued to be seized throughout 1970, but in 1971 this ceased and it once again became possible to buy it at kiosks.

The relations between the ordinary press and the police are exceedingly bad. An increasingly vicious circle of police violence against journalists, leading to adverse press comment on the police, has become firmly established in recent years. A much publicized case in 1971 of a policeman with a forged press card, masquerading as a journalist at the University of Aix-en-Provence further exacerbated the bad blood between journalists and policemen. All journalists seem to be potential victims of police 'enthusiasm', although naturally those working for opposition-orientated papers are at greater risk.

Most mass-circulation French dailies are rather depoliticized, especially in the sense of not being associated with a particular party. Of the ten newspapers with the largest circulation listed in table 24, none is a party paper. The top three Paris dailies are generally pro-government but in a rather diluted form, while *L'Aurore* and *Le Monde* are generally anti-government. The largest provincial papers tend to be 'apolitical', which means that criticism of the government is rare and muffled. As in local politics, so with the local press, the emphasis is on what unites rather than on what divides. Newspapers with a recognized partisan slant include the provincial *La Dépêche du Midi* at Toulouse (radical), *L'Est Républicain* at Nancy (opposition centrist) and *Le Provençal*, Defferre's Marseille socialist daily. Of the national dailies, *L'Humanité*, the communist party's organ, has a circulation of about two hundred thousand, while the UDR's *La Nation* limps along with a meagre thirteen thousand. However, although *La Nation* has few readers, it has numerous listeners, thanks to the disproportionate space it receives in the daily review of the press on the radio.

Table 24
Average Number of Copies Printed of the
Ten Leading French Daily Newspapers (first quarter of 1968)

Paris		Provincial	
France-Soir	1,238,622	*Ouest-France* (Rennes)	706,368
Le Parisien Libéré	831,362	*Le Progrès de Lyon* (Lyon)	541,711
Le Figaro	515,157	*Le Dauphiné Libéré* (Grenoble)	503,833
L'Aurore	424,588	*La Voix du Nord* (Lille)	430,356
Le Monde	407,804	*Sud-Ouest* (Bordeaux)	399,052

About three-quarters of French homes take a daily newspaper but they are read mainly for relaxation rather than to acquire political information. Despite the growth in the French population by one-fifth since 1939, newspaper circulation has only increased by one-twelfth and the number of papers has fallen drastically (see table 25). As a result of the disruption of the distribution of Paris newspapers during the German occupation, and the increased interest in local news, the provincial press outstripped the Paris press in total circulation after the war and has maintained its substantial lead. The relative importance of this provincial press is a corrective to the highly centralized character of French political and administrative institutions, particularly if one bears in mind that the number of separate local editions of each paper may exceed sixty. However, the Parisian political class concentrates its attention upon *Le Monde*, arguably the world's leading newspaper, together with weeklies like *L'Express* and *Le Nouvel Observateur*. In a class by itself is *Le Canard Enchaîné*, the finest and best informed satirical weekly in the world (with a circulation of over three hundred thousand copies), which played a major part in discrediting the UDR and Chaban-Delmas, leading to his dismissal as prime minister in 1972. Apart from such isolated cases, which keep alive the old crusading French journalistic tradition, the bulk of the press endeavour to make a profit through being innocuous; newspapers do not seek to mould opinion or to exert political influence.

Table 25
Number and Total Circulation of Paris and Provincial
Daily Newspapers, 1939–66

| Year | Paris | | Provinces | | Total Circulation |
	Number of Dailies	Circulation	Number of Dailies	Circulation	
1939	39	6,000,000	175	5,200,000	11,200,000
1946	28	5,959,000	175	9,164,850	15,123,850
1952	14	3,411,965	117	6,188,010	9,599,975
1958	13	4,373,459	110	7,294,020	11,667,479
1966	13*	4,384,032	72	7,879,348	12,263,370

* Fell to 11 in 1972.

Since the second world war, and especially since the advent of the fifth republic, while newspapers like *Le Monde* and *Le Figaro* have achieved greater independence from private financial and political interests, the radio and television services have been increasingly subordinated to the state, being converted into the government's docile propaganda instrument. The traditional view that monopoly control of a public service is an essential attribute of state sovereignty is widely held among the French political élite, though not by the general public. The reluctance to accept opposition as legitimate has meant in practice that French governments have used radio and television to expound official views to the exclusion of those of the opposition. Prior to the outbreak of the second world war radio had been controlled by an official of the ministry of postal services but under the fourth republic it was usually controlled either by the prime minister or the minister of information. The latter ministry was created during the second world war and from 1958–69 the minister of information combined the functions of government spokesman and tutelage over the state radio and television service, known since 1964 as ORTF. By 1969 it was recognized that for one minister to discharge these two distinct roles meant the subordination of radio and television to the government and the ministry of information was abolished.

In July 1968, following the 'events' of that year, the *Service de liaison interministérielle pour l'information* (SLII) was also abolished. This secret committee of about ten officials from the major ministries met daily at eleven o'clock from 1963 to 1968, under the chairmanship of an official of the ministry of the interior, to coordinate information for the benefit of the ministry of information and the prefects. It also decided which politicians would appear on television and the subject-matter of broadcasts. The assistant director of television news always attended to receive instructions on the matters to be emphasized or played down, until May 1968 when as part of the revolt of ORTF staff against government manipulation, he ceased to do so. (He was subsequently one of seventy-two who were discharged as a reprisal in August 1968.) The SLII was replaced in December 1968 by an interministerial committee for information, similarly composed, which claims to confine itself to providing information without actually seeking to interfere in radio and television programmes. It receives feedback from the public through officially commissioned opinion polls, the more favourable of which it allows to be published.

It would be naive to believe that the abolition of the SLII in 1968 and of the ministry of information in 1969 made ORTF politically unbiased. It is the ingrained practice of self-censorship, deriving from dependence upon the government, that has resulted in the perversion of radio and television. Successive reforms have changed the letter of the law whilst the spirit has remained the same. The 1964 Act, which claimed to make the ORTF independent of government to ensure the impartiality of political information, signally failed in this respect owing to the inability of the governing board to carry out its functions. How could it guarantee the ORTF's independence when this board was constituted so as to ensure a permanent majority of government nominees, half of whom were civil servants representing the major ministries? (In 1968, two were members of the personal staff of the prime minister and one the head of the minister of information's personal staff!) The director-general was in effective control and he exercised it according to government directives. The frequency with which directors-general have come and gone since 1958 suggests that even complete pliability has not guaranteed security of tenure. Part of the reason may be that they have been under pressure not merely from ministers but from ministerial staffs, senior civil servants, prefects, pro-government deputies and influential mayors. The result was that the 1964 Act safeguard, which at the instance of the council of state required the government to make clear when it was using radio and television for ministerial purposes, has been circumvented.

Although the custom has been to deny that the ORTF shows political bias, Alain Peyrefitte a former minister of information who became secretary-general of the UDR in 1972, had the audacity to justify its partiality by claiming in 1965 that its function was to counterbalance press bias in favour of the opposition. The same justification could no doubt be adduced in favour of the daily press review at 8.30 am on 'France-Inter', in which the extensive quotation accorded to the UDR's *La Nation* is coupled with disjointed excerpts from the opposition press enveloped in polemical commentary by the ORTF 'reviewer'. Competition from the 'peripheral' commercial radio stations (so called because they are nominally situated beyond France's borders in Luxembourg, the Saarland, Monte Carlo and Andorra) means that the French listener has some freedom of choice. However, the independence of these stations should not be exaggerated as the French government is a shareholder in all of them either through Havas, in the case of Radio Luxembourg, or through SOFIRAD (*Société financière* *de radiodiffusion*) in the case of Europe 1, Radio Monte Carlo and Sud-Radio.* The two larger commercial stations, covering northern France, Radio Luxembourg and Europe 1 (in which it does not have a majority shareholding) are furthermore dependent on the French post office for permission to link their studios in Paris with their transmitters abroad. So, although they express themselves more freely on political matters and have generally been rather more generous to the opposition parties, they have to be careful not to provoke suppression. In the last quarter of 1970 the listener ratings were as follows: France-Inter, 28 per cent; Europe 1, 24·2 per cent; Radio Luxembourg, 17·8 per cent; Monte Carlo, 2·8 per cent; Sud-Radio, 0·7 per cent, making a total of 44·5 per cent of French listeners to commercial radio compared to the 28 per cent who receive their news bulletins from state radio.

Despite the enduring importance of radio as a source of political information, the coverage of television had by 1970 reached 70 per cent of the French population and would reach almost all French families by 1975. The number of television sets in 1972 already exceeded the circulation of the daily press. Although the use of television for propagandist purposes was even more uninhibited than in the case of radio, especially by the twenty-three regional television stations set up by Peyrefitte in 1965 (with regional prefects daily suggesting what to comment upon and whom to interview) there is little evidence that it has helped the governments of the fifth republic. The frequency with which ministers appeared and the total exclusion of the opposition leaders in fact proved very counter-productive at the 1965 presidential election. The opposition candidates achieved great impact when each received a total of two hours on television and two hours on radio to expound their programmes. Since then, ORTF has administered homeopathic doses of opposition politicians to the French public throughout the periods between elections to counteract the attractions of novelty. At the 1968 general election, the parties making up the majority coalition received equal time with those of the opposition. However, the relative fairness

* The French government owns 17 per cent of Radio Luxembourg; 35 per cent (but 46 per cent of voting shares) of Europe 1; 83 per cent of Radio Monte Carlo and 99 per cent of Sud-Radio. See *Rapport de la Commission d'Etude du statut de l'ORTF* (known as the *Rapport Paye*), 1970, pp. 50–53.

shown during elections was more than compensated for by the bias between elections, both in general political reporting and more specifically in the selective transmission of debates in the national assembly and from party congresses. The rule followed by ORTF on broadcasts of political matter is that spokesmen of the government, the pro-government parties and the opposition parties each receive one-third of the time, which works 2 : 1 in the government's favour.

Opposition resentment at such discrimination came to the boil in April 1968 when a censure motion attacked the government for 'confiscating the ORTF for its personal propaganda' to the exclusion of the opposition and those such as Giscard d'Estaing, who was at the time giving the government only critical support and was punished by being banned by ORTF. Although this motion was defeated, the May 'events' quickly embroiled the mass media in political controversy as the commercial radio stations were accused by the government of helping to provoke and spread the student riots by their incendiary reporting. Forced to act as a fire brigade rather than an accurate news service, the cream of the ORTF journalists unprecedentedly criticized their organization for failing to report properly and pilloried the television news in particular for 'failing to resist government pressure'. They followed this by joining the general strike, demanding an end to government interference in ORTF, and held out until mid-July, long after the manual workers had ended their strike. Not only did they lose their fight for an impartial and independent ORTF. On the pretext of reducing staff, the government chose the beginning of August (when most of France is on holiday) to dismiss the ringleaders of the strike, administering a lesson on the dangers of seeking to restore dignity and independence to the profession of ORTF journalist.[25]

After de Gaulle's withdrawal in April 1969, the interim president Alain Poher made the independence of ORTF one of the planks in his electoral platform and Pompidou countered this by promising to abolish the ministry of information and to liberalize ORTF. After the election, Pompidou's prime minister assumed responsibility for the reform of ORTF. Chaban-Delmas immediately created two independent news services, one for each of the television channels, putting the first channel (with more viewers) in charge of a journalist with a reputation for independence, whilst the second channel was placed under a notoriously partisan Gaullist from the radio news service. (This attempt to secure a more independent television news was a step for which Chaban-Delmas subsequently suffered much criticism from the more intransigent UDR members and was a contributory cause of his dismissal by Pompidou in 1972.)* News increased to 21 per cent of all television programmes in 1970. Chaban-Delmas had also promised, as part of his plan to restore credibility to ORTF, that the spokesmen of all political parties represented in the assembly and organized interests represented in the economic and social council would have the right to make regular appearances on television. In March 1970, ORTF inaugurated a very modest application of this promise, and in August 1972 the new director-general instituted a system of quarterly party political broadcasts, in which government and opposition parties (with at least thirty parliamentary representatives) collectively receive equal time.

Chaban-Delmas also set up a committee on ORTF reform which reported in 1970. It did not seek to make any fundamental changes in the relations between ORTF and government. However, it did advocate the recognition of a 'right of reply' comparable to that enjoyed since 1881 by anyone attacked in the press. (Any named person can require a newspaper to publish a rebuttal within three days in the same part of the newspaper, in the same print and of the same length as the original article.) When the senate tried to incorporate such a right into the 1964 Act, the government prevented it, but the new director-general promised to institute a right of reply. The Paye Report also implicitly acknowledged the bias in regional television by suggesting that safeguards against political interference should exist in each region as well as at the centre.[26] It gave no convincing reason for refusing to transfer responsibility for ORTF to the minister of culture, as suggested by the senate, preferring instead to leave control in the highly political hands of the prime minister. Admittedly, one is not reassured by the remark made in the United States by André Malraux, minister of culture from 1959–69 : 'How can

* The new director-general (see p. 150), immediately abolished these independent news services with the result that the independent journalist in charge of the first channel service resigned while the notorious Gaullist was appointed head of the first channel.

one govern a country where the government doesn't have a television monopoly?'

A year after the Chaban-Delmas attempt to change ORTF's image from that of a slanted, pro-governmental propagandist institution into a reliable public information service, an opinion poll (see table 26) limited to television indicated that a substantial degree of suspicion remained. It appears that just over one-third of the French population are satisfied with the political information they receive from ORTF, just under one-third are dissatisfied and nearly two-fifths (which includes rather more women than men) have no opinion. It is perhaps worth adding that when asked about the honesty with which television reports on economic issues like prices, wages and unemployment, the number who are dissatisfied leaps to 41 per cent, whereas only 30 per cent consider the reporting on these matters to be honest. There may well be a connection between this finding and the consistent unpopularity of the government's economic policy in recent years.

Table 26
The Honesty of French Television Treatment of
Political Subjects, October 1970 (%)*

Political Activities of	Honest	Insufficiently Honest	No Reply
Government	39	33	28
Trade unions	37	29	34
Parliament	35	20	45
Youth movements	34	26	40
Political parties	32	30	38
Opposition leaders	29	31	40

* Source: IFOP in *Le Nouvel Observateur*, 2 November 1970, p. 34, and *Sondages*, 1971, nos 1–2, p. 103

Resistance within the UDR to the attempts by Chaban-Delmas to allow ORTF more freedom found its spokesman in René Tomasini even before he became the party's general secretary. In June 1970 he criticized the ORTF for concentrating its attention on the 'negative' features of French life and hoped that it was not due to '*un plan concerté d'intoxication du pays*'. In the following February he moved on from his speculative conspiracy theory to a direct attack on the prime minister, who had been 'misled' in handing over television news on the main channel to 'the enemies of freedom' who deliberately played up 'the negative aspects of French society, the bizarre, exceptional, scandalous, morbid, pessimistic, unpleasant and demoralizing'. Whereas he was compelled to retract his accusations against the judiciary, the then UDR general secretary did not withdraw his remarks on ORTF, confident that he was not only reflecting rank and file feeling but had the tacit support of the president of the republic. The more extreme elements, represented by the Dijon committee for the defence of the republic, followed up Tomasini's attack with a call for the resuscitation of a ministry of information and 'a governmental news service'. Ironically, Tomasini was forced to resign as UDR general secretary shortly after his anti-liberalization campaign was crowned with a measure of success in 1972.

The opportunity to reverse the trend towards greater ORTF objectivity came in 1972 when a senate supervisory committee investigated a television 'secret advertising' scandal in which a number of prominent personalities were implicated. President Pompidou (who held television directly responsible for the poor result of the April 1972 referendum owing to inadequate 'psychological preparation' of the electors) assumed control over an area of policy previously left to the prime minister. He asked the junior minister for civil service matters, Philippe Malaud, to prepare a reorganization of ORTF and this was done very quickly so that legislative action could be completed before the end of the parliamentary session in June 1972. The 1972 ORTF Act reaffirmed the public service monopoly character of television. Power was concentrated in the hands of a director-general, appointed by the government for three years. He would also be chairman of the fourteen-member governing board, half of whose members were also government nominees, while the other seven represented the ORTF staff (three), the viewers (the national assembly and senate each choosing one representative), the press (one) and journalists (one). As the director-general has a casting vote, the government has a built-in majority on the governing board. One of the first decisions of the Messmer government in July 1972 was to appoint as director-general a UDR deputy, Arthur Conte, known to be close to President Pompidou and outspokenly anti-communist. With the 1973 general election in sight, President Pompidou decided that it was essential to use ORTF for the purpose of returning a majority of his political friends. The fact that M. Malaud's office has been redesignated 'civil service and information services' suggests the prelude to a resurrection of the ministry of information function abolished in 1969.* Thus a modest experiment in liberalizing the television service did not survive the temptations of short-term partisan expediency.

One should perhaps stress that despite all that has been said in this chapter about the weaknesses in the protection of civil rights in France, and despite certain superficial resemblances to the Soviet police state, individual Frenchmen stand an incomparably better chance than would the Soviet citizen of surviving relatively unscathed in their encounters with authority. France is, despite all its authoritarian features, fundamentally a liberal democracy in which personal rights are not automatically sacrificed to *raison d'état*. She has a stubborn libertarian tradition of popular resistance to authority. There is a great deal of truth in the quip that whereas in Britain everything is permitted except what is forbidden, in the Soviet Union everything is forbidden including what is permitted, whilst in France everything is permitted including what is forbidden. However, for civil rights to receive greater weight in relation to the requirements of public order or the convenience of public power, the balance of political forces will have to shift away from the UDR which is susceptible to the temptations of domination.

* Malaud became minister of information in April 1973.

6 Economic Policy: By Whom and How It Is Made

Owing in part to the belated nature of her industrialization and exposure to international competition, official France – unlike Britain or the United States – did not even pay lip service to market values until the late 1960s. French governments had for centuries alternated between policies of passive protection and active promotion – state-sponsored capitalism and state capitalism – based upon close collusion between the private sector and its public senior partner. The legendary timidity of the mass of French family firms meant that it was public rather than private enterprise that innovated and took risks. Despite the dramatic industrial revolution through which France has been going in the last two decades, and is still undergoing, the weight of this long-standing *dirigiste* tradition still makes itself felt in the sense of dependence upon government, which French businessmen more or less explicitly acknowledge. In November 1968 the president of the CNPF asserted that far from the growth in foreign competition requiring a withdrawal of the national government's protective and supporting intervention, it was a further justification of such assistance. 'The salient feature of this new phase of our economic development is the decisive role that states will be called upon to play. International competition will involve the whole nation. Left to themselves, firms cannot face this competition alone.'[1]

That this view is shared not merely by a majority of businessmen but by the French public in general is evident from table 27. If public attitudes are grouped into four categories, nonintervention or *laissez-faire* (to give it the French name that paradoxically was so inappropriate to French public policy) can be eliminated as of negligible importance. Now, less than ever, is such doctrinaire liberalism popular in France. A third of the public favour state economic intervention limited to selective, piecemeal action to deal with particular problems which cannot otherwise be satisfactorily settled. Support for this view increases with age, suggesting that it is likely to decline in the future. The two types of comprehensive state intervention win a clear majority of public support, with the purely indicative approach being much less popular than a direct administration of the economy by the

Table 27
Public Attitude Towards the Scope and Type of State
Economic Intervention, 1970 (%)*

Reply	Laissez-faire	Type of State Economic Intervention			No Opinion
		Selective	Comprehensive		
		Corrective	Indicative	Directive	
All	2	33	20	36	9
Sex					
Men	3	35	23	36	3
Women	2	32	18	36	12
Age					
21–34	2	23	24	44	7
35–49	3	32	24	35	6
50–64	2	39	15	32	12
65+	1	42	17	28	12
Occupation					
Farmer	2	31	22	32	13
Shopkeepers and craftsmen	2	35	26	33	4
Professional and large business	1	38	32	27	2
White-collar employees	1	31	25	39	4
Workers	4	29	16	42	9
No occupation	2	40	16	31	11
Party vote					
Communist	4	37	16	38	5
Socialist and radical	3	32	28	36	1
Opposition centre	3	41	26	27	3
Independent republican	2	33	20	31	14
UDR	0	32	17	43	8

* Source: adapted from SOFRES, *Les Français et l'Etat*, p. 59.

government, backed by the full force of the law. There is disproportionate support for persuasive planning among men, the under-fifties, bigger businessmen and the professions and in the non-communist left and left-centre. A more assertive and if necessary coercive type of public intervention finds support particularly among the young, workers and the UDR. When asked whether the French government intervenes too much in the nation's economic life, 23 per cent feel that it does while 40 per cent reply that it does not intervene enough. What is striking about these findings is that despite the variations between sex, age, occupation and party that they reveal, the propensity to support 'strong' state intervention cuts across all these categories and provides a cultural underpinning to the political behaviour, especially of those in authority, that we have described and will discuss below.

The political coordination of state economic intervention

Overall economic coordination is carried out in France through an elaborate network of mainly informal and *ad hoc* interdepartmental committees and interministerial committees and councils.* The most important of these is the economic interministerial committee, which usually meets weekly on Tuesdays under the chairmanship of the prime minister, its only other permanent member being the finance minister. Ministers and senior civil servants attend when invited but its main function is to resolve conflicts between the prime minister, the minister of finance and the spending ministers, prior to endorsement by the cabinet. These conflicts will arise when the prime minister supports expenditure demands that have been rejected by the minister of finance. Particularly in the latter half of June each year, the prime minister spends a lot of time settling disputes that have arisen between the spending ministries and the finance ministry in the preparation of the budget. The disputed matters are reported to the government's general secretariat, where they are examined by its economic adviser and by the economic and budgetary advisers on the prime minister's personal staff. Issues which cannot be settled amongst officials are then dealt with by the prime minister, the minister of finance and the

* See above, p. 97.

minister concerned, the finance minister winning about 90 per cent of such conflicts. The prime minister's decision is final unless either the spending minister or the finance minister chooses to appeal to the president of the republic; or the president – informed by his economic adviser, who is present at such interministerial meetings – elects to make his own decision through an inter-ministerial council at the Elysée. The decision not to devalue the franc in 1968 was very much the personal decision of President de Gaulle; the decisions to devalue in 1969 and not to revalue in 1971 were taken by President Pompidou. At a press conference on 22 December 1971, President Pompidou made his intimate involvement in economic policy clear when he declared: 'You can be certain that the prime minister, the minister of economic affairs and finance and I myself are attentively following the situation day by day and that, if necessary, we would take the measures required to maintain the level of employment and expansion at a satisfactory rate.'

Apportioning influence over economic policy decisions among the triumvirate of president, prime minister and finance minister in general terms can only be done in a very crude way. By contrast with the fourth republic, when the finance minister was in a dominant position, especially in budgetary matters, under the fifth republic the president and prime minister have played a much more active role. The finance minister has been forced on to the defensive, compelled to provide the resources to meet com-mitments of which the president or prime minister approve. President Pompidou appears to intervene much more extensively than did President de Gaulle, while Pompidou's first prime minister, Chaban-Delmas – given his general coordinating role and the ultimate responsibility for national and regional economic planning – was as active as were Debré and Pompidou. Shorn of the regional planning function in 1972, Messmer was clearly intended to be a weaker prime minister. The low water mark of the finance minister's influence under the fifth republic occurred between January 1960 and January 1962, when the former governor of the Bank of France, Baumgartner, was frequently short-circuited by the Prime Minister.* This was the period when the National Plan was being given great emphasis by president

* He replaced M. Pinay, in circumstances described briefly in chapter 4, p. 90.

and prime minister, but by 1963 the new finance minister, Giscard d'Estaing, used the inflationary situation to substitute his ministry's deflationary stabilization plan for the Fourth Plan. (It has been claimed that the 1963 stabilization plan was imposed by de Gaulle on Giscard, that Pompidou saved the latter from being dismissed in 1963 but that in 1966 he was made the scapegoat for the political consequences of the deflation.[2]) There has since been a partial restoration of the traditional financial veto over the expenditure proposals of all the other ministries, which are treated as irresponsible advocates for their sectional clientèles. The consequence has been a partial usurpation of the coordinating role of the prime minister by the finance minister with the president intervening as ultimate arbiter.

An important element in this restoration of the traditional power of the finance ministry was the revival of the pre-Keynesian principle of the balanced budget. This aim was inspired by Jacques Rueff, an economist who had the ear of President de Gaulle. In addition to influencing de Gaulle's views on international monetary policy, Rueff's liberal conservatism encouraged the government in 1963 to adopt a commitment of long standing in Federal Germany: that public expenditure should not increase at a faster rate than the national product. This was the prelude to the 1964 application of the aim of a balanced budget in the preparation of the 1965 budget, utilized by Giscard d'Estaing as part of the public relations façade for the stabilization plan curb on public expenditure. Balanced budgets have owed much to the artifice of selective inclusion and exclusion of items. The fundamental purpose of this fictional balance was not merely to impress the conservative electorate with the housekeeping rectitude of the finance minister; it was to disengage the treasury from its previous task of substantial short-term borrowing from the public and to channel these funds into long-term investment in public and private corporations, a role transferred notably to the *Caisse des Dépôts*.* It was the prelude to a neo-liberal attempt to free these corporations from the detailed control of the finance ministry over their investment policy and to reduce the tendency of the French public to affix political blame upon the government for economic mishaps. How-

* See below p. 165.

ever, the deflationary policy followed by Giscard – inspired in part by the Rueff–de Gaulle desire to compel the United States to conform to the discipline of the gold standard – contributed to de Gaulle's poor showing in the first ballot of the December 1965 presidential election and to Giscard's dismissal from office in January 1966.

Table 28
Who Should Take the Blame When Things Go Badly? (%) *

Responsible	Sphere of Public Policy			
	Order	*Education*	*Prices*	*Taxation*
President of the republic	36	26	16	14
Prime minister	36	28	20	11
Minister of finance	1	2	38	54
Assembly deputies	5	14	5	6
No reply	22	30	21	15

* Source: IFOP poll, 21 September 1971, published in *L'Express*, 27 September 1971, p. 13.

To whom does the French public attribute the power to take economic decisions? Table 28 indicates the public's assessment in 1971 of the way in which responsibility should be apportioned between the president, prime minister, finance minister and assembly deputies on four major issues of public policy. There is a marked difference in allocation between the two economic issues (prices and taxation) and the two non-economic issues (order and education). Whereas most blame is attributed almost equally to the president of the republic and the prime minister on the non-economic issues, when it comes to economic matters the position is more complex. Here, the finance minister is singled out as the main culprit, with the president and prime minister nevertheless sharing some of the blame. The assembly deputies are rightly exonerated from responsibility except in the matter of education, where the unanimous vote in favour of the Faure Act of 1968 is held against them. (The large number of abstentions on this question may be due to public inability to express the view that the real culprits were either the ministry of education, the students or the teachers.*) As to the main beneficiaries of the influence

* See below, chapter 7. Considering the importance sometimes attributed in the problems encountered to inadequate financial provision for education, the negligible blame attached to the finance minister is interesting.

exercised, the same poll indicates that 59 per cent (79 per cent of the government's opponents and 35 per cent of its supporters) regard President Pompidou's policy as primarily favouring big business. The public impression of presidential bias is significant when it is linked with the fact that the finance inspectors, who form the élite of the finance ministry, as well as occupying other top posts in the civil service and public corporations, frequently move while still in their prime into private business. This facilitates administrative as well as political concerted action in the management of the public and private sectors.

The ministry of finance

In France, as in Britain, there have been several unsuccessful attempts to avoid the tendency of overall economic policy to be subordinated to a ministry with a financial emphasis. In both countries, two major attempts were made by left-wing governments (in France during the popular front government of 1936–7 and when Mendès-France was minister of the national economy in 1944–5). The aim was to plan the economy in a medium-term perspective and not simply to steer the economy through unpredictable squalls with the aid of the annual budget. In all four cases, the failure to check the power of the ministry responsible for the nation's finances restored the priority accorded to short-term budgetary and balance-of-payments considerations over the planned growth of the national economy, free from lurches between 'stop' and 'go'. However, before Britain embarked on the first of its postwar failures, in France the birth of the planning commissariat in 1946, which was to acquire a modest but respected and independent position vis à vis the finance ministry, ensured that medium-term planners would be tolerated and then accepted into the exclusive club of economic decision-makers. In 1963 the creation of the office of regional and spatial planning delegate general represented an extension of medium-term planning from a purely sectoral phenomenon – dealing with particular industries or public services – into an assessment of the implications of national economic decisions for particular regions considered as intermediate structures between the central government and the local authorities. However, the absorption of the rival ministry of the national economy into a ministry of finance and economic affairs and then into the current ministry of the economy and finance did not represent the centralization in an overall coordinating ministry of the power to make economic policy. The staffs of the planning commissioner, and until 1972 the regional planning delegate general, were answerable to the prime minister. This enabled him to challenge any attempt at economic omnipotence or omnicompetence by his rival for overall control under the president. Nor have these changes meant that the re-entitled ministry has ceased to be primarily a ministry of finance, which is the name that is still currently used.

The superiority complex of senior finance ministry officials is based upon the fact that the ministry is in a stronger strategic decision-making position to all other ministries, who come as supplicants for financial favours. Corresponding to this relationship, the finance ministry's divisions and bureaux contain officials whose function is to supervise or short-circuit the activities of every other ministry. Thus the sub-divisions of the budget and treasury divisions concerned with the nationalized industries may in practice take over the tutelage role assigned to other ministries. We have seen that finance usually gets its way in the interdepartmental committees which meet to resolve disputes. Furthermore, its senior officials represent the best of ENA. They colonize other parts of the machinery of economic authority. Thus, of the seventy finance inspectors who left their corps during the first decade of the fifth republic (apart from the nineteen who took over divisions or sub-divisions of the ministry of finance) twelve went to senior administrative posts in other ministries; twelve joined the personal staff of a minister (six joining the staff of the minister of finance or his minister of state for the budget); seventeen became managers of public corporations (eight in banks); and six took posts abroad (three in the EEC).[3] If to the inspectors are added the many finance civil administrators who move to prominent positions in other ministries or public agencies, a very powerful network of influence over economic decisions enables those in command at the Rue de Rivoli to count confidently upon securing acquiescence to their wishes.

However, the ministry of finance is too large and complex to be the cohesive and monolithic organization frequently depicted. With a staff exceeding 130,000 officials, all but 4 per cent of whom belong to the ministry's field services, the finance ministry would be more appropriately described as a federation of divisions, each of which is itself sub-divided into autonomous bureaux which the minister's personal staff make valiant attempts to coordinate. The finance minister's *cabinet* is headed by a director* who is not only the coordinator of the work of the ministry's divisions but the person whom other ministers initially contact, the director being almost permanently in his office whilst the minister of finance is frequently away. In recent years the *cabinet* has varied in size between under twenty (Giscard) and about forty (Debré). To keep the minister informed of the main economic issues and provide liaison with the most important divisions, about ten specialists are assigned particular duties within the *cabinet*. Treasury, budgetary, tax, industrial policy and planning, prices and incomes, internal trade, foreign economic relations and agricultural policy are regular candidates for such special treatment, indicative of the importance attached to them. Those selected are usually drawn from the ministry's divisions as men marked out for promotion. A specialist, who usually comes from the budget division, is responsible for expenditure estimates and overall budgetary coordination in the *cabinet*, with the revenue side being handled by the tax specialist. They report through the director of the finance minister's *cabinet* rather than the minister of state for the budget who deals primarily with the interministerial and parliamentary aspects of the budgetary process.

Figure 2 presents a simplified representation of the central organization of the finance ministry, with attention focused on the major divisions concerned with national economic policy. The finance inspectorate audit the finances of most state institutions (except nationalized industries) and concern themselves with the efficiency as well as the legality of public expenditure. After five years service they are free to leave and they often go off to positions of power inside and outside the finance ministry. They have, for example, enjoyed a semi-monopoly of the top posts in the treasury, budget, foreign economic relations and taxation divisions since the second world war. The finance inspectors supervise the very extensive field services of the finance ministry, notably those concerned with taxation and public accounts. At this stage of their career, these Napoleonic creations are concerned with the rigorous enforcement of the central rules, and as such they deprive

* See above, p. 111.

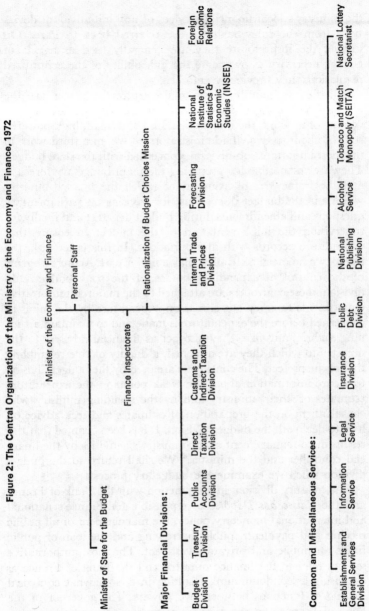

Figure 2: The Central Organization of the Ministry of the Economy and Finance, 1972

Minister of the Economy and Finance

Personal Staff

Minister of State for the Budget

Finance Inspectorate

Rationalization of Budget Choices Mission

Major Financial Divisions:

Budget Division

Treasury Division

Public Accounts Division

Direct Taxation Division

Customs and Indirect Taxation Division

Public Debt Division

Internal Trade and Prices Division

Forecasting Division

Internal Trade and Prices Division

National Institute of Statistics & Economic Studies (INSEE)

Foreign Economic Relations

Common and Miscellaneous Services:

Establishments and General Services Division

Information Service

Legal Service

Insurance Division

National Publishing Division

Alcohol Service

Tobacco and Match Monopoly (SEITA)

National Lottery Secretariat

the ministry's local financial services of any initiative, all deviations from the rules having to be referred back to Paris. On leaving the inspectorate they are generally used as agents of change necessary to overcome the inflexibility of the centralized regulations they previously enforced.

The finance ministry's two main centres of power are the treasury and budget divisions (see figure 3). Considering the volume of its work, the budget division has a small, high-powered staff of about sixty civil administrators, of whom a third work in the most important sub-division, concerned with the state budget. They are responsible for preparing the main budgetary forecasts and the framework of assumptions which the finance minister will use in the budget discussions; for advising on parliamentary questions and amendments during budget debates; and finally for supervising the implementation of the budget to ensure that expenditure accords with appropriations. In this latter task, the thirty-two financial controllers play a major part. Acting as agents of the control of expenditure' office of the state budget sub-division, these controllers are attached to the major administrative departments to carry out checks on expenditure by the ministry concerned before the expenditure is made and to maintain a running audit. Janus-like, they also act as financial advisers to the ministry to which they are attached, a duality of role resembling that of the prefect. The controllers are used by the budget division to secure information about the weak points in the expenditure estimates of 'their' ministry and by the spending ministry who consult them on the preparation of estimates and seek advice on how to deal with the budget division. It has been claimed that this results in co-management of the ministry's activities by the financial controller and the minister.[4] We shall return to the budget division when we examine the budgetary process.

The treasury division, in conjunction with the Bank of France and the *Caisse des Dépôts*, is responsible for France's national and international monetary policy, the management of all public receipts and payments, public borrowing and the loan of public funds for public and private investment. The most authoritative sources refer to the finance ministry and the Bank of France as exercising a 'condominium', resulting in a 'somewhat equivocal sharing of functions between two powers. The governor of the Bank of France and the minister of finance are sometimes com-

Figure 3: Internal Organization of the Ministry of the Economy and Finance: Budget and Treasury Divisions, 1970*

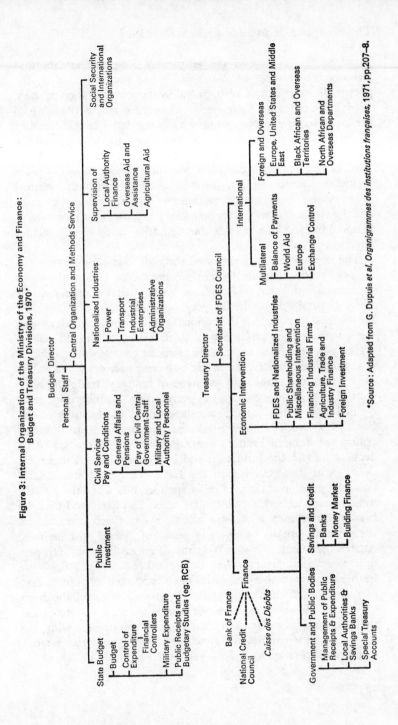

*Source: Adapted from G. Dupuis et al. *Organigrammes des institutions françaises*, 1971, pp.207–8.

pared to the pope and the emperor.'[5] Despite the fact that treasury control over the Bank of France was increased by the popular front legislation of 1936 and by its nationalization in 1945, French governments have remained faithful to the intention of the bank's creator, Napoleon, who commented to his treasury minister : 'I want the bank to be sufficiently in the hands of the government, but not too much. . . .'[6] It has been felt, as with the Bank of England, that complete government control would place 'monetary power' at the disposal of the short-term political interests of ministers, while autonomy would enable the traditional guardians of monetary orthodoxy to protect the longer-term national interest and increase the confidence of foreign monetary circles.

The condominium is exercised through four committees : the national credit council, the banks control commission, the stock exchange commission and the franc area monetary committee. Of these, all presided over by the governor of the Bank of France, by far the most important is the national credit council, which advises the government on all aspects of its monetary and credit policy. Its forty-five members include the planning commissioner, officials of the finance ministry, the major economic ministries, the public credit institutions and representatives of industry, trade and agriculture. However, owing to overlapping membership, 'the council is virtually a supplementary board of directors of the Bank of France'.[7] Although nominally merely an executant of policy, the Bank of France's general directorate of credit plays a decisive part in the formation and implementation of monetary policy, with the governor of the bank being in a particularly powerful position at times of crisis, such as 1968 when the government needed to borrow substantial sums. The likelihood that the bank and the finance ministry will see eye to eye is increased by the governor usually being an inspector of finance, although the current incumbent, Olivier Wormser, is an ex-diplomat. His predecessors Baumgartner (1949–60) and Brunet (1960–69) were former finance ministry officials. Their long periods in office also explain the influential role played by the governor of the Bank of France. However, he does not possess the autonomous power that enabled the German Bundesbank president – with the approval of the cabinet at a meeting in which he participated – to topple a prestigious federal economics minister in 1972.

The *Caisse des Dépôts et Consignations* is another Napoleonic creation, although it did not acquire its present name until 1816. Since the second world war – thanks to the decline in the burden of financing the long-term national debt (owing to inflation) and the rapid increase in the funds of savings banks which form 90 per cent of its deposits – it has become the most important treasury agency in the selective financing of public and private investment. It has concentrated on its traditional role, the long-term financing of local authority public works programmes at low rates of interest; but low-cost housing has now overhauled the provision of other types of public investment. (This building society function is discharged through a subsidiary called scic.) All these loans are undertaken within the framework of the investment priorities fixed by the national plan and the economic and social development fund, the *Caisse* only lending money to institutions other than the central government if they are in receipt of a public subsidy accorded by the finance ministry's economic intervention sub-division. Formally, the *Caisse* is thus the plan's investment bank, with the finance ministry possessing a veto power. Nevertheless, the *Caisse* encourages ministries and local authorities – with the collusion of the ministry of the interior – to over-invest relative to the limits imposed by the finance ministry and the plan because it will usually supply the funds to make up the difference between what is authorized and what is spent.

The *Caisse* has created a number of subsidiaries, notably the *Société Central pour l'Equipement du Territoire* (scet). Launched in 1955 at the instance of the finance ministry, it provides the financial and logistical support for urban development joint public-private enterprises, in which the public sector never own less than 50 per cent or more than 65 per cent of the shares. They have played a major part in equipping an increasingly urbanized and industrialized France with housing and industrial estates which are beyond the capacity of individual local authorities. In the process, the *Caisse* (through scet) has been able to exercise a coordinating influence over housing policy that rivals that of the responsible ministry.[8] scet's creator was the then director-general of the *Caisse*, François Bloch-Lainé, precursor of the new-style interventionism of the finance official, whose career illustrates the pivotal role in a planned economy of the finance ministry. An inspector of finance who rose to be director of the treasury division (1947–52) he then served for some fifteen years at the head of the *Caisse*. He became the leading advocate of the notion of a concerted economy, prior to heading the most important nationalized deposit bank, the *Crédit Lyonnais*. He has written of the *Caisse* that it is 'close to the treasury but not identified with it' and recalls the quip : 'The *Caisse des Dépôts* does nothing of which the government disapproves, but it does not do all that it requests.'[9] However, refusal to comply is rare and is more likely to occur in the buying of shares on the stock exchange, where the government may suggest that it help sustain a flagging market or save a French firm from a foreign takeover bid.

In France, the public sector controls nearly two-thirds of credit and nearly half national investment (15 per cent being carried out directly through public enterprises). The treasury division is responsible, through an office in its economic intervention subdivision, for all state shareholdings, though the *Caisse* may act as a holding company on its behalf and always collects dividends due to the state. The treasury instructs the state representatives – civil servants who are appointed by the minister of finance – on the policy to adopt at board meetings but they generally act as sleeping partners. The economic intervention sub-division plays a vital role in determining both industrial and regional policy by virtue of its influence over industrial investment. It thereby reduces the ministry of industrial development and the regional and spatial planning delegacy to the humble role of sorting out the more valid requests for investment funds, saving it the trouble of dealing with private industrialists directly. Furthermore, it acts as banker vis à vis the investment projects that will be supported in connection with the national plan through the economic and social development fund (FDES) for which it provides the secretariat, refusing to transfer this very important source of financial power from the finance ministry to the planning commissariat which has a less piecemeal approach.

It would be difficult to exaggerate the coordinating role of the FDES in the field of economic policy. This is reflected in its composition. Its management council meets twice yearly under the chairmanship of the finance minister. It includes as regular members the ministers of regional planning, public works and housing, industrial development, agriculture and labour (with other ministers attending when directly involved); the planning commissioner, the regional and spatial planning delegate, the directors of four finance divisions (treasury, budget, forecasting and prices); the governor of the Bank of France, the president-director-generals of the *Caisse* and of three other public banks. The council discusses the most important national investment decisions, with the director of the treasury division introducing each item on the agenda and the finance minister summing up the discussion. Although it is only an advisory body, the fact that all the important people concerned are present gives it decision-making significance in practice.

Most of the detailed work is transacted in fifteen specialist committees which deal separately with the long-term financing of sectors dominated by nationalized firms (which took one-third of all FDES loans in 1967 and half the total in 1968); aid to private firms; the capital investment programmes of ministries; agriculture; housing; the cinema industry; and foreign aid. On these committees, finance representatives play a less dominant role, the planning commissariat providing either the chairman (in the case of the committee on loans to the private sector) or secretariat for most of them, the relevant ministry introducing the matters for discussion.[10] Although there has been a deliberate reduction in the proportion of total investment financed through the FDES, it still provides the finance minister (who authorizes the allocation of funds that will be advanced either through the special treasury accounts or by a public bank) with a stranglehold on the volume and distribution of investment. The FDES council supervises the implementation of investment programmes assisted by public funds and publishes a detailed annual report of the extent to which they conform with the plan's objectives.

The planning commissariat and DATAR

The complementary nature of the processes of industrialization and urbanization, and the need to concert them in a medium and long-term perspective at the national and regional levels, involves going beyond the triangle of ministry of finance, FDES and *Caisse des Dépôts* to include the planning commissariat and the regional and spatial planning delegacy. The Monnet Plan, which just managed to catch the ebb tide of resistance innovation in January 1946, succeeded where the attempts at a ministry of national economy had failed because it did not challenge the authority of the finance ministry or other administrative agencies and concentrated upon medium-term industrial modernization through planned investment programmes. The First French Plan was initially insulated from the finance ministry's anti-inflationary attentions by the fact that the funds for investment were derived from the American Marshall Plan and Monnet, the planning commissioner, enjoyed excellent relations with the American government.[11] As well as avoiding a challenge to the finance ministry's monopoly of short-term economic policy, the planning commissariat initially concentrated upon relatively non-controversial issues. It mobilized a business and trade union consensus in support of the Plan's targets, although the CGT withdrew from this when the communists were excluded from the government in 1947. By dint of its modesty and prudence it reduced its administrative and political enemies to a minimum. This helped to ensure that whereas the loss of power by the Labour Party in Britain sealed the fate of a planning experiment that had already lost most of its impetus, the swing to the right in France did not result in the abandonment of national economic planning.

Despite the changes that have subsequently occurred, French planners have never forgotten that their survival and success within the process of economic policy-making has owed more to their skills in political negotiation than to economic expertise. With the fifth republic tendency of the president and prime minister to take a much more active interest in planning; the elevation of the Plan's achievements into a prominent place within government propaganda; the appointment of close collaborators of the prime minister to the key post of planning commissioner (Ortoli in 1966 and Montjoie in 1967); the movement of both a planning commissioner and a regional and spatial planning delegate into ministerial office in 1967; the overt politicization of planning became incontrovertible whereas it had previously been played down. The coincidence between the final stages of the preparation and parliamentary approval of the Fifth Plan and the presidential election campaign of 1965 ensured that the politically oriented policy directives of the government would be given controversial prominence. The planning commissioner, whose politically neutral prestige had hitherto been used by the government to secure public identification between its proposals and the public interest, emerged as the instrument of political will rather than the conciliator and arbitrator between official policy and group interests. He was the committed champion of the government's preferences rather than the detached advocate of the dictates of economic rationality.

The independence of the planning commissariat from close political control should, therefore, not be exaggerated. While it has never been straightforwardly subordinated either to the prime minister (between 1946–54 and since 1962) or the finance minister (1954–62), the commissiariat's freedom of action is limited. Coordination with short-term economic policy was facilitated when it was linked with the ministry of finance, whilst overall coordination is promoted by its ability to invoke the authority of the prime minister. The commissariat is represented on the many bodies through which public economic policy decisions are taken. The commissioner may be summoned to cabinet meetings and has regular discussions with the president, prime minister and finance minister. He sits on the government bench in the assembly and senate when the Plan is being debated and will advise and prompt his political masters. In the economic and social council he is likely to bear the brunt of the debate on the government's behalf. In all three chambers he and his senior staff are closely questioned by the relevant committees prior to the floor debate. Because the planning commissariat's work is essentially concerned with formulating problems and influencing decisions at the preparatory stage, as well as coordinating and supervising decisions whose implementation will be undertaken by others, it has been able to retain its modest size of some fifty *chargés de mission*. They work in a relatively informal way, being organized in 'horizontal' economic, financial, social, regional and urban teams, and 'vertical' agriculture, industry and transport teams. The spending ministries regard the planners with favour to the extent that they can gain their support in battles with the finance ministry. Without such support they would expect to be defeated but when the dispute can be elevated to the point at which the prime minister is involved, the support of 'the Plan' may prove decisive.

Given the planning commissariat's success as a type of

' "missionary" rather than "managerial" administration',* it was natural in the early 1960s, when it was considered necessary to strengthen central politico-administrative coordination of regional planning without upsetting existing decision-makers, that the commissariat should serve as a model. There is in the regional and spatial planning delegacy – the *Délégation à l'Aménagement du Territoire et à l'Action Régionale* – the same small size, informality of style and diversity of recruitment, though in the case of DATAR the thirty or so *chargés de mission* come mainly from the spending ministries and the prefectoral corps. Its greater tendency to recruit members of the *grands corps* facilitates political and administrative coordination by providing high level contacts with ministerial *cabinets*, central ministries and regional prefects.

Younger and still less institutionalized than the commissariat, DATAR has been more obviously political from the start.[12] A fifth republic creation of which Pompidou is proud, it was headed from 1963 to 1967 by a prominent Gaullist grey eminence, Olivier Guichard, who had been a close collaborator of de Gaulle before becoming one of Pompidou's closest aides and ministers. The nature of DATAR's activities also involves it more directly and practically in political controversy. It is called upon to deal with sensitive local employment problems and has at its disposal a regional intervention fund – *Fonds d'Intervention pour l'Aménagement du Territoire* or FIAT† – for promoting industrial decentralization which it was accused in 1967, with some justification, of using for the 'aménagement électoral du territoire'. As a result of this great politico-administrative involvement, the regional and spatial planning delegate, like the planning commissioner, although formally a civil servant, is more influential on major public policy matters than are many ministers. In 1967, Prime Minister Pompidou created a new post of minister delegate for planning and regional development and appointed the head of DATAR (Guichard) minister of industry, while the planning commissioner (Ortoli) was made minister of public works and housing. Subsequently, Guichard has held the offices of minister delegate for planning and regional development (1968–9) and minister of education (1969–72) before being appointed head of the new

* See above, p. 39.
† Although it amounts to only 1 per cent of the state investment expenditure, it is important because it serves a pump-priming role.

ministry of regional planning, public works, housing and tourism. Ortoli has been briefly minister of education (1968), minister of finance (1968–9) and minister of industrial and scientific development (1969–72), prior to becoming Pompidou's man on the EEC commission. As men on whom President Pompidou can implicitly rely, they are likely to continue to illustrate the heights to which the top national and regional planning posts may lead.

In the mid-1950s, when planning regions were designated and official action commenced, the finance ministry and the planning commissariat played the most active role but when the inflexible centralist Debré was replaced by Pompidou as prime minister in 1962, the need for a coordinated implementation of regional planning was finally recognized. (Had the full implications of Pompidou's surreptitious acquisition of wider powers as prime minister been appreciated at the time France would have been less surprised that he has become such an assertive president.) The highest level of effective coordination is achieved through a permanent regional planning cabinet committee at whose monthly meetings outstanding problems are settled. The agenda is prepared by the delegate. When regional planning was attached to the prime minister these meetings were sometimes preceded by contacts between his personal staff and DATAR officials. So close was the collusion between DATAR and the prime minister's *cabinet*, and so well aware of this were the ministries concerned in regional planning, that the mere threat by DATAR to refer a dispute to the prime minister was often sufficient to secure acquiescence.

DATAR clearly has to ensure that regional planning not only works in harmony with the ministries but also with the planning commissariat, which has the main responsibility for the regional policy guidelines and the regionalization of the national Plan. DATAR and the commissariat work together closely on the unwieldy national commission for regional planning of seventy-seven members, one of the Plan's 'horizontal' commissions of which the delegate is vice-president, with DATAR *chargés de mission* frequently acting as *rapporteurs* for its working parties. The conflicts that may arise owing to an overlap of functions between DATAR and the commissariat is clearest in the work of the Plan regionalization committee (whose chairman is the planning commissioner) and of the commissariat's regional staff. Each member of this staff is responsible for regular contact with several regional prefects and all the bodies indicated below them in figure 4. However, the DATAR officials have much closer contacts with the regional institutions. The regionalization of the budget since 1963 has not merely strengthened links with the finance ministry and the spending ministries in Paris but has improved DATAR's ability to control the overall coordination of regional planning where it counts – on the ground. The 1972 'delegation' of regional planning to a new ministry, however, probably means that the president will in future play an even greater part in settling disputes which arise between national and regional planners.

The budgetary process*

Because the budget is the detailed annual presentation in financial terms of present government activity and what it hopes to undertake in the coming year, it has traditionally occupied a pivotal place in public economic decision-making. From its figures, the government's economic policy can be inferred. It is also an excellent vantage point from which to observe how government works and who exercises decisive influence, both in the routine administration of agreed policies and in the initiation of controversial ones. As financial control over taxation and public expenditure was the principal instrument by which parliaments enforced the accountability of governments, the fifth republic's drastic modification of the power relationship between executive and legislature has transferred the emphasis in the budgetary process from the autumn parliamentary scrutiny to the winter-summer administrative and political executive preparations and decisions. Although the assembly finance committee had never been as potent an influence on the budget, even in the heyday of parliamentary sovereignty, as the budget division of the finance ministry, the tendency to make the annual budget the 'handmaiden' of the quinquennial Plan (Debré *dixit*) over which parliament has almost no control, effectively concentrates public economic power in the hands of a political and administrative élite. While the 1959 reform of financial procedure

* At numerous points in this section, I am deeply indebted to the excellent Oxford D.Phil. thesis by Guy Lord, *The French Budgetary Process*, presented in 1969 and published in a shortened form in 1973 at Berkeley, by the University of California Press.

Figure 4: The Decision-Making Structure of French Regional Planning, 1972

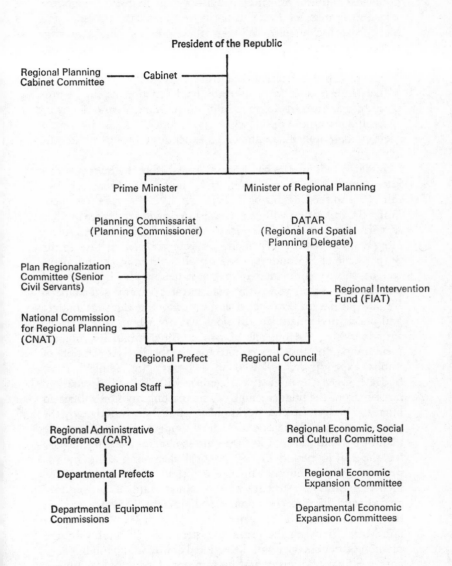

installed an executive-dominated budgetary process which subordinated the defence of particular interests to the government's public expenditure priorities, it did not include in the budget the substantial areas of local authority, nationalized industry and social security finance. Without these items – separately controlled by the finance ministry – the budget ceases to ensure financial coordination, and overall parliamentary control through the finance bill is frustrated. Furthermore, the government has reduced the budget from its traditional function as the centrepiece of government accountability to parliament into a formal accounting framework in which governments annually report their predetermined taxation and expenditure proposals to the legislature.

Budget preliminaries commence a year before the budget comes into force. The finance ministry's budget division asks the ministries to send details of their last budget, the basis for calculating the funds that will be necessary to provide the same services at current prices. These *services votés* (continuing commitments already approved by parliament) are voted *en bloc*. Although the 87 per cent of the budget made up of continuing commitments can be subsequently altered, bygones tend to be bygones and politico-administrative scrutiny concentrates on proposed changes. By late January a dozen civil administrators in the state budget and public investment sub-divisions, each of whom is responsible for supervising the budgets of two or three ministries, prepare memoranda for the budget director on the likely evolution of public expenditure, followed in February by detailed draft budgets for each ministry. Together with other information, notably from the finance ministry's forecasting division (discussed later) the budget director works out a detailed draft budget by the end of March. Alongside the draft budget prepared by the planning commissariat, this forms the economic policy framework for the spring period of top political decision-making by the president, prime minister, finance minister and their aides. (The finance ministry's estimates of the annual rate of expenditure growth and of price inflation are characteristically lower than those of the Plan.) There are a series of high level meetings in late March between the prime minister, assisted notably by the planning commissioner and the regional and spatial planning delegate, the finance minister and his minister of state for the budget, with the president of the republic's economic aide in attendance, to decide the guidelines of budget policy. Modifications may be made by the president at an interministerial council in early April. The priorities having been settled and the percentage increase (not exceeding that of the gross national product) in new civil and military expenditure having been decided, investment estimates are fixed in relation to the Plan's objectives. In May-June the president, prime minister, finance and defence ministers conclude the period of major decision-making by settling the defence estimates. The overall balance of the budget, the allocation of resources between current and capital expenditure (the latter linked with the Plan), as well as expenditure priorities have now been fixed.

The spending ministries are concurrently preparing detailed estimates. This work is left to civil servants, only surfacing politically when major disputes occur. Each ministry's budgetary strategy is usually in the hands of the budget bureau (habitually called *Service du budget et des affaires financières*) and the minister's *cabinet* but all the central and field services are involved in the exercise. As it has no authority over the divisions, the budget bureau's role is confined to evaluating the cost of proposed policies. The resolution of conflicts for scarce resources is left to the minister, his *directeur de cabinet* and budget aide. By the beginning of April a draft budget is submitted to the minister with an evaluation of the relative advantages of each choice and an estimate of the likely attitude of the finance ministry. The minister's verdicts result in a new draft, setting out the general aims, the anticipated cost, and justification of each specific expenditure proposal, which is sent to the finance ministry's budget division by the end of April. The head of each ministry's budget bureau and the relevant official in the budget division discuss the draft, setting aside any issues on which they cannot agree, and report to their ministers. The minister of state for the budget will have at least three meetings with each spending minister : on current expenditure, on capital projects with the Plan, and on other investment projects. Any outstanding proposed expenditures are either settled by the finance minister or referred to the prime minister's *cabinet*, who advise him on his decision, where the matter ends unless the spending minister appeals to the president.

The detailed allocation of each ministry's estimates leads to tough negotiations with the finance ministry's budget division. The precaution of referring the budget beforehand to the financial controller* for his comments helps to reduce the conflict with his parent ministry but the budget division's strategy is to place the spending ministry on the defensive by attacking many of its estimates and questioning the timeliness of its projects and the adequacy of the information supplied. The substantial cuts suggested at the start are intended to make the spending ministry concentrate on defending the efficiency with which they discharge their existing activities and allow the budget division to appear generous when it eventually concedes some new expenditures. The humiliation of spending ministers is reflected in complaints like: 'It is not right that the minister of education should in fact be the subordinate of financial officials who have no political responsibilities'; while a former minister of agriculture attacks that ministry's unbearable subordination to the finance officials, 'involving in addition a daily subjection over frequent decisions on products, prices, credit and markets'.[13]

The spending ministry's strategy has four salient features. It seeks to prevent the reduction of its past programmes, even when funds voted were not spent. When unable to secure priority, it tries to get an average share of increased public expenditure. It uses the Plan and the commissariat against the budget division where possible. Finally, foreign comparisons cannot fail to be relevant: either France is behind and must make up its leeway or France is ahead and must preserve its lead. By August the final readjustments are made and by early September each ministry's draft estimates are distributed to the parliamentary committees. The cabinet having approved the Finance Bill, the finance minister commends it to the public through a press conference.

The budget must be submitted to parliament before the beginning of October, the assembly having a maximum of forty days and the senate fifteen days to debate it on first reading. Article 47 of the constitution goes on to provide that if parliament has not reached a decision on the budget within seventy days, it can be enforced by ordinance, the procedural presumption in its favour protecting the government from the use of delaying tactics against it in parliament. The executive seems mainly concerned that the

* See above, p. 162.

budget should pass quickly and unscathed through parliament (by the end of December, the French financial year beginning in January). The government does not seek legislative help in improving financial control. Provided it is willing to set aside a hundred million francs (about 0·05 per cent of the budget) to make a number of minor but politically popular concessions to its own parliamentary supporters, the government can secure the legitimation of its budget by parliament. Finance ministers deliberately make provision for such concessions that allow deputies to boast of their victories at his expense.

Insofar as parliament continues to have an influence, it is largely exerted through the assembly and senate finance committees. In the assembly the budget is carefully examined by a *rapporteur général* and over forty assistant *rapporteurs*. Its finance committee holds about fifty meetings a year, including hearings before the budget. Thus, for the 1968 budget the finance minister was examined for ten hours, with shorter periods for the minister of state for the budget and spending ministers. In the budget debates, ministers (notably the budget minister) and committee spokesmen each take up a quarter of the time, leaving half the time to be shared among the parliamentary groups. Two hundred and twenty-two amendments were proposed in the debate on the 1968 budget. Two-thirds of the sixty-six carried were suggested by the government, usually at parliamentary prompting, and fourteen were proposed by the finance committee. However, the changes made are generally insignificant, provoking exasperation by deputies at a ritualistic budgetary process reduced to 'litanies, liturgies and lethargies', in which the government only talks to its supporters, an exchange limited to small talk at that.[14] Ambitious parliamentary intervention, such as the 1971 attempt to end the scandal of massive evasion of death duties (facilitated by the 1952 Pinay loan) is overcome with minimal concessions, thanks to the support of a reliable parliamentary majority.

Controversial debates are generally the result of the activities of well-organized pressure groups. For the 1972 budget, the Concorde project was debated by ten times fewer deputies than were the agriculture estimates, a reflection of the enduring electoral importance of rural France and the capacity of the farm organizations to exert pressure. When the farmers, small shopkeepers or ex-servicemen, who are regarded with sympathy by the UDR, exert pressure, the government will avoid an open clash by requesting a suspension of the debate to allow a settlement behind the scenes. Usually, this amounts to concessions on minor points, with the budget as a whole being passed by an *en bloc* vote. Although forbidden by Article 40 of the constitution to propose increases in expenditure or reductions in taxation, deputies still seek to please their electoral clientèle. They are encouraged in this attitude by the government, which accepts some of these amendments in sharing out the tiny fraction of the budget which, as has been seen, it is prepared to yield to parliamentary initiative. Failure to exert parliamentary control over estimates has not led to an attempt to exert *ex post facto* checks along the lines of the House of Commons public accounts committee. French parliamentarians regard such work as of no political or electoral significance. Yet it is estimated that owing to the greater ease with which the government can alter its expenditure after the budget has been voted, 40–50 per cent of the sums involved are modified by regulation.[15] Another result is that budgets voted in overall balance are nevertheless in deficit at the end of the financial year. The government, therefore, remains in undisputed control over all aspects of the budgetary process, the major disputes occurring within the executive.

The economic planning process

The main links between the annual budget and the quinquennial plan, between finance ministry and planning commissariat, are provided by the forecasting division and the national statistical and economic studies institute (INSEE). The latter provides the general statistical data necessary for national and regional planning, as well as undertaking forecasting work based upon past economic performance. Its programming sub-division provides the main projection on which the National Plan discussions are focused. It devised the over 1,000-equation econometric simulation model FIFI (which stands for physico-financial) that played a vital part in the preparation of the Sixth Plan (1971–5). Three-quarters of INSEE's staff serve in eighteen regional offices but its one thousand Paris officials include a hundred *polytechniciens* who provide the econometric expertise. Its current head, Jean

Ripert, spent eighteen years at the planning commissariat and became chairman of the manpower commission for the Sixth Plan. He is well fitted to orient INSEE's work to suit the needs of economic planning and to preserve official statistics from the accusation of being slanted to suit the government.[16]

The finance ministry's forecasting division, hived off in 1965 from the treasury division, was an attempt to establish a high-powered challenge to the planning commissariat, based upon the work hitherto carried out by the treasury's economic and financial studies service (SEEF). The forecasting division prepares the 'economic budget', which represents the short-term assumptions on which the budget for the coming year is planned. Each autumn, and again each spring, the forecasting division prepares an economic and financial report (the latter aspect being mainly the work of the treasury and budget divisions). It indicates the current year's performance and next year's growth perspectives for production, consumption, investment and foreign trade that underlie the Finance Act to which it is appended. This 'economic budget' should provide the vital link between short- and medium-term economic forecasting and the economic policy pursued, without which the objectives of economic planning are unlikely to be achieved. French planning's objectives are fixed for the end of the five-year period – 1975 in the case of the Sixth Plan – without describing the itinerary by which they are to be attained.

The finance ministry's reluctance to undertake medium-term financial commitments has been partially corrected by a Sixth Plan innovation, in which the forecasting division and INSEE played a leading part. More than a year before the meetings of the planning commissions, eight working parties of finance ministry officials met to agree on a common standpoint and prepare the working papers that shaped the discussions of the planning commissions. However, as a group of thirteen members of the planning commissariat and INSEE have deplored, the price of greater commitment by the finance ministry to the medium-term Plan has been to shift more and more of the real bargaining out of the planning commissions, on which organized interests are represented, into a purely administrative negotiation.[17] The challenge by the forecasting division to the planning commissariat for centralization of the information necessary to forecast economic policy wilted with the departure of Debré from the finance

179

ministry in 1968. The forecasting division turned its attention to the rationalization of budgetary choice (discussed below) as another way of strengthening the finance ministry's control over all other ministries.

The forecasting framework, which embodies at a very early stage the government's political choice between the alternative possibilities available, seeks to confine all subsequent discussion within a statistical straitjacket, the government's preferences being treated as the only economically rational ones. The popularity of the term 'indicative planning' has tended to place a misleading emphasis upon the 'generalized market research' and 'reduction of uncertainty' aspect of concerted forecasting, rather than the Plan as an instrument for working out and monitoring the carrying out of the government's social and economic policy in the medium term. French national and regional planning goes beyond the rational calculation of what is collectively possible or probable, as revealed by projections and forecasts, to a government attempt to reconcile them with the politically preferable. This is done by a strategic use of all the instruments of economic and social policy in conjunction with extra-governmental organizations, who have the capacity to facilitate or frustrate public action, to secure the achievement of more or less explicit quantitative and/or qualitative objectives. The politically explosive nature of some objectives – such as the willingness to tolerate a higher rate of unemployment or to accept a rapid rate of exodus from agriculture to industry and services – means that some of the government's targets will not be stated clearly. However, while seeking to bamboozle its opponents, the government must not mislead itself. So, like a systematic tax evader, it must keep more than one account of its activities. Nor is the planning process comprehensive, several substantial but politically sensitive categories of public expenditure, such as defence, social security, foreign aid and farm income supports, having so far evaded the Plan's grasp. Nevertheless, although the National Plan is partly a public relations exercise, it provides a relatively accurate guide to the ideological and practical orientation of French economic policy and – with important reservations in areas such as those indicated above – can be taken at face value.

Despite the efforts made to give the French public some sense of participation in the planning process, or even some awareness that it is taking place, the results so far have been modest. Thus, in a period when the mass media were devoting plenty of attention to the preparation of the Fifth Plan, the number of Frenchmen who *claimed* to have heard of it rose from 33 per cent in October 1964 to 45 per cent in August 1965, and less than one-third thought that their personal living standards were involved in the attainment of the Plan's targets.[18] Table 29 gives a more flattering picture of the importance attributed to planning. Twice as many attribute to it a great impact on their personal standard of living compared to those who dismiss it as unimportant. In

Table 29
Public Perception of the Plan's Influence on
Personal Living Standards, 1970 (%)*

(a) Degree To Which One Is Personally Affected	Government Activity in General	Planning In Particular
Very great	25	21
Rather great	44	36
Rather unimportant	18	18
No importance at all	9	10
No opinion	4	15

(b) Occupation and party	Plan's Importance Is				
	Very Great	Rather Great	Rather Unimportant	No Importance	No Opinion
Occupation					
Farmers	19	30	21	6	24
Shopkeepers and craftsmen	26	39	20	9	6
Professional and large business	30	45	15	6	4
Employees	30	37	20	5	8
Workers	18	37	18	11	16
No occupation	17	35	17	14	17
Party Vote					
Communist	21	26	24	19	10
Socialist and radical	27	40	17	8	8
Opposition centre	21	44	22	10	3
Governmental centre	13	46	29	4	8
Independent republican	32	40	11	15	2
UDR	21	40	19	5	15

* Source: adapted from SOFRES, *Les Français et l'Etat*, pp. 84, 87.

occupational terms, businessmen in large firms and the professions attach the most importance to planning, whilst farmers, workers and the retired are the most likely to express no opinion. Politically, supporters of the independent republicans and the non-communist opposition are most inclined to attach importance to planning, while the communists are most disposed to play down its significance. Despite the UDR tendency to treat the Plan as a major propaganda weapon in parliament and at elections, its supporters are well below average in attributing importance to planning and are most inclined to express no opinion on the subject.

The preparation of a Plan is a long and elaborate affair. Only the salient features of the national (not regional) part of the process for the Sixth Plan are set out below.

The Preparation of the Sixth Plan (1971–5)

1. *The Technocratic Phase (October 1966–September 1969)*

   (i)   Preparation of the mathematical model (FIFI) and the main medium- and long-term projections of the French economy's development by INSEE and the forecasting division.
   (ii) The planning commissariat establishes thirteen long-term (1970–85) study groups in early 1968, reorganizes the planning commission structure and decides their agenda.
   (iii) To prepare the financial aspects of the Plan, not included in FIFI, eight Finance-Plan groups (set up in 1965) meet between March 1968–September 1969.

2. *The Guidelines Phase (October 1969–June 1970)*

   (i) The planning commissions and working parties (who begin their work a year late owing to the May–June crisis of 1968) meet from October 1969–March 1970 to investigate the alternative policies to deal with the problems assigned to them.
   (ii) In January 1970 the government discusses five alternative growth rates (eventually choosing 5·9 per cent) and makes some preliminary decisions.

(iii) The planning commissariat staff prepares a draft Guidelines Report to be discussed first by the president, prime minister and finance minister, then the cabinet, in March–April 1970, leading to the publication of a Guidelines Report.

(iv) The economic and social council is consulted on the Report in April–May 1970 and in June the national assembly and senate approve the guidelines to the Sixth Plan.

3. *Programming the Government's Policy Directives (June 1970– June 1971)*

(i) The government issues its policy directives on the preparation of the Sixth Plan in June 1970.

(ii) The planning commissions and working parties meet from July 1970–March 1971, preparing reports that are 'synthesized' by the staff of the planning commissariat into a draft Plan in March 1971 under the influence of more precise government directives.

(iii) President Pompidou puts the finishing touches to the text of the Plan which has previously been examined by the prime minister in an interministerial committee.

(iv) The economic and social council is consulted in May 1971 and parliament approves of the Plan in June 1971, six months after the Plan was scheduled to commence.

The 'closed' phase prior to autumn 1969, when the relatively open consultative phase began, was characterized by the work of (mainly finance ministry) civil servants. The constraints on policy that emerge from this phase already embody the political priorities of the government but neither the planning commissions nor parliament share in this, the longest and most crucial preparatory phase. The functional and political representatives of the people are involved in discussing the guidelines only after the Sixth Plan has already taken shape in the earlier phase. Traditionally the most important role in this phase has been played by the planning commissions. For the Sixth Plan, there were seven 'horizontal' or general commissions: general economy and finance, employment, social transfer payments, research, economic information, regional planning, overseas departments. There were nine production commissions: industry, agriculture, food, transport, telecommunications, trade, crafts, tourism. There were nine public service commissions: education, social services, health, housing, towns, rural areas, water, cultural affairs, sport. There were also a number of 'intergroups' concerned with the old, leisure, building, etc. The most important of all commissions is 'general economy and finance', whose chairman is the planning commissioner. It synthesized the work of all the others and had three very important sub-committees devoted to competition, finance and foreign trade. Under business pressure, a very powerful new industry commission was created for the Sixth Plan, combining the activities previously undertaken by eight commissions. Its more detailed work is undertaken by twenty-two industrial sub-committees. In fact the full commissions meet infrequently, most of the discussion taking place in working parties, with civil servants and businessmen generally occupying the key positions of chairman and *rapporteur*. About 4,500 people are involved in these consultative activities. Businessmen and officials from employers' organizations outnumber trade unionists by three to one and are better equipped to influence the proceedings. The civil servants, who form about one-quarter of those involved, use these discussions to obtain reactions from the organized interests to their proposals and information of a technical nature.

The political parties and major interest groups get their best opportunity to express their views in parliament and in the economic and social council. Whereas the parliamentary debates tend to degenerate into parochial, constituency-oriented speech-making, the ESC makes a more serious assessment of the Plan's basic assumptions and often challenges the Plan's strategy and its priorities, without going as far as to present a counter-plan. The trade unions are usually in a minority, the business-farmer majority generally supporting the government. The CFDT, ardent advocate in the early 1960s of democratized planning, has become utterly disenchanted with the planning process. In September 1970 it informed the planning commissioner that it would boycott the work of the planning commissions at the national and regional levels and adopted an attitude of intransigent hostility in the ESC debate on the Sixth Plan. It regards the Sixth Plan's emphasis on international competition and industrialization as evidence of a sell-out to private industrialists.

Despite de Gaulle's phrase about it being an 'ardent obligation', the French Plan has never had the force of law, and even the ardour has been dissipated. Parliament merely passes a one-sentence approval of the Plan as a 'guide' to public economic policy and a 'framework' for public investment programmes. The parliamentary votes are rather predictably along pro and anti-government lines. For the Fifth Plan, the assembly voted in favour of the guidelines by 353 to 120 and approved the final version by 283 to 184, while the senate passed the guidelines by 190 to 75 but rejected the final Plan by 152 to 96, only to be over-ruled. In the case of the Sixth Plan, matters went more smoothly. The assembly voted in favour by 351 to 95 (guidelines) and 349 to 99 (Plan), while the senate approved by 109 to 88 and 131 to 97. These debates are an improvement on the first four Plans, when parliament either did not vote on the Plan at all (First and Third Plans) or only discussed it whilst it was being implemented (Second and Fourth Plans). Still, it cannot be gainsaid that parliament plays a negligible role in the planning process and the executive is determined to keep it that way.[19]

None of the French plans has to date been implemented without a major hitch, and the first two years of the Sixth Plan's implementation suggest that it will run true to type. The First Plan's targets were achieved a year late; the Second Plan, thanks to Edgar Faure's 'eighteen-month plan' of 1953–4, exceeded its targets; the Third Plan was scaled down by an Interim Plan covering 1960–1, only for the results to be nearer the original targets; the Fourth Plan was modified by the 1963 'stabilization plan'; while the Fifth Plan was going badly until it was unexpectedly rectified by the May–June 1968 crisis and devaluation in 1969. Furthermore, aggregate data conceal substantial disparities in the more detailed targets. (This has prompted a reduction in the number of detailed targets for the Sixth Plan, the official reason being the increasing forecasting difficulties due to the growing importance of foreign trade which is notoriously unpredictable.) Since the Fourth Plan, improvements have been made in getting public investment programmes and budget authorizations into step but serious divergences between Plan and performance, measured by annual expenditure, still occur. The court of public accounts in a 1966 Report stated that from one-quarter to one-third of the funds annually allocated to ministries were not spent until up to four years later, the ministry of education being especially prone to sluggishness. The delay either held back currently budgeted investment schemes or led to the abandonment of the previous programmes. The delay also exacerbated the effects of inaccurate cost estimation, with the result that less could be achieved with the funds allocated. Finally, new projects were given priority without foreseeing the effects on existing projects.[20]

The alliance of the finance ministry's budget division and the spending ministries, who wish to be free to grant/withhold investment funds outside a multi-annual framework, means in practice that the Plan's investment programmes are regarded as merely ideal targets to be achieved 'other things being equal'. Chaban-Delmas, prime minister from 1969 to 1972, promoted the signature of contracts intended to secure greater respect for the Plan's objectives in the public corporations and the private sector. For his part, President Pompidou has tried to restore some lustre to the Sixth Plan by prefacing the Guidelines Report with ringing Gaullist phrases such as 'the Plan should be the affirmation of a national ambition'. However, he has failed to restore a belief that the Plan is seeking a 'particular French conception of society'. The 'new society' towards which France is moving may be new to France but it bears a marked resemblance to old industrial capitalism elsewhere.

Costing public expenditure and rationalizing political choice

The current disenchantment with governmental planning has led to a revival of support for market criteria in which the virtues of competition and cost-effectiveness take pride of place. The government is invited to concentrate on making the public sector more businesslike, and 'management' has become an anglicism with wide currency. French state intervention has, despite the rhetoric, always improvised in an incremental manner rather than been comprehensively planned. It has been established that in implementing their industrial policy the finance ministry and planning commissariat did not keep a 'detailed record of just what industries and branches had received exactly how much [state financial assistance] or why. Such a situation implies a lack of systematic criteria for giving aid, inattention to the measurement of results accruing from the help provided and thus the lack of at least a sound *economic* basis for providing further state aid.'[21] The realization that the planning process has not had so innovative an effect on the way in which administrative and political decisions are taken and carried out as was hoped in the early 1960s, led in 1968 to the adoption of a new nostrum : the planning, programming, budgeting system (PPBS) from the United States. Because the initiative was seized by the finance ministry and because the budget, in the words of the man mainly charged with promoting the new development, is the 'symbol and summit of the public decision system', the 'fundamental political act',[22] it became known in France as the rationalization of budgetary choice (RCB).

Whereas both budgeting and planning traditionally relied upon an advocacy and bargaining process in which priorities were decided by the ability of groups to exert pressure and gain the necessary political support, the new approach seeks to replace 'muddling through', the historic legacy of expedient short-term adjustments between politicians, bureaucrats and organized interests, by a 'decision process as it rationally should be'.[23] In the United States, where national planning was ideologically unacceptable, the adoption of a management technique devised by the Rand Corporation and applied in the defense department by McNamara from 1961 led President Johnson in August 1965 to generalize it prematurely throughout his administration with rather limited results. In France, as in the United States, a major motivation has been to avoid a further rise in public expenditure (owing to the unpopularity of increasing taxation) by selecting and programming projects more efficiently. Even more important, though less stressed, has been the political decision-makers' desire to have a freer hand in reallocating resources annually. The extent to which the budget is already committed by past decisions, and expenditures unrelated to quantified objectives, seriously inhibits the government from switching resources to secure greater cost-effectiveness. Although, as in the United States, it was the defence ministry that in 1965 first became interested in programme budgeting, the finance ministry characteristically took command from the moment it was decided to generalize the experiment.

In January 1968, Finance Minister Debré encouraged all the ministries to begin the process of 'rationalizing budgetary choice'. Initially fostered by the forecasting and budget divisions, an RCB mission was established in May 1968 at the finance ministry to overcome the resistance that was anticipated to an attempted administrative and budgetary revolution. Defence, expenditure on which had been falling from its pride of place since the end of the Algerian war in 1962 and was to be overtaken in 1971 by education, made a major contribution in restraining the growth in public expenditure. As unproductive expenditure *par excellence*, it was a prime candidate for cost-utility scrutiny. As well as using RCB techniques in the preparation of the Third (1971–5) Military Plan, the defence ministry was able to present its 1972 budget in RCB form, with a preface by Debré in his capacity as defence minister. The tasks of the armed forces were related to the resources used to carry them out. Defence was split into nine major programmes, each divided into eight cost categories. There were five strike forces : nuclear, frontier defence (ten times more men than the nuclear force but only twice as expensive), internal security forces (gendarmerie, etc.), overseas forces and general use forces (e.g. air transport). In addition there were four logistical programmes : research and development, personnel services, equipment, central administration. Experimentation with RCB has been undertaken in other ministries with a technological emphasis, such as the ministry of public works and housing. In such ministries as foreign affairs, justice and education, little progress has been made, either because they do not have quantifiable objectives or because of strong administrative resistance.[24] As minister of education, Guichard confessed his embarrassment in March 1970, describing his budget preparation as a 'particularly delicate exercise, consisting of precise requests for resources to attain imprecise objectives, based upon inadequate statistical and forecasting services'. The reorganization of the education ministry he carried through in 1970 was, as we shall see in the next chapter, intended to remedy these defects.

It is much too early to assess this latest attempt at counteracting the incrementalism and immobilism of French public administration. At present the RCB experiment is being conducted in a very piecemeal and pragmatic fashion, each ministry being allowed to go its own way and at its own pace, without much coordination. If it were generalized along uniform lines, RCB would greatly stregthen both the finance ministry and the planning commissariat, the latter through the greater effectiveness of budgetary plan implementation that would result.[25] The danger of RCB developing into a twentieth-century, Colbertist, centralist instrument of *raison d'état* seems not to have gone very far as yet. The explicitness and evaluative quantification of objectives required will doubtless prove too demanding. This heroic style of economic policy-making will probably be transformed out of recognition by the consensus-building 'irrationalities' of political expediency, interest group pressure and bureaucratic routine. Whatever the outcome of the battle for power that pervades the reform of decision-taking procedure, one may rest assured that the finance ministry will emerge in its customary pivotal position, if one excludes the unlikely transfer of the budget division to the prime minister. Meanwhile, France's high rate of economic growth since the second world war suggests that the political and administrative architects of public policy have served their country well, although the benefits have been shared unequally. With industrial investment increased by 60 per cent between 1969–71 and exports in 1970 representing nearly 30 per cent of French industrial production (compared with an average 23 per cent between 1965–8) France will probably continue to improve her relative position in the 1970s.

7 Elusive Autonomy: Education and Public Enterprise

While it is not customary to consider state education in conjunction with the industries and services that are collectively described as public enterprise, in problems of organization and management, in economic and budgetary importance, education raises similar questions to those that occur in the nationalized sector. However, because of the key role that it plays in the processes of political socialization and social stratification, education is a far more central task of government than running the railways or coal mines. This pride of place has been reflected in the close control that successive French governments have exerted over education, conceived either as the matrix of political and social stability or as the instrument of political, economic and social modernization. These functions potentially bring the state educational system into conflict with the family and Church, which have been rival socializing agents. Furthermore, the development of an industrial society has meant that new demands are made by the economic system, affecting both the scale and content of the education provided. In these circumstances, government's relation to the educational service becomes a matter of pervasive importance.

Governments are reluctant to relinquish centralized control over education as an instrument of public power. However, it is increasingly difficult to insulate education from intervention by parents, Churches, businessmen or local authorities. By the early 1960s, senior ministry of education officials were themselves questioning the traditional combination of close central control and isolation from social pressures and were speculating about the possibility of promoting autonomy relative to government and reducing it relative to society. Insofar as the main proponents of nationalized industry in France were inspired by a desire to socialize without bureaucratizing, to increase the public service role of the nation rather than the power of the state, there has been a comparable search for a type of public institution which is responsive to public demands without being subordinate to the government. However, the attainment of autonomy has proved elusive, both in education and in public enterprise.

Dualism and division in French education

While the state attained a dominant position over education in the nineteenth century, the whole of pre-revolutionary education was dominated by the Church, with its emphasis on protecting the young against corruption by society rather than upon preparation for a productive role within it. Although secularized, education's traditional function of preserving and transmitting a timeless culture, transcending the changing demands of society, economy and polity, has survived almost intact. However, the Napoleonic and republican traditions each gave a different twist to the fundamental task of indoctrination inherited from the Church. Over and above the encyclopaedic emphasis of French education, the schools imparted a religious respect for the language and a pride in national identity and France's cultural achievements. As half the French population did not speak standard French before the mid-nineteenth century, the primary school teachers were regarded as missionaries of national unification dedicated to the rigorous elimination of regional languages and local dialects. This work of linguistic proselytization and cultural assimilation was facilitated by the Imperial University established by Napoleon in 1806: a hierarchical, centralized state monopoly control of all schools and teachers, whose political function Napoleon clearly formulated. 'My main purpose is to have a means of controlling political and moral opinion. . . . As long as people are not taught from childhood whether they should be republican or monarchist, catholic or atheist, the state will not fashion a nation; it will be based on vague and uncertain foundations, constantly exposed to disorder and change.'[1]

The restoration monarchy transferred the educational monopoly to the Church. Despite a period of liberalization under the July monarchy, the 1848 revolution convinced the conservatives of the need to promote Catholic schools as an anti-revolutionary bulwark. The notorious Falloux Act of 1850 increased the number of Catholic primary schools fivefold in the next thirty years but a powerful secularist retort came in the 1880s, establishing a free, secular and compulsory system of publicly provided education. Ideally, it sought to overcome France's ideological split by seeking to enforce neutrality and equal respect for all beliefs, especially through state control over school textbooks whose use could be forbidden by the minister of education on the ground that they were not neutral. This threatened a colourless uniformity and conformity with official truth, leading to a Catholic demand for 'freedom' now that the Catholic hierarchy no longer controlled public education. However, the bitter anticlerical struggle that followed the post-1882 replacement of 'moral and religious' by 'moral and civic' instruction in the primary schools meant that civic education was regarded as an opportunity to indoctrinate the young with a secular republican ethic underpinning the new régime.

At this time the primary school teachers were the anticlerical equivalent of the priesthood, providing – along with the Masonic lodges – the rudimentary organization that the radical party, which did not have an organized mass following, needed at the local level. Especially in the rural areas, the primary school teachers wielded great power, acting as the mayors' secretaries and chief assistants in some twenty-five thousand communes at the turn of the century. However, as the fervour went out of the anticlerical struggle in the first half of the twentieth century, the role of civic education declined into its present bloodless formalism. It consists of dogmatic normative abstractions mixed with legalistic descriptions of the political and administrative organization of France, proceeding from the commune to the national government, with international affairs being reached by the end of secondary education. The limited time and teachers' enthusiasm devoted to civic education – which is sometimes simply replaced by history and geography – is significant in a country whose teachers are likely to be socialists or communists. The relative neutrality of French state education is evidenced by the fact that its products imbibe patriotism rather than any clearcut partisan orientation. However, a 1963 investigation into the political attitudes of secondary school children in Catholic and state schools showed that although the non-political Pasteur emerged as the leading national hero for both groups, he rated higher in state schools, while St Louis and de Gaulle achieved better results in Catholic schools. Male and state school pupils were predominantly favourable to the French revolution, whilst female and Catholic school pupils were equally divided for and against.[2] Far from civic education being the vehicle for political indoctrination, the universal indifference with which it is regarded indicates conclusively that one must look elsewhere for the pedagogy of political commitment.

What are the dimensions of the strictly educational cleavage between Catholic and state education? Some 15 per cent of those in full-time education frequent private, i.e. generally Catholic establishments (which account for 91 per cent of private pupils and students). The proportion varies substantially : about 15 per cent of kindergarten and infant pupils as well as primary pupils; about 17 per cent of general secondary pupils but 25 per cent of the select *lycées*, 38 per cent of the technical students (mostly non-Catholic schools) and a mere 5 per cent of the university and *grandes écoles* students. The regional variations are very great, ranging from under 10 per cent in Burgundy to over 50 per cent in Brittany. (The three Alsace-Lorraine departments, detached from France between 1871–1918 when Church and state were separated, are a special case, exempted from the anticlerical legislation of that period.) The financial straits to which the Catholic schools were reduced by the late 1940s led to a vigorous campaign for state aid by the 'free school' lobby organized by a secretariat whose constituent elements were a one and a half million strong National Federation of Ex-Pupils and a 750,000 strong Parents Union. Its main political lever was the Parliamentary Association for Free Education, drawing on the right and centre parties. The resistance to using public funds to subsidise Catholic schools was organized by the National Committee for Secular Action, whose main supporters were the 500,000 state school teachers of the National Education Federation – notably the primary school teachers of SNI – the 1,200,000 family strong Federation of Parents of State School Children, the Educational League, over half of whose 2,700,000 membership are children, the major trade unions and left-wing political parties.

The battles between these two lobbies culminated in the 1959 Debré Act when the ascendant right legislated in favour of the Catholic school lobby. However, prime minister Debré was keen to resolve the dispute once and for all by a non-sectarian compromise which would promote rather than frustrate national unity. The Act provided that Catholic schools which were prepared to offer a public service on a par with state schools should sign contracts with the ministry of education which could be of two types. They could either conclude an 'association agreement', whereby the Catholic school would teach according to the regulations and curricula of state education, in return for public payment of the staff and the expenses of running the school; or they could enter into a 'limited agreement' under which the state paid the teachers' salaries, approved their appointment and inspected them but had no influence over the curriculum. Despite bitter opposition from the secularist lobby and its political allies (who threatened nationalization of all schools that accepted public subsidies when the left returned to power), the 1959 Act was quickly passed by large majorities in both the assembly and senate. The agreements were prepared by the prefect in each department, in conjunction with regional and local officials of the ministry of education; the resort to prefects indicating a distrust of the traditionally secularist education ministry and reliance on the prefects' political sensitivity. Although up to 1964 the prefects had rejected some 1,700 applications to sign a 'limited agreement' and nearly a hundred proposed 'association agreements', a large majority of Catholic primary schools signed a 'limited agreement' while secondary schools favoured the 'association agreement'. By 1970 the situation was as shown in table 30, with only 12 per cent of all pupils attending Catholic schools having refused to sign either type of agreement. Nevertheless, the state's financial support did not prevent a steady fall during the 1960s in the percentage of children educated in Catholic schools.

In the decade following its passage, the Debré Act's fundamental ambiguity over whether it would perpetuate scholastic segregation or facilitate gradual integration into state education,

Table 30
Agreements Between Catholic Schools and the State, 1970 (%)

Type of School	Type of Agreement		
	Limited	Association	None
Primary	89	5	6
Secondary	27	52	22

was resolved in favour of the former alternative, at least in the short run. The 'limited agreement' had been instituted for a trial period and a decision could not be postponed beyond 1971. In the preceding years, the Parliamentary Association for Free Education (which in 1970 boasted a membership of 264 deputies – an absolute majority – and 136 senators) had pressed the education minister to make these 'limited agreements' permanent but he hesitated to provoke the left-wing state teachers in the wake of the 1968 crisis. However, President Pompidou was worried about the fact that the crisis in Church authority threatened to deprive the right of its traditional support and he sent the minister of state for education to talk to the Vatican in November 1970. Although the prime minister and the education minister agreed, at an interministerial meeting in December 1970, to postpone the problem by proposing that the 1959 settlement simply be extended for another nine years, President Pompidou intervened personally to impose the solution that was adopted by parliament in April 1971. The 'limited agreements', that in 1970 applied to 1,200,000 children, would be made permanent in the primary schools, where they predominated. Schools that had signed 'association agreements', involving 600,000 children, mainly in secondary schools, would also continue as before but Catholic secondary schools would not be able to benefit from 'limited agreement' status beyond 1979. Thus a former state school teacher and son of an anticlerical school teacher (Pompidou) repeated the mid-nineteenth century exploit of an atheistic liberal (Thiers), each paying an educational price to exorcise their fears of revolution. The share of the education ministry's budget devoted to Catholic schools rose from 4 per cent to 8·6 per cent between 1961–70 and can be expected to rise further. Although a swing of the political pendulum may lead to nationalization of state subsidized Catholic schools, a majority of the public now seems to favour a preservation of their autonomy and their continued subsidization.

The dualism of French education has not been due to religious cleavage alone but to class divisions as well. The place of Latin in the secondary school curriculum illustrates both the religious and the class sources of divisiveness in French education. Latin's symbolic importance should not be underestimated. 'The feeling that the French have always had that they are the true heirs to

Table 31
Public Attitudes Towards Private vs.
Public Education in France, March 1968 (%) *

Replies by Party Preference	All	Communist	Socialist	Centre	UDR
1. Abolish private schools	5	13	11	0	1
Integrate them into the public system	34	34	37	42	35
Leave them as they are	53	47	47	54	57
No reply	8	6	5	4	7
2. Increase subsidies to private schools	29	24	20	39	40
Maintain subsidies to private schools	39	27	41	46	39
Reduce subsidies to private schools	14	34	23	7	5
No reply	18	15	16	8	16

* Source: adapted from *Sondages*, 1968, no. 2, pp. 57–8.

Roman culture has been reinforced by religion. Latin is the language of Catholicism,'[3] although it is being replaced by the vernacular. Furthermore, Latin has traditionally provided a barrier between the non-vocational education of a leisured middle class and working-class education for menial tasks of production. That it still has influential supporters is evident from an instruction published in the Official Bulletin of the ministry of education in 1967 which claimed that Latin constituted the main medium of contemporary thought! Latin has been a major obstacle to the development of comprehensive secondary education and Edgar Faure as education minister, in the wake of the 1968 events, postponed the Latin option to the eighth year, to provide two years of common secondary studies. It appears that Pompidou made pre-presidential electoral promises to reverse the Faure decision (which would itself have had only a slight desegregation effect) and this was partially done, Latin commencing in the second year of secondary education. Just as President de Gaulle had areas of public policy which he particularly reserved to himself, President Pompidou's intervention showed a propensity to overrule both his prime minister and education minister in the educational sphere.

As some of the bitterness ebbs from the religious obstacle to national unity, social inequality becomes a central issue between left and right, with the left acting as the champion of the one and indivisible republic. The class cleavage in French education was, until the extension of the school leaving age beyond primary education, a clear one between elementary mass education for manual employment and republican citizenship and secondary and higher education to train the economic and political élites. The working classes were taught obedience to their social betters by what H. G. Wells, in the English context, described as education 'of the lower classes, on lower-class lines, with specially trained inferior teachers'. Despite a formal commitment to equality and respect for a classless general culture presupposing the existence of a neutral general interest, French education has reflected, reinforced and legitimized the class divided nature of French society. The meritocratic 'career open to talent' has been almost exclusively of benefit to the middle classes, with 'democratization' of the educational system being mainly due to pressure by the lower-middle class to gain access to the institutions that have hitherto been the preserve of the church-going upper-middle class. For example, there is a close correlation between religious belief and the class character of the senior civil service, practising Catholics being disproportionately likely to attain such posts, especially in the *grands corps*.[4]

Despite all the rhetoric about general culture, the economic, administrative and political élites have maintained a quasi-monopoly of recruitment to prestige professional training in the *grandes écoles* and in the law and medical faculties of the universities, which control access to prestigious economic, administrative and political positions in French society. The discontinuous ladders to social advancement by educational merit ensure that an apparent equality of opportunity can be combined with a maintenance of inequality, the high failure rates in French education being a tribute to its social as well as its educational selectivity. On a socio-educational index of inequality, members of the upper-middle class are twenty-four times more likely to secure a higher education than members of the working class.[5] The minister of education himself admitted to the national assembly in 1969 that scholarships, though numerous (about 130,000 annually) were of such modest size that they played no part in increasing equality of opportunity as between social classes. France is still ruled by élites based upon birth and wealth, although privileged status usually has to be ratified by education, which permits a small proportion of school-made men to work their way to the top. There is no sign that the educationally conservative Pompidou will permit any breach in a severely selective system which has the merit of allowing the occasional individual, such as himself, to achieve the French equivalent of elevation 'from log cabin to White House'.

A ministry in search of a policy

Education is the most spectacular example of the French practice of undertaking reform only under the pressure of revolutionary crisis, thereafter stabilizing the new order in a system impervious to change. Although the monolithic, one and indivisible University of France, embracing all educational institutions and controlled from Paris, lost its Napoleonic Grand Master, the attempt at monopoly control over the educational process survived, a prey to the creeping paralysis of bureaucratization from the third republic onward. This obsessive preoccupation with universal regulation led the teachers, in self-defence, to convert the rules into a stubborn protection of their vested interests. So, although in the 1960s the ministry of education at times issued on average three circulars a day, securing compliance was quite another matter. It had, for example, failed in 1959 to obtain a reduction in the very long school holidays in France and was to fail again in 1969, on both occasions owing to resistance by the teachers' organizations.

The ministry of education, which in a centralized system was the sole potential source of innovation, was faced on issue after issue with an insoluble problem. Sweeping reform – alone acceptable because it respected sacrosanct national uniformity – proved impossible owing to corporate resistance; while piecemeal reform – which might have avoided a head-on collision with opponents – was ruled out as the source of arbitrariness and diversity such as existed in the decentralized English system. Other Napoleonic legacies were the emphasis upon nation-wide examinations to ensure central control over selection to the élite; the damaging fragmentation between teaching, research and professional education – each entrusted to separate institutions – the central role being accorded to the *grandes écoles* who embodied the Napoleonic ideal of the 'engineer-administrator';[6] the draining away of all

talent to form a hyper-centralized, Parisian intellectual élite. However, although the Paris-based public service cornered the scarce
resource of trained intellectual talent, we have seen that the
ministry of education has not been successful in obtaining its
share.*

We have already, in this and in the preceding chapter, had
occasion to raise the question of whether education policy is made
at the ministry of education or whether it is at the mercy of the
president of the republic, prime minister and finance minister.
The qualitative and quantitative 'under-administration' of education – only 2 per cent of its budget is spent on the central administrative services – coupled with the scale of the demands made
upon it – owing to the centralized nature of the system – have
resulted in its partial dismemberment. A new ministry (culture)
and a minister of state under the prime minister (youth and sport)
have been hived off, while less important functions were transferred to the ministries of industrial development and health.
Much more significant is the fact that the most important matters
concerning education are often decided at interministerial meetings at the instance of the president, the prime minister and his
staff – notably in the context of planning – or of the finance
ministry in the budgetary context.

President Pompidou's first education minister, Olivier
Guichard, nevertheless claimed in 1970 that he had been given an
impossible task: 'There is no political or administrative post in
France that is as monstrous as that of national education minister.
The notion that a politician can supervise 811,000 civil servants
and a budget of 27 milliard francs with the help of a skeletal headquarters staff is far-fetched.' Until 1972 (when the post was
abolished) a minister of state for education received responsibility
for a number of matters: principally university and school building (subject to great political pressure), technical and vocational
education (insofar as this has not been 'usurped' by the prime
minister's staff) continuing education, libraries and private education. However, if important matters arose in his sphere, the
minister probably intervened anyway and the civil servants were
quite capable of playing off the ministers and their personal
staffs against each other. So, the minister's burden had not been
significantly lightened by the existence of a junior minister.

* See above, p. 110.

Overall policy formation has been no senior official's responsibility in the education ministry apart from the shortlived experiments with a director-general from 1944 to 1946 and a secretary-general from 1963 to 1968. The minister's private office has sought ineffectually to impose a measure of coordination on compartmentalized divisions, preoccupied with short-term practical problems. Despite the nearly three-fold improvement in ministerial stability achieved under the fifth republic, as indicated in table 32, the fact that between 1959 and 1972 there were ten ministers of education (and four interim ministers) indicates that there has been no improvement in that ministry. However, the turnover of division directors at the education ministry has been doubled, so on average they serve only two rather than four ministers.

Table 32
The Relative Duration (in years) of Ministers and Division Directors†

Ministry	1944–58		1958–66	
	Minister	Division Director	Minister	Division Director
Finance	0·8	4·3	2·2	3·3
Foreign affairs	1·6	2·7	8·8	3·0
Justice	0·8	3·3	2·9	3·0
Interior	1·2	2·8	2·2	3·7
Agriculture	1·1	5·4	2·2	3·2
Industry	1·2	4·7	2·9	3·8
Labour	0·9	5·2	2·9	3·0
Education	1·2	5·0	1·2	2·3
Average*	1·1	4·1	2·9	3·4

* Including ministries not mentioned above.
† Source: J. Siwek-Pouydesseau, *Le personnel de direction des ministères*, p. 73.

In 1963 the minister of education created the post of secretary-general. He entrusted it to a non-academic in an attempt to impose coordination on a ministry where almost all the important posts were held by academics and teachers, which bolstered its corporatist, compartmentalized and conservative character. The post was abolished by Edgar Faure in 1968, dismissing its incumbent with the phrase 'because he was irreplaceable, I have decided not to replace him'. Faure acted to placate the irate ministry officials and rectors who bitterly resented the secretary-general's authoritarian 'meddling in their affairs'. Until then the secretary-general had tried to run the ministry singlehanded. 'Every day, two hundred officials reported to him. He dictated on average twenty-five circulars and personally signed the correspondence of the seven main divisions. Over five years, he organized three hundred meetings of division directors to try to establish a logical organization.'[7]

After this failure of heroic administrative leadership and Edgar Faure's reversion to the traditional pattern, coupled with reliance on an exceptionally gifted and active 'super-administrative' personal staff from his private office to galvanize the ministry into radical reform, Olivier Guichard instituted in 1970 a far-reaching reorganization of the education ministry along lines inspired by the new nostrum of management by objectives. He hoped to overcome his ministry's congenital weakness by strengthening and separating the functions of policy-making from those of policy implementation. The latter's traditional predominance had led to the loss to others of the elevated function of taking decisions of major consequence. Faced by the 'largest administration in the world except the red army', Guichard aimed at 'putting new life into a system whose taste for initiative had been destroyed by a century and a half of centralization' devoted to the regulation of action rather than to its stimulation.[8] The ministry's gerontocratic general inspectorates which, in theory, might have been agents of innovation and feedback, worked as bulwarks of traditionalism because they concentrated on checking that the Parisian centre's directives were being respected to the letter at the provincial periphery.

The new structure – set out in figure 5 – sought to restore the ministry's role as a leader and an effective policy-maker by remedying its under-administration at the highest level, notably through the appointment of three director delegates. Aided by small staffs, these director delegates (objectives) – responsible for higher education and research, elementary and secondary education, counselling and continuing training* – were to formulate policy programmes based on feasibility studies of cost made by

---

* Great importance is currently attached to this because pupils are counselled in their choice of education and employment and are offered subsequent opportunities for further training and retraining.

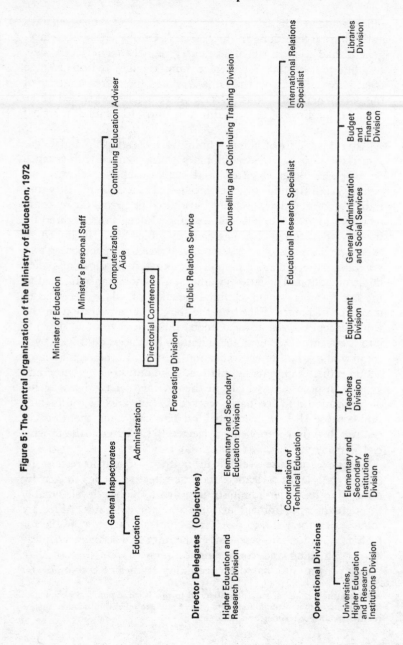

Figure 5: The Central Organization of the Ministry of Education, 1972

the forecasting division and the operational divisions. The director delegates (objectives) would work out the timing of these strategic plans in relation to budgetary provision from 1973 and issue general instructions on implementation to the seven operational division directors. The main difficulty arises in the attempt to elevate the objectives directors above the operational directors, regarded as too preoccupied with improvising expedients to deal with immediate problems. Guichard's original intention had been to appoint politician minister delegates who clearly would have been the hierarchical superiors of the operational directors but he did not receive cabinet approval of this proposal. Compelled to fall back on the idea of civil servant director delegates, there is a serious likelihood that power in the new structure will remain with the operational divisions, leaving the director delegates to ratiocinate about objectives in the void. It will require a sustained impetus by successive ministers and their personal staffs to secure the *de facto* subordination of day-to-day management to the programmes and objectives. More effective coordination may be secured partly through regular meetings between the minister's personal staff and the director delegates, partly through the full directorial conference, which has a permanent secretariat. A new public relations department was also intended to facilitate intraministry communications. However, the attempt to transfer management techniques which originated in American industry to the most bureaucratic of French civil service ministries must be regarded as a hazardous venture. Guichard himself was well aware that the success of his reform would require patience and sustained commitment over the long haul. With his replacement by Fontanet in 1972, the success of his innovation will turn particularly on whether or not the director delegates survive long enough to ensure priority to objectives over management.

Other traditional barriers to educational reform have been the previously influential primary and secondary school teachers' organizations. Under the fourth republic their power was so great that the ephemeral education minister's name was sometimes confused with that of the general secretary of the primary teachers (SNI) or secondary teachers (SNES) unions, which constituted respectively over two-thirds and one-tenth of the National Education Federation's membership. A senior official recalled that 'even the directors were inclined to be more attentive to the behests of the unions than to the minister's orders, as it was very likely that the latter would finally reflect the former'.[9] The strength of the SNI – which organizes 90 per cent of state primary schoolteachers – is based on its local share in educational management but it is as centralized in its organization as the education ministry. Although of predominantly left-wing political convictions, the teachers were in favour of radical reform or revolution in every sphere other than education, where they submitted to change only when their desperate attempts to defeat it had failed.

Under the fourth republic the teachers dominated the hierarchy of advisory councils, culminating in the higher national education council, which blocked rather than initiated innovation. In 1964 the Gaullists passed an Act eliminating the rebellious teacher majority in the HNEC. It is now composed of twenty-five education ministry officials; up to twelve officials from other ministries, including the planning commissioner; at least thirteen representatives of trade unions and employers, parents' associations and students; twenty-five teachers' representatives and five representatives of private education. The minister of education is chairman. However, not content with reducing the HNEC to a rubber stamp, the minister seldom even bothers to consult it. (When in 1971 the minister wanted advice on secondary school teaching he set up an *ad hoc* committee.) The president of the national committee for secular action resigned from the HNEC in protest against the fact that it had not met for fifteen months and was not consulted about the 1971 Bill on aid to Catholic schools. Nevertheless, the HNEC plays an important role in disciplinary proceedings against teachers and students, another example of the corporative character of the education service. In addition to quashing decrees issued without consultation of the HNEC where this is required by law, the council of state hears appeals in cases concerning expulsion from school, refusal of a scholarship, or denial of admission to a university, thus reflecting the judicial protection afforded by the centralized educational system.

The ministry's field services are run by twenty-five rectors, the regional educational prefects who were created by Napoleon in 1808 to represent the central government and guarantee that unity of education which has been both the pride and despair of France. It is only since the beginning of 1972 that the 'academic regions' have been aligned with the standard regional pattern, which is indispensable to effective regional planning of educational expenditures. However, the Paris region has been divided into three academic regions, the attempt to control 1,700,000 pupils, 180,000 students and 80,000 teachers having finally been recognized as extravagant. Prior to 1950, almost all decisions were taken by the ministry in Paris. As the volume of work grew with the numbers educated, piecemeal deconcentration developed until in the 1960s a policy of timid but systematic transfer of decisions to the rectors was adopted. This change received its greatest impetus after the 1968 crisis and especially following on the 1969 appointment as minister of a former delegate general for regional planning, whose role in entrenching prefectoral powers we have already encountered. Like the prefect, the rector commands the channel of communications (information, advice, decisions) between the field services and the minister.

Although the rector must be qualified to teach in a university, his appointment is at the discretion of the cabinet. As the central ministry has come to see itself as the echelon that conceives, advises and supervises, delegating detailed management to the field services, the rector has become a decision-maker rather than a mere transmitter of orders from Paris. While the centre fixes the number of posts of each type allocated to the academic regions, the rector and his skeleton staff – about 130 in an average-sized academic region – decide to which institutions the posts are attributed. He supervises and inspects the educational establishments in his region and vets their budgets. However, it is realized that to avoid congestion at the regional level, a further stage in the deconcentration process is imperative; delegation to the end of the command hierarchy, the ninety-five academic inspectors who run the education ministry's field services (especially primary education) in the departments. At both the regional and departmental level there is a problem of reconciling the prefect's desire to achieve overall coordination and the traditional separateness of educational organization. The regional prefect decides the secondary school building programme, while the prefect is chairman of the primary education departmental council which decides the number and allocation of primary schools in his department. For most other matters, however, the academic inspector can escape the prefect's attempt to monopolize administrative power. Subordination to the prefect would probably compromise the collaboration between the primary schoolteachers union (SNI) and the primary school inspectors in the matter of promotion to coveted posts in the towns. This practice maintains the high level of recruitment to the SNI but their participation in joint management at the local level undermines their challenge to official authority at the national level. Applying the experimental technique used in advance of the 1964 decrees reasserting the role of the prefect, Guichard selected Grenoble and Toulouse as 'pilot rectorates' to try out ways of extending the delegation of decision-making to suit local needs as against the traditional rigid application of centrally fixed standards. However, it is open to question whether any measures short of decentralization – from which France has hitherto recoiled – will overcome the inflexible, sluggish and standardized way in which French education is administered.

About 80 per cent of all funds for education are spent by the central government, the remainder being spent by local authorities, firms and families. Not merely has education tripled its share of budgetary expenditure between 1952 and 1971, a share which had slightly *declined* between 1912 and 1932. The education ministry steadily overhauled the defence ministry's share of the budget in the twenty years after 1952, starting at only 18 per cent of the defence ministry's expenditure, reaching 53 per cent in 1962 (when the Algerian war ended) and surpassing it in 1971. However, President Pompidou warned that education could not expect to go on increasing its share of public expenditure and he supported the defence minister's desire to halt any further relative decline of military expenditure. Whilst, as we have seen,* the defence ministry was the first to present its budget objectives, the education ministry is alone in having reorganized itself on the basis of this principle. It retrospectively calculated the education budgets for 1969–72 along programme budget lines. Thereafter, a joint working party drawn from the ministry's budget and forecasting divisions – which assist the director delegates in the definition of objectives – became responsible for preparing a programme budget in advance of and serving as the guideline for the traditional education ministry budget.

Education budgets have been more concerned with the minimum provision necessary to meet immediate needs rather than

* See above, p. 188.

with satisfying the full requirements anticipated by the education planning commission. The main problem appears to be that in the planning context education has been considered primarily a consumer of public expenditure rather than a productive investment. Until the Third Plan (1958–61) education was neglected. Despite the obvious implications of the post-second world war population increase, the Church-state struggle over subsidies to private schools monopolized attention. The backlog that resulted has not yet been made up. Successive crises prompted piecemeal reforms that changed educational priorities during the Plan, with consequent disorganization and delays in building programmes on which the planners concentrated their attention. There was no educational strategy only annual improvisation. These expedients were negotiated between the ministries of finance and education, although the Fourth Plan (1962–5) did make an attempt to deal belatedly with the educational impact of the demographic 'explosion'. This lack of effective educational planning accounts for the fifteen-year postponement of the effective implementation of the 1959 commitment to increase the school leaving age to sixteen. The increasing importance attached to industrial competitiveness and restraining tax increases in the Fifth (1966–70) and Sixth (1971–5) Plans led to a drastic cut in the rate of increase in educational investment compared with public services regarded as contributing more directly to the priority aim: roads, telecommunications, research. The May 1968 crisis prompted economies in public expenditure that resulted in substantial under-fulfilment of the education targets.

The preparation of the Sixth Plan marked an important turning point, with the education ministry no longer being content to leave it either to *ad hoc* committees like Rueff–Armand in 1960 or successive educational equipment planning commissions to make up for its lack of a coordinated set of future policy objectives. Edgar Faure, then education minister, took the decision to secure greater control over the work of the education planning commission (as it was called for the first time). He obtained the appointment of a rector as its president and its general *rapporteur* was given an office alongside the minister's personal staff. More important, twenty national planning groups internal to the education ministry were charged with advance preparation of the commission's work and regional educational planning groups were also established to fulfil the same function at their level. Coordination was undertaken by the minister's personal staff through meetings of the chairmen and *rapporteurs* of these groups, on which the ministry's divisions were represented where relevant. The ministry's planning staff – which became part of the new programming sub-division – was represented on all groups. Their reports formed the basis of the education planning commission's work, which in RCB* style worked through three sub-committees concerned respectively with objectives, means and evaluations. They focused attention on the cost of the high failure rate at all levels of French education.

Unfortunately, the new planning zeal of the education ministry coincided with a desire on the part of the government (notably the president of the republic and the finance minister) to reduce its commitment to educational expenditure. There was a larger gap than usual between the needs calculated by the planning commission and the resources allocated in the Plan and made available in successive budgets. Having failed in its effort to secure priority for education in the Sixth Plan's preparation, the education ministry is now, nevertheless, in a better position to allocate the resources available to secure the Plan's implementation. The forecasting division seeks to fix objectives early enough to allow its programming sub-division to calculate the cost and calendar the necessary decisions. Computers speed up the allocation of resources where they are most needed.[10] Deprived by a political choice of plentiful funds, the education ministry is devoting greater attention to sharing out penury efficiently.

The dynamic conservatism of an Imperial University in crisis

The late eighteenth-century revolution that replaced birth by competitive examination as the main criterion for selection to fill important posts in France, helped to conserve the dominance of the ascendant bourgeoisie in ways which have provoked a revolt of rising frustrations. The happy few were recruited and trained outside the university system through the *grandes écoles*, the exclusive caste of school-made leaders being preserved from the cultural factory of mass education into which the university system degenerated as a concession to official egalitarian rhetoric.

* See above, p. 187.

Far from increasing social mobility, early selection through competitive examinations helped maintain the traditional social structure by providing it with an impersonal and respectable justification. In practice, examinations merely confirmed the advantages acquired by birth into a particular social class and sanctified it as merit. The centralized and standardized nature of the educational system was a further obstacle to the sort of innovation that would have spared France the decline in science which she underwent in the nineteenth century and the cultural and institutional cataclysm that threatened to engulf much more than higher education in 1968. For too long the revolutionary trilogy inscribed on public buildings had proved a hollow mockery. 'An educational system which rests on the ideal of equality but in which failure is the lot of most people, which teaches fraternity but stresses competition, and which celebrates liberty but offers most individuals only limited options, is a source of chronic social tension and hostility.'[11]

There have been many interpretations of the 1968 crisis that commenced at the Nanterre campus of the University of Paris and rapidly developed into a generalized crisis of paternal, educational, industrial and political authority. It culminated in a reassertion of presidential authority and the reaffirmation of the electoral process as the source of legitimacy in a liberal democracy. Conspiracy theorists stressed the role of the ultra-leftist groups, while devotees of the 'generation gap' emphasized youthful revolt. The feeling that the source of discontent was at the deeper level of values was expressed by those who talked about a rejection of the consumer society, the emergence of a cultural revolution or a 'crisis of civilization' (Malraux *dixit*). A more traditional analysis interpreted the 1968 crisis as either a spectacular example of a familiar type of class conflict, exemplified by the general strike, or a political crisis that was resolved by holding a general election to allow the voters to decide who should govern. Although all these interpretations contribute something to an eclectic view of the 1968 May-June crisis, it was no accident that the educational system – and more especially the University of Paris – should be the link in the chain that snapped under strain. It exemplified, in an extreme form, the hyper-centralized and authoritarian character of French institutions, too petrified to cope with new pressures.

The University of Paris was part of a system subjected to escalating demands for access to higher education – particularly from lower-middle class parents – reflected in the rapid increase in the numbers that had achieved the minimum university entrance qualification (the *baccalauréat*) at secondary school. Those who wished to preserve the traditional system proposed to stem the tidal wave by severe selection, pointing out in addition that there would not be enough posts of high status for the numbers of graduates that an unselective entry would disgorge. The threat that selection would be imposed by the government in 1968 contributed to an atmosphere of panic which initially ensured a sympathetic public response to the eruption of student demonstrations, particularly after student confrontations with the police. When the incidents that sparked off the crisis occurred, the university's lack of autonomy and the absence of an effective student union organization with whom negotiations could take place precipitated a political crisis, involving in turn the education minister, the prime minister, the president of the republic and finally the régime itself. When the régime was finally rescued from collapse, de Gaulle recognized that a fundamental reform of the educational system had become inevitable and called on the astute Edgar Faure to take on the role of education minister with the task of rapidly remedying the university system's combination of apoplexy and paralysis. To avoid the political consequences of a cultural revolution, the most adept exponent of dynamic conservatism was summoned to persuade a reactionary parliamentary majority to accept the minimum changes that the circumstances required, under the guise of re-establishing order as well as undertaking overdue reform.

To grasp the exceptional character of Faure's achievement, one must realize that the normal incubation period for a major educational reform since 1945 has generally been about nine years; the time during which a crisis has persuaded the interest groups and public opinion to accept change and allowed the minister to galvanize his sluggish bureaucratic machine into coping with the problem. However, there have been illustrious predecessors – notably Jules Ferry, the only premier simultaneously to hold the education portfolio – who have presented major items of reform legislation within weeks of taking office. Appointed minister on 12 July, Faure prepared his University Guidelines Bill in August, secured its acceptance by the government in September, followed by the parliamentary debates in October and promulgation in early November. Faure was helped in the Bill's preparation by the brilliant team of collaborators who formed his private office but it was he personally who wrote out the first draft of the Bill. Imagination having failed to seize power in the spring of 1968, Faure was determined that the powerful should show themselves capable of imagination in the autumn. For this he needed the support of the president and the prime minister against those, such as the minister of the interior, who saw the problem essentially as the repression of conspiratorial groups, and the arch-centralist Debré, then finance minister. Faure received remote but decisive encouragement from the president; more hesitant backing from the prime minister (particularly unenthusiastic when it came to implementing the 1968 Act). This support sufficed to see him through when allied with a sympathetic press, his own indefatigable exertions and a mesmerizing eloquence projected by radio and television, notably during the direct transmission of the parliamentary debates.

The Bill was the subject of laborious pre-parliamentary discussions and compromises between Faure's closest collaborators – attacked by the Gaullist right as 'leftists' – and those of the prime minister and finance minister. Faure had consulted an unprecedented number of representatives from various educational organizations, many of them anathema to his UDR parliamentary majority. Unable to deliver a frontal attack on the Bill's principles – the creation of an autonomous, pluralistic, participatory and multidisciplinary university system – because they had been approved by de Gaulle, the UDR backbenchers focused on Faure's suspect entourage or on especially sensitive details in his proposals, notably the postponement of Latin in secondary schools and the supposed violation of the neutrality of state education through tolerance of political discussion inside universities. The amendments made before the Bill went to parliament – by the higher national education council, the council of state and the government – left its major guidelines intact but the finance ministry and the council of state, as guardians of centralist administrative orthodoxy, played a major role in restricting the universities' financial autonomy and in curbing the powers of the new national council of higher education and research. The national assembly's cultural affairs committee suggested and the assembly adopted further amendments reducing the much debated 'participation' of students in the running of the new universities. Faure's tactical ingenuity throughout was calculated to depoliticize the issue as much as possible, relying upon the sympathy of the left-wing opposition and the discipline of the right-wing majority to create at least a semblance of consensus. Many of the assembly amendments passed, particularly those from the PDM (whose leader was a former Faure aide), were prepared with the help of the minister's personal staff and used to reverse concessions reluctantly made in cabinet. When the Act was passed, after thirty-two hours debate in the assembly (by 441 votes to 0) and twenty hours discussion in the senate (by 260 votes to 0), Faure appeared to have achieved his desired aim of unanimity, as the communists – who abstained – were to play the most active part in seeking to make the Act work.[12]

However, it was one thing to persuade parliament to pass the University Guidelines Act unanimously; it was quite another to secure its faithful implementation. As the assembly's UDR *rapporteur* on the Act, former rector Capelle, had written of the pre-1968 situation, a French university was 'a mere juxtaposition of various subjects, each represented by one professor, isolated in his field'. One cannot understand the bitterness of the attack on the 'mandarins' unless one appreciates the servitudes occasioned by the primordial significance of 'the professorial chair, connoting a domain of knowledge belonging literally to one man who reigns over it as an absolute monarch until he has reached retirement age'.[13] In place of the Napoleonic professor, the new Act put councils composed of teachers (including non-professorial staff) and students based upon 632 departments (called UER) which would be united into universities of a manageable size. The elected university councils in turn choose a president, a professor on whom devolves the responsibility for effective management of the university and for preventing each department from resuscitating the impervious aversion towards interdisciplinary ventures. However, whilst the 1968 Act proclaimed the autonomy of the universities to be designated (forty-three provincial universities and thirteen Parisian universities), its explanatory memorandum made clear that there would be limits to this autonomy, of a financial, administrative and pedagogical character.

Predictably, these limitations on university autonomy have been applied in a restrictive fashion. The reassertion of the education ministry's power, exercised from Paris and by the rectors, as the guardian of central administrative and pedagogical uniformity, and the finance ministry's role as the authority on financial rectitude, has prevented the decentralization that was a fundamental aim of the Act. The university teachers, traumatized by the speed and scale of the changes, have generally facilitated the reduction of autonomy to a fiction by their pusillanimous preference for passing awkward responsibilities on to the central ministries as a way of minimizing conflicts within the university. However, when it came to electoral participation, the university teachers voted massively whilst students – especially in arts and social sciences – abstained in large numbers, a fact which in part reflected the hostility to the reform of a significant fraction of active students. The main beneficiaries of this indifference were the communists, who were able to win a large number of the student seats on the departmental and university councils.

Edgar Faure had hoped that he would be left in charge of education for the crucial years necessary to see his reform through. De Gaulle's replacement by Pompidou deprived him of this opportunity, the new president making it clear that there had been sufficient dynamism to placate the reformers. Priority had to be given to conservatism to satisfy the UDR voters.[14] Although participation was also introduced into primary and secondary schools, the 1968 Act's promise that the reorganization of higher education was merely 'the first stage of a general reform of education' was not to be fulfilled. Still less would the very significant omission, even at the height of the crisis, of the *grandes écoles* from the reformed university structure, be repaired. The new minister devoted himself to making the ministry of education a more efficient organization. The implementation of the 1968 Act was left largely to the rectors, exemplars of the centralized nature of the French administrative system, confirming that France is not hospitable to experiments in pluralistic autonomy.

Nationalization as state capitalism

In contrast to Soviet Russia, where public ownership of the means of production is the doctrinaire rule, and the United States where it is the doctrinaire exception, in Britain, Italy and France a substantial public sector developed in the twentieth century within a mixed economy that remains predominantly in private ownership. Whereas in Britain the private sector has traditionally enjoyed greater prestige and power than the public sector, in France the situation is reversed, with pervasive consequences for public policy. While the large private firms in Britain are the senior partners in the mixed economy, in France it is public enterprise that sets the pace. Although there has been a recent rehabilitation of the market and of competition in the EEC context, France has never officially adopted the ideology of free competition. The long-standing tradition of state intervention took the form of public enterprise as early as the seventeenth century and the state capitalism that subsequently developed owes more to mercantilism than to socialism. This helps to explain the relatively high degree of public satisfaction with the nationalized industries, the lack of denationalization backlash when the right has been in power, the widespread support for further extensions of public ownership; these attitudes cutting across all parties and classes. In 1966, 46 per cent regarded the performance of the major public enterprises as satisfactory, 32 per cent as unsatisfactory, with 22 per cent not replying; while in 1968 more people favoured nationalizing the space and electronics industries, as well as all banks, than opposed this.[15]

It was the semi-revolutionary fervour of the Liberation France of 1944–6 that engendered the mood of pro-nationalization consensus to which the bulk of the public sector owes its existence. Although a left-wing parliamentary majority, active trade union pressure and a widespread desire to punish unpatriotic industrialists played their part, it was under de Gaulle's aegis that France not only extended public ownership but established a comprehensive social security system and started national economic planning. De Gaulle made it clear in his memoirs that his aim was not to end the exploitation of man by man. 'It is to the state that it falls to build the nation's power, which henceforth depends upon the economy. The latter must be directed, all the more so because it is deficient, because it needs to renew itself and because it will not do so unless prevailed upon. Such, in my view, is the principal motive for the measures of nationalization, control and modernization taken by my government.' Most of the legislation setting up the major public enterprises was adopted swiftly by the constituent assembly in the months after de Gaulle resigned in 1946 but with his support. The Coal Act passed unanimously; the electricity and gas industries were nationalized by 512 votes to 64, the largest insurance companies by 487 to 63, and the main deposit banks by 521 to 35. Furthermore, the preamble to the fourth republic constitution declared: 'Any property or enterprise which has or acquires the character of a national public service or of a monopoly must come under collective ownership.' Although this has been reaffirmed in the fifth republic's constitution, even in 1946 it was more a justification of the extensive nationalization programme just carried out than a prescription for further public ownership. Thereafter, French governments have preferred to establish joint enterprises, usually with a controlling state shareholding. However, the 1972 joint socialist-communist programme included the outright nationalization of nine major firms in the chemical, electrical and aluminium industries as well as the armaments firm of Dassault and state acquisition of shares in the three largest steel firms. A public opinion poll in September 1972 suggested that nationalization would not substantially affect the way people voted in the 1973 general election. Only 21 per cent said that the nationalization programme would incline them to vote for the left, 16 per cent would be inclined to vote against, 42 per cent were indifferent and 21 per cent did not reply.[16]

A satisfactory definition of the public enterprise sector in France has so far proved impossible. If one takes as criteria the state's controlling share ownership (which may be less than 50 per cent) and the firm's accountability to and supervision by government officials, one still has not succeeded because of the extensive secondary and tertiary shareholdings by public enterprises that have largely escaped both public notice and public control. Subsidiaries are immune from investigation either by the commission responsible for checking the accounts of public enterprises or by parliamentary finance committees, the senate finance committee making a formal protest in July 1972 against the government's refusal to allow such inquiries into the use of public money. The assembly's finance committee special *rapporteur* on public enterprises estimated that in 1971 some six hundred firms involving thirteen different ministries were concerned. These are firms in which the state directly or indirectly owns at least 30 per cent of the shares but the number exceeds a thousand if all holdings are included. It was calculated in 1965 that the Electricity, Gas and Renault Corporations each owned shares in over a hundred firms, though in the case of the last two, 40 per cent of their holdings were of less than 1 per cent of the firm's capital. The number of public enterprise holdings were increasing annually by an average of thirty, so that the public sector has been incrementally expanding with minimal controversy. There is no ministry of state holdings such as exists in Italy to control the expanding number of partly or wholly owned public enterprises nor, as in Federal Germany, to sell off a public enterprise like Volkswagen. It is left to a unit within the finance ministry's treasury division to manage the French state's shareholdings.* The 1967 Nora Report, which attempted to provide an overall government strategy for public enterprise, deplored the lack of an instrument with the power to apply this strategy. It suggested a strengthening of the unit in the treasury so as to assert more effective control.

The weight of the public enterprise sector in the French economy can be indicated in various ways. Narrowly defined, public enterprises directly purchase 8 per cent of goods and services, supply 10 per cent of national production, contribute 13 per cent to the national income, pay 15 per cent of the wage bill, make 15 per cent of the nation's total investments and 40 per cent of investment by firms. Compared with Italy and Federal Germany, French public enterprise has a larger turnover and volume of investment, though it employs a smaller percentage of the working population than in Italy. Its average share of the national economy (based on an arithmetic mean of the percentage of turnover, investment and employment) worked out in 1968 at 18·2 per cent compared with 15·9 per cent for Italy and 12·9 per cent for Federal Germany. However, one cannot identify a criterion that accounts for the peculiar collection of industries which have been nationalized in France. There are both monopolies and competitive firms; heavy and light industries; those vital for national security and others that are not; firms crucial to steering national economic development and others that are not; enterprises dependent on state subsidy (the *Les Invalides* of capitalism) and others that make profits. Nevertheless, two

* See above, p. 159.

major types of public enterprise may be distinguished for our purpose: those in the administrative economy sector, which are public service monopolies, and those in the competitive, market economy sector, approximating most closely in their behaviour to private business.

The public service monopolies are constituted principally by the power and transport corporations, which together account for some 60 per cent of the value added by nationalized industries and 70 per cent of their manpower and investment.[17] It is this infrastructural, public utility sector that has primarily been used by government as an instrument of both long- and short-term public policy. It was also this sector's technological dynamism after the second world war that helped galvanize both private industry and government into an acceptance of rapid economic growth as the norm. The main fuel and power corporations consist of *Charbonnages de France, Electricité de France* and *Gaz de France*. The coal corporation has had to deal with the industry's rundown, which has hit the main centres of the Nord and Lorraine especially hard. The government has reacted by formulating a national fuel policy that includes a slow-down in the phasing out of high-cost coal to diminish localized unemployment at the price of substantial subsidies to cover running costs and investment. The electricity corporation was also compelled in 1966 to provide an indirect subsidy, contracting to triple its French coal purchases until 1978 at up to 50 per cent above world prices. Electricity (which has a number of common services including a joint distribution network with the Gas Corporation) plans to increase its share of national fuel consumption from 28 per cent to 45 per cent between 1965 and 1985, when nuclear power is expected to become the main source of electricity. This involves the Atomic Energy Commissariat, which of course is also heavily engaged in military work. The largest employer among the nationalized industries is the SNCF railway corporation which, together with Paris Transport, has had to be heavily subsidized to meet deficits caused by government intervention to keep down prices and maintain uneconomic services that make political sense but reduce their accounts to financial nonsense.

In the market economy public sector, by contrast, the government has generally left its wholly or partly owned firms much more to their own devices. There are exceptions to this rule, notably the petroleum enterprises ELF–ERAP and TOTAL–CFP, which supply about 40 per cent of France's consumption, in competition with the major multi-national enterprises. Like British Petroleum, they are joint public-private enterprises but the contrast in national attitudes is exemplified by the fact that whereas the British government has not asserted its management rights despite majority ownership, the French government effectively controls CFP even though it owns only 35 per cent of the shares. After the immediate postwar interlude of outright nationalization, the French government has reverted to its prewar technique of establishing joint enterprises with private business, which often merely disguise effective public control through techniques such as preferential voting rights on the board, possession of a suspensory veto over board decisions, and government nomination of or approval of the appointment of the managing director. So the state is no ordinary shareholder. Despite the fictional character of these joint enterprises' autonomy, in practice the government has sought to allow them some of the managerial and financial flexibility enjoyed by private firms, while using them for surveillance of the private sector and as a stimulant to competitive vigour, so frequently absent in French private business.* Now that France can no longer be isolated from the international market, an administrative economy style of management, preoccupied with providing a public service rather than selling goods against stiff competition, is judged no longer appropriate. The French government expects these public enterprises to set private business an example in entrepreneurial drive.

In addition to the petroleum enterprises mentioned, some major transport firms also come into this competitive sector, notably Air France and Air Inter (domestic flights) and two merchant shipping firms which account for half the French merchant navy. However, the market economy sector principally flourishes in the three main industries outside power and transport. First the state acquired a firm grip on deposit banking and insurance when it nationalized, in addition to the Bank of France, the four major banks with 55 per cent of bank deposits and thirty-four insurance companies (since amalgamated into three) doing 62 per cent of the

---

* See p. 165 on the role in urban development played by such joint enterprises, the *Caisse des Dépôts* forming partnerships between local authorities and private business.

business, to neutralize the political as well as economic influence exerted by private financial interests. In 1966 the number of state deposit banks was reduced by amalgamation to three. They were instructed to invest directly in industry and to establish merchant bank subsidiaries and generally to use public money for the promotion of industrial mergers and competitiveness. The three state banks – *Banque Nationale de Paris*, *Crédit Lyonnais* and *Société Générale* – control 60 per cent of all bank branches and deposits; together with the *Caisse des Dépôts* and the Post Office they handle over 80 per cent of all bank deposits in France. In addition SNCF and the nationalized insurance companies have created their own banks. Secondly, the state owns half the aerospace industry – paradoxically the civil aviation half – through SNIAS, a 1969 amalgamation into a joint enterprise (two-thirds public). The private sector is dominated by Dassault, producing miltary aircraft and therefore closely involved in French foreign and defence policy. Its owner is a UDR deputy, the firm making substantial contributions to UDR election expenditure.

Finally, the French motor car industry is lead by Renault, which moved from third place when it was privately owned to first place after nationalization. 'It is impossible to prove that the industry has performed better than it would have if Renault had remained under private ownership, but those respects in which the firm's choices differed from the private companies' were consistently in directions favourable to consumers and to the expansion of the French economy.'[18] As well as its impressive record in product innovation and increasing exports, Renault has played an important role in improving working conditions. It pioneered the concession of a third and then a fourth week's paid holiday to its employees, against the opposition of both private business and the government, which correctly anticipated that longer holidays would quickly spread throughout French industry. Table 33 indicates the relative satisfaction of the French public with their major nationalized industries, although between 1966 and 1968 there was a notable shift from both the satisfied and unsatisfied to those of neither opinion.

The last thing that the CGT pioneers of nationalization wanted to bring about was state capitalism. Their 1919 programme was a functionally representative version of the anarcho-syndicalist vision of workers' control in which the miners – not the minister –

Table 33
The French Public's Attitude Towards Selected Nationalized Industries (%) *

	Satisfied		Unsatisfied		No Answer	
Reply	1966	1968	1966	1968	1966	1968
Railways	49	—	28	—	23	—
Coal mines	30	20	35	28	35	52
Electricity and gas	54	42	25	24	21	34
Insurance companies	26	25	23	20	51	55
Deposit banks	30	27	17	14	53	59
Renault	49	35	19	20	32	45

* Source: *Sondages*, 1968, no. 1, p. 39, and 1969, nos 1–2, p. 88.

would run the mines. However, the attempt to create autonomous public corporations after the second world war quickly succumbed to political and administrative pressure for a reassertion of state control. Characteristically, it was Debré who gave the most frank and forceful expression to the view that only the government was entitled to act in the general interest :

The state must not be divided up. There cannot be nationalized industry policies independent of state policy. One might even say that the existence of a nationalized sector imposes on the state, if for no other reason, a transport, credit, fuel, insurance, social security and public employees policy. A significant part of the faults attributable to the nationalized sector is due to the fact that the state, represented by the government, has not been sufficiently conscious that being 'boss' it should deliberately formulate a policy and guide the enterprises over which it has assumed responsibility.

Debré was proud of the fact that when he was in office he had increased the prime minister's control over managerial appointments in nationalized industry and set up an interministerial committee which was consulted before any wage agreement was concluded in a nationalized industry. His rejection of the idea of a nationalized industries ministry is based on the view that 'it is indispensable to maintain and even reinforce [the nationalized firms'] allegiance to the ministry for whose policy they should be an instrument and sometimes the main instrument.'[19]

The nationalized industries lost their autonomy long before Debré became prime minister. The fears that they would become 'states within the state' and that their deficits would impose an excessive financial burden on the government, were utilized by those who wished to reassert traditional state control. The managements are so curbed by regulations and supervision that one is reduced to speculating whether their profusion indicates a lack of autonomy or really signifies the failure to impose effective state control. Superficially, it would appear that interventions by various state agencies 'are so numerous and direct in all matters concerning investment, finance, charges, remuneration, production and sales objectives, that managerial discretion is better defined by subtraction than by enumeration'.[20] Government control is exerted both from outside and from inside each nationalized industry. Externally, a few officials in the finance ministry's budget, treasury, prices and forecasting divisions, together with the relevant sponsoring ministry, take most of the public enterprise's major decisions. They do so to suit national economic policy rather than the objectives of the enterprise, whose management suffers as a consequence. As the last word usually rests with the finance ministry, it was decided in 1966 to improve coordination within the divisions concerned by holding meetings of their directors. The sponsoring ministries – notably the ministries of industrial and scientific development and of regional planning, public works and housing – are much more sympathetic to 'their' public enterprises, officials and managers generally having both been trained at *Polytechnique*, but they are in a weak position compared to the finance ministry, where the budget division plays the crucial part if a subsidy is to be granted, whilst the treasury division decides if an investment loan is requested.

Inside the public enterprises, there are two kinds of state surveillance. In a few corporations there is a government commissioner – usually the director of the relevant division in the sponsoring ministry – who provides liaison and exercises on the spot supervision, as well as representing the sponsoring ministry on the board. More generally, there are either state supervisors or supervisory commissions, loosely attached to the finance ministry, who tend, however, to become spokesmen for the enterprise to which they are attached for a long time. Actual ministerial interference in the running of a nationalized industry generally depends upon two factors : the size of the corporation's income and capital, in absolute terms and as a proportion of its total revenue and investment programme, provided by the government; the volume and intensity of the political pressures by business, trade unions and local authorities, directly or through members of parliament. Under the fourth republic, sub-committees of both assembly and senate finance committees tried to exercise parliamentary control but from 1958 until 1971 this practice was virtually discontinued. An attempt by the assembly finance committee to exert control was ruled unconstitutional in 1964 but in 1971 the assembly finance committee appointed a special *rapporteur* concerned with general parliamentary supervision over the nationalized industries. However, France is still a long way from having a select committee on nationalized industries such as exists in Britain. Only 2 per cent of parliamentary questions concern public enterprise. Parliament annually receives the general report of the public enterprise accounts audit commission but its searching comments seldom result in severe sanctions. The debates on the sponsoring ministries' budgets provide the main occasion for parliamentary scrutiny of the nationalized industries.

The attempt to nationalize whilst avoiding state management was to be achieved by confiding power to a tripartite board where functional representation was to express the aspirations of the inter-war CGT towards economic democracy. In 1919 the CGT, considering that it could not realistically demand outright workers' control, accepted a formula coined by the economist and cooperative propagandist Charles Gide: a board equally representative of the state, the workers and the consumers, a formula which directly challenged the view that the sovereign state alone represented the national interest. The functionally representative boards of directors established after the second world war failed to achieve the aim of autonomous management for a variety of reasons, including the fact that each of the three 'interests' to be represented presented problems even before the question of their cooperation in decision-making arose.[21] The most paradoxical case is that of the government nominees, given the view that the state alone represented an indivisible general interest, which was the pretext for the restoration of total government control after 1953. In practice, state representation was divided between the 'interested ministries', who became accustomed to regarding their nominees as instructed delegates representing their separate ministerial viewpoints, although they often attempt to reach advance agreement. Consumer representation, which was meaningful in terms of Gide's vision of a cooperative repub-

lic based on powerful consumer organizations, was reduced
to the representation of local authorities, consumer industries and
family associations; the government in 1953 taking over the choice
of consumer nominees to give it an unchallengeable majority on
the board, including choice of the chairman. Finally, by the time
the CGT's diluted conception of workers' control was attained, the
leading trade union had been captured by the communists, who
did not believe that it was possible to undertake socialist experiments in a capitalist context. The attempt by communist
ministers and the CGT in 1946–7 to assume control of the nationalized industries provided an early pretext for extinguishing the
hope of a socialist-style autonomy.*

Even before the government acquired both majority control and
a suspensory veto over the decisions of the public enterprise
boards, such power as remained after ministerial direction,
authorization and surveillance had passed to the full-time management and particularly to the chairman-managing director,
who embodies the Napoleonic style of managerial authority.
The board members, composed of busy part-timers, generally
delegate all their powers to the chairman-managing director,
retaining a residual advisory and supervisory role. The appointment of chief executives, like that of the government board
nominees, provides ample scope for political patronage. This
ensures that the propensity to technocracy is based upon a combination of expertise and political reliability. The transfer by
pantouflage of technocrats from the civil and military *grands
corps* of engineers and finance inspectors (the latter dominating
the state banks) has provided the personnel to run the nationalized
industries with a high degree of efficiency, although the osmosis
between the supervising ministries and the management that
sometimes results has its dangers. In 1960 *Polytechniciens* provided 70 per cent of the senior executives of the railway corporation and 22 per cent of the Electricity and Gas Corporations;
while 44 per cent of the Coal Corporation executives were from
the *Ecole des Mines* and 55 per cent of Renault executives had
studied at the *Ecole des Arts et Métiers*.[22] In 1972, out of the forty-
four chairmen-managing directors of the twenty largest public

---

* In the case of social security, the extinction of genuine autonomy was delayed
until financial problems provided the pretext for the 1967 reorganization, under
pressure from private business and the finance ministry.

enterprises, thirty came from the senior civil service, twenty-three from the *grands corps*. At a lower level, colonization by graduates of ENA is widespread. They occupied fifteen senior posts in ELF–ERAP, fourteen in ORTF and eleven in Renault.

Public enterprise, through the severance between ownership and control, has allowed an executive élite to subordinate these large-scale organizations to the discipline of efficiency defined in terms of technical criteria, making it the best example of techno-bureaucratic management. A new sort of autonomy has developed, a technocratic autonomy, in which Princes of Petroleum, Earls of Electricity, Counts of Railways or Renault have become more powerful than some ministers. In 1972 the government decided to avoid the threat of techno-gerontocracy by reducing the retirement age of the heads of nationalized enterprises from seventy to sixty-five. Although the nationalized enterprises are subject to a variety of checks, these usually concern detailed operations rather than the enterprise's strategy. Furthermore, public enterprises generally do not supply enough information to government departments about their activities, Renault justifying its taciturnity by a desire not to forewarn its competitors. A former head of the Electricity Corporation, who moved to a large private corporation, declared that there was not much difference between the role of management in the two cases, except that on major policy matters he had enjoyed more freedom of action from government when he was in the public sector.[23] We shall see in the next chapter how a *Polytechnicien* in the atomic energy commissariat was able to use its autonomy to conceive and implement a nuclear policy which was foisted upon a succession of indecisive governments under the fourth republic.

However, in the vast majority of public enterprises, where military considerations are not a major factor, managements are compelled to pursue profit to preserve their autonomy from government interference just as in the private sector the managers of an unprofitable enterprise become vulnerable. Although public firms have acted very much like the more enterprising type of private firm, this tendency was fostered from 1969 to 1972 by the efforts of the Chaban-Delmas government to implement the recommendations of the Nora Report, the author of that report spending two years as the prime minister's right-hand man. Starting from the premiss that the existing administrative economy organization made management impossible owing to excessive supervision, Nora had recommended that public enterprises should sign contracts with the government in which the quantified commitments of each party would be specified. The policy was quickly acted upon in the case of the railways, legislation being presented in 1969 to guarantee managerial autonomy within a framework of general rules fixed by the government. The Railway Corporation accepted the duty of eliminating its chronic deficit, notably through reducing its labour force by one-sixth within five years. It would be compensated for providing uneconomic services judged by the government to be in the public interest. (A more modest contract was concluded with the Electricity Corporation in 1970 and with ORTF in 1971.) By 1974, when subsidies will have been phased out, the railways are expected to run like a commercial enterprise but there will still be ministerial intervention in fares, wages and investment decisions, so the promised autonomy may be more apparent than real. The fundamental purpose of these reforms was to divest the government of the burden of financing the deficits of public enterprises which sheltered from the market test of efficiency behind their public service vocation. The government promised that the resources made available would be spent on new priorities such as improving the environment.

Although the contract signed with the railways was made to coincide with the duration of the Sixth Plan, the nationalized industries have not been noticeably more willing to act in conformity with the National Plan than are large private firms. The industrial planning commissions tend to be dominated by the representatives of the large firms, who use them to obtain financial support for their investment programmes from the government, while the real power lies with the finance ministry, the planning commissioner and the committees of the economic and social development fund.* Public enterprise investment is often the victim of the finance ministry's short-term economic management, being speeded up or delayed to suit the need to reflate or deflate the economy. Prices and wages in the nationalized industries are also an important part of the government's anti-inflation armoury. Although they are expected to 'break even', the nationalized

---

* See above, p. 167. The fund's annual Report on the civil (including the nationalized industries) investment programmes is appended to the Finance Bill.

firms' deficits have owed much to government imposition of politically motivated policies of price restraint or privileged rates for favoured industries, regions or social categories, a practice especially rife in public transport. As a major employer, the government tried in the 1960s to set an example to the private sector by imposing a 'wages policy'. The resulting lag in earnings provoked a large number of strikes in the public sector and reduced trade union enthusiasm for further nationalization.

Partly to make up for the poor industrial relations record in the public sector, and partly to give a personal twist to the Gaullist nostrum for ending class conflict (promoting 'participation' by workers in their firms), parliament passed an Act, in January 1970, on President Pompidou's instructions. Up to 25 per cent (but only 5 per cent in the first instance) of Renault's capital was to be distributed to its employees, who would have a seat on the board of directors in their capacity as shareholders, additional to six seats as workers. A public enterprise is being used as a guinea-pig to test whether profit-sharing will reconcile the French working classes to state capitalism. Assurances have been given that this experiment is not a step to denationalization on the Volkswagen precedent, the right to resell shares being restricted to other employees or to the state. The public sector has also increased the number of mergers, which have been part of the government's industrial policy, although the state's use of its power as a purchaser has been an even more important factor. Finally, public enterprise has been used – particularly in the cases of petroleum and nuclear power – as an instrument of foreign and defence policy, the subject of the next chapter.

As yet there is no firm evidence that government in France has managed, except in certain limited sectors such as fuel policy, to arrive at an integrated strategy for the very diverse collection of enterprises that it has acquired. Unless a ministry of nationalized industries, such as was suggested in 1968 by the British select committee on nationalized industries, is established, it will probably be impossible to carry out a consistent policy in the public sector. If such a policy were achieved, it would probably conflict with the official desire to increase the autonomy of public enterprises in the way that a standardized policy enforced by the education ministry has circumscribed the autonomy of educational institutions.

8 National Independence and International Mission

While de Gaulle was at the helm, the primacy of international concerns was such that the fifth republic could be characterized as pursuing 'depoliticization in domestic affairs, plus a foreign policy'. However, he was well aware of the interdependence of France's international standing with her internal political stability and economic strength. He deliberately used each in the service of the other. His first priority was to construct the political and economic springboard from which to launch an ambitious foreign policy but he was convinced that without the restoration of patriotism and national pride, France would remain prey to the divisions that had wrecked her polity and economy, thereby reducing her international stature. His ability to adopt a more assertive and independent role in foreign policy reflected the greater strength which France had already begun to acquire under the fourth republic, assisted by the conclusion in 1962 of the main decolonization process and by the changing nature of Soviet-American relations. He exploited these new opportunities with great skill until the domestic crisis of 1968 compelled him to assume a more modest posture.

De Gaulle combined an unswerving commitment to a few principles with complete flexibility in the way in which circumstances required that they be applied. Inter-state relations had power and cunning as their means and the promotion of national interests as their objective. France must be restored to her rank as a great world power – albeit not a super power – and to this end all else should be subordinated. To avoid domination by the two super-states, the smaller nation states should cooperate by forming confederations and alliances to preserve the balance of power. In particular, France should repudiate her relative international self-effacement and assert her 'immemorial vocation for influence and expansion'.[1] Alliances were seasonal, dictated by the opportunism of a government determined to preserve the sovereignty of the state in an international environment which threatened foreign penetration and domination. What was personal to de Gaulle was the style and range of intervention rather than the substance of this foreign policy, so one should not be surprised at the continuity between the fourth republic and de Gaulle, as well as between de Gaulle and Pompidou. The phrases may be less grandiose and the gestures less offensive (in both senses of the word) but the task of defending French interests in the context of internal and external pressures persists.

The foreign policy-making process

In domestic affairs, the policy process is discussed frequently but the policies themselves are generally neglected, whereas in foreign affairs the policies are described and assessed *ad nauseam* but the policy process is seldom investigated. French foreign policy in the de Gaulle era was described as being 'made in three admirably synchronized steps: it is prepared at the Quai d'Orsay, decided on at the Elysée and implemented nowhere. . . .' As well as emphasizing the extent to which the president dominated foreign policy-making, this statement draws attention to the fact that because de Gaulle's ambitions exceeded the strength he was able to mobilize, the actual successes achieved were few, even if one bears in mind that such success is rare. Pompidou, by contrast, has respected the ' "Micawber rule" – never allow commitments to outrun strength'.[2] From the very start of his presidency, he took a firm personal grip of the conduct of French foreign policy, publicly symbolized by his role in the 'summit' meetings at which the major understandings are reached and in the bi-annual press conferences at which he stated France's foreign policy. Unlike the American president, Pompidou relies upon two diplomatic advisers loaned by the foreign ministry and does not have the staff that President Nixon can call on, still less an equivalent of his special adviser on foreign affairs, Dr Kissinger. Nevertheless, President Pompidou has continued to dominate foreign policy decisions, especially those concerning the European Economic Community, calling a referendum on its enlargement in 1972 very much as a personal initiative and with a mixture of internal and international motives.* At the very time when he was reversing one of the general's decisions – his exclusion of Britain from the EEC in 1963 and 1967 – Pompidou asserted his claim to be more Gaullist than de Gaulle by calling a referendum on a foreign policy matter.

French foreign policy is controlled by a triumvirate, headed by the president, who is responsible for setting the policy guidelines and taking the decisions of major national and international consequence. The second-in-command is the prime minister, whose main task is to coordinate foreign policy with the decisions of all government departments other than the foreign ministry (especially defence and finance) and to defend the president's policy in parliament. Under earlier régimes, the office of foreign affairs minister was frequently combined with that of premier. From 1871 to 1918, 28 per cent of premiers were also foreign minister; between 1919 and 1939, 53 per cent held both offices simultaneously but from 1944 to 1958 the proportion fell to 15 per cent. Under the fifth republic, the prime minister has held no other office, so it is necessary for a minister of foreign affairs to make up the triumvirate. He is responsible for the detailed implementation and defence of the president's policy, the conduct of relations with countries in which the president takes only intermittent interest, and for routine diplomatic work. In describing the formation of his 1958 government, de Gaulle stated that he had entrusted four posts to former civil servants who 'would be more directly under my wing', including 'ambassador Couve de Murville at foreign affairs [and] engineer Pierre Guillaumat at the war office'.[3] While Couve was not a merely impassive executant of presidential directives, he has stated that during his tenure (1958–68) of the foreign ministry, he shared 'a sort of spontaneous agreement' on aims with de Gaulle and at their regular Friday morning meetings they only discussed 'ways and means and timing'.[4] Charged by Article 52 of the constitution with the negotiation of treaties and by Article 13 with the appointment of ambassadors, de Gaulle interpreted these provisions to mean that France's ambassadors abroad were his personal representatives.

The cabinet seldom discusses foreign affairs but receives a weekly review of the international situation from the foreign

* See below, p. 247.

The One and Indivisible French Republic

minister. The president will usually have consulted the prime minister and foreign minister before any major decision is made and when the decision has important military implications – such as the 1966 withdrawal from the North Atlantic Treaty Organization – the defence minister will also be involved. So, apart from reminding cabinet ministers of the official position on all foreign policy issues, and hinting at such shifts in these positions as are contemplated, the cabinet's function is to ratify decisions settled beforehand[5] by the triumvirate or at interministerial councils or committee meetings. To prepare the ground for interministerial meetings, there is close contact between the diplomatic advisers of the president and prime minister – who receive copies of the foreign ministry telegrams – and the personal staff of the foreign minister. The need to follow up and coordinate the implications of foreign policy for other ministries has increased considerably, especially since the establishment of the EEC, strengthening the role of the prime minister as chairman of such interministerial meetings. However, when it comes to overseas visits, the president travels to the political summits, leaving the prime minister to perform the role of France's commercial traveller in the foothills.

While Couve de Murville had the advantage of his long career as a senior foreign ministry official, Pompidou's choice in 1969, Maurice Schumann, had been a junior foreign affairs minister from 1951 to 1954 in five successive governments and president of the national assembly foreign affairs committee from 1962 to 1967. Although he modified his position after 1962, he never entirely repudiated his earlier commitment to European federalism, Anglophilia and 'Atlanticism' and in the 1969 government, which included a number of leading ministers who had defended these views with greater consistency, his appointment in place of the intransigent Debré was indicative of a certain reversal of emphasis in French foreign policy. However, he has remained in the background, playing 'third fiddle' to the president and prime minister. (It is significant that in 1970 whereas 84 per cent of the French public could name the prime minister, only 34 per cent could name the foreign minister.) There are two other ministers attached to the foreign ministry, one of whom was raised in July 1972 to the rank of minister delegate for foreign affairs; while the other one is specifically responsible for cooperation with developing countries.* In addition to all the usual factors that render the position of such junior ministers marginal, the existence since 1915 of a powerful secretary-general – the only such office to have survived all political vicissitudes since that date – has prevented the ministers from competing with the foreign minister's *cabinet* in the coordination and checking of the civil servants' work.

The reasons for the survival of the secretary-general in the foreign ministry appear to be the desire to maintain continuity in the conduct of foreign policy; to compensate for the frequency with which the foreign minister has to travel abroad; finally, the small and relatively homogeneous nature of the ministry. The secretary-general coordinates all the work of the ministry through his control of the communications network, his meetings with division directors and with the minister and his personal staff. The incoming diplomatic telegrams are channelled four times a day through the director of the secretary-general's *cabinet*, who sorts them and selects the most important ones for the secretary-general's attention. Whilst the minister signs the most important telegrams sent, the secretary-general signs those of lesser importance. Each morning, he holds a meeting with the directors of the political, economic and cultural affairs divisions, at which the director or assistant director of the foreign minister's *cabinet* is present. At these meetings the secretary-general comments on the telegrams received, gives instructions for outgoing telegrams and allocates the day's work. They also provide an opportunity to assess the state of all pending issues and for views to be exchanged. Once a week this meeting is also attended by the director of personnel, the head of protocol, and representatives of the prime minister's *cabinet* and of the defence minister. The secretary-general has frequent formal and informal contacts with the directors of all the ministry's divisions, personally or by telephone, to ensure overall administrative coordination. Finally, every evening the day's business is reviewed by the foreign minister, the director of his *cabinet*, the secretary-general and the director of political affairs.[6] The secretary-general is an unusually powerful official, who remains in office for long periods and exercises real influence on policy over political and diplomatic as well as administrative matters.

There is no planning staff at the foreign ministry, the assumption being that decisions have to be taken one by one and on a day-

* See below, p. 250.

to-day basis. Despite the fact that such distinctions are now increasingly artificial, the foreign ministry's two major divisions are those concerned with political and economic affairs. The former is the most important. It is sub-divided on both geographical and functional lines. There are five sub-divisions concerned with Europe (further sub-divided into western, southern, central and eastern Europe), Asia and the Pacific, North Africa, Middle East and Black Africa (excluding former French colonies which are dealt with separately) and America (North, Central and South). The three functional sub-divisions are concerned respectively with the United Nations Organization and its specialist agencies; Pacts (North Atlantic Treaty, of which France remains a signatory although she has left the integrated military organization,* Western European Union) amalgamated with atomic and space affairs; information and press. This last sub-division prepares a daily press review for the foreign minister, his closest collaborators and certain embassies abroad. It 'supervises French radio's broadcasts beamed abroad and the general interpretation of international affairs' given in home broadcasts and as such provides valuable assistance to diplomatic activities by 'helping French opinion to understand and support the government's action. . . .'[7] The economic and financial affairs division keeps the foreign ministry informed about the economic implications of its foreign policies and other ministries about the foreign political implications of their activities. Its work, which frequently involves participating in interdepartmental meetings, has increased substantially with the EEC. It works especially closely with the finance ministry's foreign economic relations division.

France has always given an especially high priority to projecting its culture abroad, reflecting the nineteenth-century reality that France was the cultural centre of the universe and French was the language of diplomacy. Since then the pretence of French cultural pre-eminence has become increasingly difficult to maintain and the civilizing mission has appeared to be as unrealistic as it is arrogant. French foreign cultural policy is officially organized by the foreign ministry's cultural relations division, rather than through a semi-autonomous public body like the British Council. The contrast, for once, is more apparent than real because French

* France still has a military liaison mission attached to NATO military headquarters and participates in ten NATO agencies, notably the air early warning system.

cultural and educational establishments abroad are staffed by secondment from the education ministry and call on the services of independent-minded French intellectuals, while the British Council is very much under the thumb of the Foreign Office cultural relations department. However, France is the country which maintains the largest number of educational establishments outside its borders, over 1,500 employing more than thirty thousand teachers. These institutions are regarded as the cultural equivalents of consulates in the commercial sphere. We shall return to this subject in dealing with France's relations with the French-speaking world in general and its former colonies in particular.

About a thousand of the ministry's staff are based in Paris, while three thousand are distributed over 125 embassies and 140 consulates abroad. Most of them are accredited to particular countries, where their function is twofold. They collect information that will be telegraphed to Paris and which forms the basis on which policy decisions are made. They protect French interests and citizens, promote trade (including, in the case of military attachés, the arms trade) and conduct relations with the government of the country in which they are located. Embassy work is political, military, commercial and cultural, the military and commercial attachés reporting back to their parent ministries (defence and finance). Diplomats are now sent on courses devoted to trade, science, strategy and armaments. The prestigious political work has declined in relative importance owing to the greater centralization of control at the Quai d'Orsay and more frequent direct summit dealings. There are also the very important permanent missions abroad, notably those attached to the United Nations and the EEC. French membership of the security council renders a permanent UN mission essential, the work – contacts in the corridors, speechmaking – being parliamentary rather than diplomatic in character. The permanent representative at Brussels not only provides liaison with the EEC and Euratom but also plays a direct part in running the EEC through the committee of permanent representatives. The French diplomatic corps does not enjoy the British foreign service's higher status relative to the home civil service. Its top echelons are recruited from ENA but it is below the finance inspectorate, council of state and court of accounts corps in the pecking order, owing to the more limited opportunities to transfer to remunerative positions in public or private corporations or to membership of the personal staff of a minister.

Because foreign policy is conducted in the 'closed politics' context of discreet negotiation rather than the open debate characteristic of legislation, parliaments have generally been unable to intervene effectively in this part of the policy-making process. Even under the third and fourth republics, when executive-legislative relations were dominated by the legislature, foreign affairs – except for isolated cases like the 1954 assembly rejection of the European Defence Community treaty, when the government was neutral – have always been a special case of almost undisputed executive control. So the fifth republic's reversal of the previous relationship in the executive's favour has merely served to bring the formal position into line with the real situation. Parliament has generally been content with an *a posteriori* oversight, leaving the initiation and conduct of foreign policy to the government. Apart from the anodyne provisions for asking parliamentary questions or debating a government foreign policy declaration (where no vote is taken) parliament may be asked to ratify a treaty, unilateral amendment of which is, however, impossible. The main instruments for a more searching investigation of the government's foreign policy are the foreign affairs and finance committees of the assembly and senate. The foreign minister or a junior minister testifies several times each year before the foreign affairs committees and the chairmen of these committees may enjoy close contact with the minister and the ministry, having access to incoming but not outgoing telegrams and so being better informed about foreign developments than about French policy. Annually, the discussion of the foreign ministry's budget provides an opportunity for the finance committees to raise policy matters but although foreign affairs and finance have traditionally attracted the most eminent parliamentarians into their ranks, they are likely to be little better informed than are the readers of *Le Monde* or *Le Figaro*. The UDR has an assembly study group on foreign affairs, through which it hopes to receive confidential information, but it is both inactive and ineffective.[8]

It is the president of the republic, not the foreign minister, who holds press conferences to survey current international problems and announce major policies, providing the best source of information in a field where publicity is the public relations façade that conceals rather than reveals the serious discussions between the select few. Whereas de Gaulle openly confessed that the questions were arranged in advance by his press officer and answered so that the press conference replies 'added up to the affirmation of a policy' calculated to 'rouse the national spirit',[9] Pompidou has allowed the journalists to choose the questions they ask; but the purpose of the exercise has remained unaltered. From time to time, when he wishes to put the French position on an international issue of current concern, the foreign minister receives a handpicked group of French or foreign journalists for a confidential chat. More routine contacts with the diplomatic press are left to the head of the foreign ministry's press service, who holds a press conference each day at midday. The press resent the fact that the fifth republic's accentuation of the tendency for foreign policy decisions to be concerted in private rather than debated in public has weakened their informative role. For the journalist there are two kinds of diplomat: those who know but don't tell and those who tell but don't know. Whereas the government would like the press to act as a formative influence, mobilizing public support for national policy, the press interpret the news in partisan ways. The newspapers polarize attitudes through controversy rather than promote an acquiescent consensus.

French public opinion has little impact upon foreign policy. Nevertheless it is of some interest to acquire a worm's eye view of the activities and priorities of the tiny élite who interpret what is in the national interest. When asked in 1969 who *should* take foreign policy decisions, we saw in chapter 4 that 25 per cent (35 per cent in the case of UDR voters) thought this to be the function of the president, 51 per cent attributed it to the government (64 per cent among independent republican voters) and 17 per cent (32 per cent of communist voters) selected parliament. Foreign policy is the sphere in which the executive is accorded greatest influence and if a description of reality rather than a statement of personal preference had been requested, table 16 (p. 97) suggests that parliament would have made an even more modest showing. When asked in 1970 whether the government attached more importance to home or foreign policy, half replied foreign policy (going up to two-thirds in the case of communist and socialist voters), 29 per cent said home policy (rising to 37 per cent in the case of UDR and independent republican voters), while 21 per cent expressed no opinion.[10] Given the greater importance attached by the electorate to issues of home policy, this poll clearly indicates an awareness that their leaders have a different order of priority. When asked with which side France should be allied in the Russo-American global conflict, table 34 indicates that an increasing proportion of the French people, even while de Gaulle was still in power, favoured the United States (particularly in the case of the centrists and the UDR voters). While those favouring the Soviet Union remain a modest 6 per cent (but 26 per cent of communist voters) the majority consistently favours a neutral position (nearly three-fifths of socialist and communist voters). The United States has also consistently – and by a large margin – headed the list of countries which Frenchmen consider to be France's best friend, a finding confirmed by a survey among French schoolchildren who identified the Soviet Union as France's leading enemy.[11]

Table 34
*Foreign Alliances and the French Public, 1967–9 (%)**

Ally	July 1967	July 1968	March 1969
United States	13	19	24
Soviet Union	10	6	6
Neither side	57	53	52
No reply	20	22	18

* Source: *Sondages*, nos 1–2, 1969, p. 47.

The objectives of French foreign policy

Until the second world war, France – unlike Britain and Germany – tried to be both an imperial and a continental power. Under the fourth republic, although she made a remarkable recovery from the national and international consequences of defeat and occupation, France accepted a more modest role based upon a reluctant acquiescence in three 'necessities'. First, the cold war between two coalitions led by the United States and the Soviet Union persuaded all except the communists and Gaullists to accept American leadership within an Atlantic Alliance. The resentment of an Anglo-American (with an increasing emphasis on American) directorate over NATO pre-dated de Gaulle's return to office but the fourth republic governments felt powerless to challenge this subservience. However, to the extent that they attributed French subordination to the lack of nuclear weapons, steps were taken to equip France with the means to assert herself, it being assumed that this would be primarily within an integrated NATO alliance. Secondly, Franco-German reconciliation was only possible within the context of an integrated Western European Federation in which France would play the dominant role as long as Britain was not present to counterbalance potential German hegemony. The Soviet danger, which dwarfed the fear of a partitioned Germany's military power; the elimination in 1955–6 of the one remaining Franco-German territorial dispute in the Saar; the hope that European unity would help solve France's economic troubles, end her industrial inferiority complex and prepare her to face international competition : these factors dictated French policy on the European continent. In the process, Germany ceased to be France's main enemy and became her principal ally, well before de Gaulle explicitly adopted this policy as an expedient in the early 1960s. Finally, France's defeat in Vietnam pointed to the necessity of decolonization but this policy proved difficult to reconcile with the ideology of assimilation. It was the fourth republic's indecisive move toward Algerian independence that led to its demise and de Gaulle's return to power. This in turn accelerated the process of decolonization – except temporarily in the case of Algeria – and shifted the French position vis à vis the United States and Europe to an assertion of France's independence rather than an abdication from it through acceptance of a one-sided interdependence.

It was this more vigorous affirmation of French national interest – conceived as a self-evident truth vouchsafed only to him – coupled with the 'realistic' approach to inter-state relations recalled at the outset of this chapter, that were the hallmarks of de Gaulle's conduct of foreign policy, rather than any reversal of the fourth republic's legacy. The bewildering contrast between the obstinacy with which he clung to fundamentals and the pragmatism with which he rung the tactical changes should not blind one to the calculated mixture of brutality and subtlety in his statecraft or to the resourcefulness with which he used his limited resources to achieve great power status for France as an end in itself. The appearance of inconsistency and the reality of limited success in attaining his grandiose objectives did not worry the general public unduly. They were content to be 'spectators of French prestige achieved by a single man', particularly as they thought they were not required to make any effort and that de Gaulle would provide them with a flattering prestige on the cheap.[12] However, when they began to grasp the fact that there was a stiff price to pay in foregoing personal well-being, they showed in 1968 and 1969 that they placed their standard of living well above humiliating the United States and welcomed Pompidou as president in the belief that he would conform more closely to their order of priorities. The subsequent change in style rallied those sections of the French élite which had been disturbed by de Gaulle's tendency to ostracize France's allies and fraternize with her opponents on the old dictum : 'God protect me from my friends; as for my enemies, I can deal with them myself.'

The pro-American sections of the élite and France's allies were flabbergasted at the severance of the military connection with NATO and 'the implementation of new relations with the so-called eastern European states, towards détente, entente and cooperation' as de Gaulle put it in his 1966 Kremlin speech. As neither of these policies has been reversed by Pompidou, it is important to see them as an enduring response to the 'end' of the cold war and of the Soviet military threat. De Gaulle's failure to institutionalize political cooperation within an EEC led by France, and Germany's demonstration that she was willing to act as America's 'Trojan horse' in Europe as the price of support against the Soviet Union, resulted in acceptance of a *rapprochement* initiated by the Soviet government in 1964–5. This move was attractive to France as a lever to be used against America and Germany, while to the Soviet Union the French rejection of nuclear armament for Federal Germany and her recognition of the Oder-Neisse frontier (although not of Eastern Germany as a permanent fact) made her a valuable friend within the capitalist camp. France and the Soviet Union shared a common interest in reducing the economic and military dependence on the United States to which many European politicians had accustomed their countries under the guise of anti-communism. Rejecting an ideological vision of world conflicts, de Gaulle regarded Soviet Russia as part of privileged western civilization confronted by the underdeveloped east, of which China was the formidable potential leader. In the long run, eastern Europe would recognize its vocation as part of a 'European Europe' and meanwhile bilateral contacts of all kinds ought to be increased to facilitate this process. This strategy led to a substantial increase in commercial, cultural, scientific and technical cooperation, underpinned by regular meetings of the Franco-Soviet commission, twice yearly political consultations at foreign minister level and visits to Moscow and Paris by Pompidou and Brezhnev. Whilst this policy has been especially applauded by the French communist party, it is generally popular and has led to an improvement of the Soviet Union's image in France.

The French acceptance that the cold war threat from Soviet Russia had disappeared, coincided with the decision to wage a gold war on the United States, to end the exorbitant economic influence which the inconvertible dollar enjoyed in the international monetary system. This decision was widely misconstrued as an anachronistic appeal to restore the gold standard (which would favour the Soviet Union and South Africa as major gold producers), whereas de Gaulle's intention was to halt the American export of inflation and the American ability to buy up large parts of foreign economies with money borrowed from these countries. This offensive was halted by the May 1968 crisis, when in the space of seven months France lost half her currency reserves. France was forced to devalue in 1969. Nevertheless, de Gaulle achieved a posthumous victory when the United States was finally compelled to devalue the dollar, the announcement being made at a meeting between Presidents Nixon and Pompidou at the Azores in 1971. The credit for this 'humiliation' should go to the Vietnam war rather than to Pompidou. He has used his personal control over monetary policy to restore France's gold reserves rather than to force an American devaluation, consistent with his general inclination to reintroduce more friendliness into France's relationship with her oldest ally, the first country he visited after being elected president.

Whereas France was able to extricate herself fairly easily from American military domination, the frequent changes in attitude towards foreign – especially American – investment in the form of takeovers of key industries, indicate the difficulty facing a national effort at controlling the inroads of the multi-national –

mainly American – corporations. From 1959 to 1963 the French governments encouraged American investment on the ground that it would be more advantageous if foreign firms chose France rather than her Common Market competitors. This fatalistic policy was reversed in 1963, the restrictions being prompted particularly by the spectacular takeover of the leading French computer firm, Machines Bull, by General Electric. Prime Minister Pompidou's attempt to secure joint EEC control over American investment at that time was rejected by France's Common Market competitors and French firms have not offered effective resistance, even in the period when their government has been most determined to avoid economic satellization. In 1966 came a new reversal of official policy towards foreign investments, owing to the transfer of projects to other EEC countries, in some cases just across the French border, and the conviction that American techniques and managerial skills would be valuable in the task of converting France into an industrial society. It is noteworthy that Debré, the ardent nationalist who was prime minister during the early, more liberal, phase of French policy, was from 1966 to 1968 in the key position of finance minister when a less restrictive policy was adopted.

Unwelcome publicity for the new policy of selectively accepting American investment in France was provided by the unedifying battle over the location of a small Ford plant, which became involved in a 1970 Bordeaux by-election. Neither of the main opponents at this election intended to take the seat if he won : prime minister Chaban-Delmas because this was incompatible with holding office and Servan-Schreiber – the journalist and secretary-general of the radical party who had done most to publicize the dangers of American economic penetration in his book *The American Challenge* – because he had already won an assembly seat at a by-election in 1969. The spectacle of these two men – one the prime minister – competing for the favours of an American capitalist as the means of winning the votes that would come from 1,600 jobs created, was eloquent testimony to the French failure to do more than temporarily slow down the increasing volume of American investment (already 15 per cent of French private industry in 1964 and concentrated in key sectors) and to veto particular takeovers as unacceptable. Nevertheless, whereas American investment increased between 1963 and 1968 by 175 per cent in Belgium and 113 per cent in Federal Germany, it grew by only 55 per cent in France. In 1970 France championed a modest European industrial policy. Meanwhile, the French government's policy of promoting national industrial champions is increasingly confined to industries with important military implications for national independence : computers, petroleum, nuclear energy, electronics, space and aviation.

Before looking in greater detail at French policy in the EEC and its special relationship with its former colonies, let us glance at the formerly stormy relations with the United Nations, dismissed by de Gaulle as a 'thingumabob'. France's main quarrels with the UN in the early 1960s concerned three matters. There was bitter resentment against what was regarded as interference in France's internal affairs, notably in respect of decolonization. The 'usurpation' by the general assembly and secretary-general of the role of the security council – over whose decisions France, as a permanent member, enjoys a veto power – gave great offence, especially in the case of the Congo military intervention. France, like Soviet Russia, refused to meet its share of the cost of UN peace-keeping operations until 1972, when as a conciliatory gesture President Pompidou authorized payment so as to help the UN in its financial difficulties. The end of the Algerian and Congo wars led the French government to resume active participation in the work of the UN general assembly from 1965. It provided a suitable forum through which France could cultivate its new popularity with the non-committed Third World countries, helped by the fact that nearly one-quarter (30 out of 127) of the states represented at the UN were French-speaking. The UN preserves France's great power status, which is flattering to the national ego although it is a reflection of the past rather than of present or future realities.

A confederal Europe: an ideology and a strategy

Whereas de Gaulle sought to play a world role, Pompidou has concentrated on giving a lead in the EEC. At a January 1971 press conference, in which he expounded his conviction that European political unity would only be attained through a cautious confederalism, President Pompidou seemed to blur old controversies by asserting that 'the quarrel over supra-nationality is a false quarrel'. Was he claiming that de Gaulle's conception of a Europe of sovereign states had triumphed over Monnet's vision of an integrated European federation or was he arguing that these conflicting conceptions could be pragmatically reconciled? In his 1950 memorandum to the French premier that inspired the creation of the Coal and Steel Community, Monnet argued for what de Gaulle was to call a 'European Europe' under French leadership, but maintained : 'It is not by an addition of sovereignties meeting in council that an entity is created.' However, subsequent experience showed that as long as national governments retained real power and responsibility, the supra-national high authority was unable to deal with serious problems, leaving member states to act in their national interest outside the ECSC framework. Ten years later, de Gaulle substituted an institutional emphasis on confederation based upon inter-state cooperation as the only realistic basis for a harmonization of national policies going beyond the limited, technocratic ECSC, Euratom and EEC treaties (inherited from the fourth republic) to a separate political union. For the foreseeable future, power would be concentrated in the council of ministers representing the member states, decisions being subject to unanimity. De Gaulle's 1960 scheme, which came to be known as the Fouchet Plan, foundered in 1962 on Belgo-Dutch opposition and Italian hesitation, inspired by the desire for prior British entry into the EEC as a safeguard against Franco-German hegemony.[13]

In January 1963 de Gaulle counter-attacked by unilaterally terminating negotiations on Britain's application to join the EEC and concluding a treaty providing for closer political cooperation with Germany as the basis for a Franco-German condominium over the EEC. The treaty transposed the Fouchet Plan provision for regular meetings of heads of the executive and foreign ministers on to a bilateral plane. It established an interministerial secretariat run by senior foreign ministry officials in the two countries to coordinate consultations at all levels, involving defence and youth ministers and delegations of the government parties in the two countries, the UDR and CDU. But the ministers in both countries successfully frustrated such coordination, demonstrating the failure of such inter-state cooperation. More serious, this attempt at partial political union was watered down – under American pressure – by the German parliament, provoking French resentment at the very lack of German assertiveness vis à vis America that they expected vis à vis France. The recognition that Germany would side with the other EEC countries on the major political issues meant that the prospect of political union was abandoned by de Gaulle, who took the view that 'if the western half of the Old World remained subordinate to the New, Europe would never be European, nor would she ever be able to bring her two halves together'.[14] The refusal of her EEC partners to accept French leadership led de Gaulle to press forward his policy of *détente* with eastern Europe. Within the EEC he secured – through the boycott of community institutions in the latter half of 1965 – the abandonment of majority voting in the council of ministers, a curb on the power of the EEC commission, and the replacement of its supra-nationalist president (Hallstein), accused of usurping the functions of the national governments.

To establish the fundamental continuity between the conception of Europe championed by Pompidou as de Gaulle's prime minister and as president in his own right, some comparisons are useful. In a speech to the national assembly just before the June 1965 EEC crisis came to a head, Pompidou foreshadowed the phrase from his 1971 press conference quoted earlier, when he asked:

What can the goal of a European policy be? Federation? Confederation? Let us not quarrel over words. In any case, no one can claim ... that all the conditions have at this time been met for a true federation . . . with a single government, a common parliament, one foreign policy, one military policy, and one financial, economic and social policy. At the present stage, there is no possibility other than to encourage a gradual *rapprochement* among the European states which will lead them little by little to harmonize their policies. . . .

Accusations of French nationalism ignored the fact that because France alone defended her own and Europe's independence, the French were the real 'Europeans'. Destined by history and geography to be the motive force of Europe, Pompidou claimed in 1967 that France was 'not its administrative, technical or institutional but its ideological motive force'.[15] The ideology was that of national independence, conceived increasingly within a European framework; an extension that was tolerable only so long as France was able either to get her own way on all major points at issue or remain free to opt out or veto any proposals to which she objected.

In his January 1971 presidential press conference, Pompidou met the question 'What kind of Europe?' with the reply : 'It can only mean building, on the basis of what exists, a confederation of states that have decided to harmonize their policies and to integrate their economies.' In line with the Monnet approach, Pompidou believed that political union, and agreement on foreign and defence policy, could only come after piecemeal, pragmatic economic *integration*, a word de Gaulle shunned like the plague. However, he remained faithful to the Gaullist view that all these decisions would have to be based on intergovernmental agreement. To facilitate such collaboration, President Pompidou proposed that each member government should include a European affairs minister – initially a Foreign Office minister – who would eventually cease to belong to a national government. On the working of the European council of ministers, Pompidou insisted – by analogy with the working of coalition government – that important decisions should only be taken unanimously, on pain of wrecking the embryo European government. In 1972 Pompidou accepted a German proposal that a modest political secretariat should be established to facilitate the coordination of policy by foreign ministers but only provided it was not linked with the EEC commission in Brussels and was located in Paris. The Gaullist fear of a European 'government by assembly' emerged clearly from President Pompidou's postponement of the creation of a 'true European parliament' – directly elected and with increased powers – until after the establishment of a 'true European government'. Confronted by governments that often seemed not to have any clearly thought out objectives or strategy to attain them, France had the advantage of knowing what it did and what it did not want.

Although the interrelationship between national and EEC officialdom has been fostered by hundreds of specialist working groups in Brussels, the French government has maintained close control over the experts who represent it, allowing them ever less discretion as the stake involved in EEC decisions increased and propensities towards technocratic decision-making had to be curbed. Instructions were more frequent and precise and were issued earlier in the policy formulation and negotiation process by the general secretariat of the interministerial committee for European cooperation. This secretariat (with a staff of seventy, fifteen being senior civil servants) is headed by a finance official, responsible to the prime minister, receiving most of his directions from the foreign ministry. (In 1967, he was also economic adviser to the president.) Coordination is achieved notably through weekly meetings called by the secretary-general, attended by ministerial *cabinet* members, senior finance and foreign ministry officials, and representatives from other ministries particularly concerned with the EEC, e.g. agriculture. A separate meeting is held each week attended by the secretary-general, the directors of the treasury and foreign economic relations division of the finance ministry and the economic affairs division of the foreign ministry (which controls the permanent delegation in Brussels). While there are problems in having such highly centralized administrative co-ordination without a minister specially responsible for European affairs to assume the political responsibilities, the secretariat's loose attachment to the prime minister allows the finance ministry to accept coordination which it would resist if the foreign ministry had full control. The secretariat has been 'the most organized and most effective coordinating mechanism' between a national government and its EEC agents, giving 'maximum manoeuvrability to the political leadership'.[16]

Under the president, the prime minister seeks to assert control over European policy through the interministerial committee for European cooperation which deals with high policy. However, the finance minister chairs the interministerial committee for the implementation of the European treaties, concerned with detailed application, while the foreign minister has sought to monopolize supervision over the relations between the EEC commission and all French ministries. The foreign ministry plays a decisive role in the key EEC decision-making bodies, the council of ministers and the committee of permanent representatives, through the monthly meetings of EEC foreign ministers and its influence over the preparation and exposition of agreed national positions through France's permanent delegation. (The committee of permanent representatives meets weekly to prepare the monthly discussions of the council.) Couve de Murville has recalled how much he relied on the director of economic affairs at the Quai d'Orsay and France's permanent representative in Brussels during his ten years as foreign minister but his regular presence at EEC council meetings was essential to gain the mastery necessary 'to make France the community's motive force that she intended to be'.[17] Under intense French pressure, it has been accepted since January 1966 that all important actions by the EEC commission should be preceded by consultation with national governments through their permanent representatives, thereby placing the foreign ministry at the intersection of the French and EEC decision-making processes. Although a few top officials in the finance, agriculture, labour and transport ministries should be included among the national actors involved in the community process, the dominant position of the foreign ministry in deciding strategy and tactics has largely insulated the European aspects of French policy from the rest of national politics, promoting 'the minimalist strategies pursued in Brussels and the minimizing of participation at the national level'.[18]

French public opinion seems much more willing to press forward towards political integration than are France's political and administrative leaders. In particular, the French people are strongly in favour of a directly elected European parliament and are willing to concede wide powers to a European government. A 1969 IFOP survey asked whether the French or European governments should take decisions in three important fields. On foreign policy, 44 per cent favoured the European government (particularly men, the younger, the wealthier, large town dwellers and the non-communist left), 25 per cent the French government and 31 per cent did not express a preference. On a European currency, 50 per cent were in favour (the same categories, businessmen and the better educated also polling especially strongly), 20 per cent were against and 30 per cent abstained; 52 per cent allocated defence to a European government, 20 per cent wished to preserve French government control, while 28 per cent expressed no opinion. Similar results were registered in a poll carried out under EEC auspices in 1970; when excluding those who had stated no preference, 65 per cent of the French people supported the idea of a European government with powers in the spheres of foreign, defence and economic policy [19]

When asked in June 1971 on which of ten issues President Pompidou had been most successful, European policy rated the highest score (38 per cent), closely followed by relations with communist eastern Europe (34 per cent); the only other issues in double figures being the maintenance of order (18 per cent) and relations with the United States (16 per cent). While 47 per cent pronounced his style as close to that of de Gaulle, 36 per cent attributed a new style to him, and 57 per cent regarded Pompidou as being more conciliatory in foreign policy (with 11 per cent considering him less conciliatory and 32 per cent conceding ignorance or indifference).[20] At his March 1972 press conference, Pompidou sought to use the popularity of his European policy to strengthen both his negotiating position in the EEC and his domestic support, by calling a referendum, using the ratification of the treaty enlarging the European community to nine members as a pretext. As well as dividing the French left, this initiative had the advantage of using a Gaullist procedure to carry through a reversal of Gaullist tactics – the exclusion of Britain from the EEC – to facilitate the fulfilment of the Gaullist plan of creating a confederal political union. De Gaulle had in 1960 advocated a European referendum in all six countries to harness the support of public opinion for his proposed confederation. Such a referendum was described at the time as a 'psychological trump card'[21] and was so interpreted when Pompidou played it in 1972.

By calling for approval of his plans for European economic and monetary union, to be supplemented by political cooperation, Pompidou intended to attract the support of those centrists who had refused to rally to de Gaulle because of their loyalty to a supra-national Europe, without losing the support of more than the most diehard Gaullists. His calculated inexplicitness resulted in a campaign of great ambiguity and confusion. Some voted 'Yes' because of continuity and others because of what they interpreted as a repudiation of de Gaulle; the communists called for a 'No' to Pompidou and the EEC; while the socialists advocated abstention or a spoiled ballot to say 'No' to Pompidou and 'Yes' to Britain and the EEC. In the event, Pompidou proved to have been too clever by half. The myriad ambiguities and *arrières pensées* underlying the 'simple question' asked led to record rates of abstention (40 per cent) and spoiled votes (7 per cent). Although the 'Yes' votes outnumbered the 'Nos' by 2 : 1, only 36 per cent of the electorate had voted in the affirmative, 1 per cent fewer than voted for Pompidou in the 1969 presidential election. The French people warned Pompidou that they could not be manipulated and mobilized for action as they had been under de Gaulle. They had welcomed him precisely because he was expected to leave them in peace and not periodically threaten them with political chaos if they did not support him. Yet his failure to make a 'Yes' vote in the referendum a matter of personal confidence partly explains the low turnout. This was the price of not taking the risk that de Gaulle ran at each referendum up to the fatal one of 1969. The French people lost their appetite for helping their president to dominate the European stage when they defeated de Gaulle. Their Europeanism is genuine but tepid. They no longer say 'Yes' to the president, even if he proposes to say 'Yes' rather than 'No' to foreigners on their behalf. They are content to leave this work to parliament while the president is determined to keep France's European strategy in his own hands.

Imperial aftermath: from colonization to cooperation

French overseas expansion was inspired by the same unitary political ideal as reigned at home. Boissy d'Anglas expressed the peculiar mixture of chauvinist pretentiousness and universalist egalitarianism characteristic of the French colonial ideology of assimilation when he declared in 1794: 'The Revolution was not only for Europe but for the Universe.... There can only be one right way of administering: and if we have found it for European countries, why should [the colonies] be deprived of it?' The sense of cultural superiority, the stress on the cultural aspect of colonialism – the French language being the instrument of France's 'civilizing mission' – over and above the crude appetite for economic exploitation, was very clearly stated in the 1880s by the principal architect of French colonial expansion, Jules Ferry. The cultural self-confidence that subsumed the French belief that just as she had assimilated the many diverse peoples that made up metropolitan France, she could convert any people in the world into French citizens, was more genuinely Roman than anything the British Empire had to offer. However, assimilation never really applied to more than a tiny élite. When they moved from principles to practice, the French were all too conscious that if they granted their overseas subjects equal democratic rights to representation in a unitary parliament in Paris, they risked becoming the colony of their colonies. So, while the ideal of assimilation was publicly proclaimed, evoking the enthusiasm of a privileged minority overseas, a select few becoming deputies and even ministers during the fourth republic, the promise of equality through integration proved to be a hollow mockery. Those territories (Vietnam, Morocco, Tunisia) that could envisage creating a viable state independent of France, did so by force of arms or through negotiation under the fourth republic. Because of the large number of European settlers in Algeria, decolonization proved a more prolonged and agonizing process, destroying the fourth republic and unsettling the early years of the fifth republic. France thus paid a high price for trying to absorb and assimilate her colonies, the absence of a tradition of colonial self-government making a peaceful transition to independence especially difficult.

In 1958 de Gaulle made one final attempt to rescue the old assimilationist relationship based on a common citizenship, common language and common control of foreign, defence, economic and financial policy, it being understood that 'common' was a euphemism for 'French'. The confederal 'Community', established by Articles 1 and 77–88 of the fifth republic constitution, was intended to maintain a close association between France and her former black African colonies, most of whom were dependent upon financial, administrative, technical, military and educational assistance from France. This dependence was accentuated by the dismantling of the West and Equatorial African federations, owing in part to de Gaulle's hostility towards federations. Another factor was the desire of the leaders in each colony to acquire the trappings of independence, accentuated in the case of the relatively wealthy Ivory Coast and Gabon by a reluctance to combine with impecunious neighbours. Although Guinea alone voted against any further association with France, the Community, with its elaborate political institutions, became a dead letter in 1960 as all its twelve members successively obtained formal independence.* France secured as a precondition the signature of bilateral cooperation agreements in all or some of the following fields: prior consultation before taking major foreign policy decisions; defence assistance against internal or

---

* These states were the Central African Republic, Chad, Congo-Brazzaville, Dahomey, Gabon, Ivory Coast, the Malagasy Republic, Mali, Mauritania, Niger, Senegal and Upper-Volta.

external threats, French troops occupying military bases to facilitate offering such assistance; access to raw materials and strategic
products (notably the uranium of Niger); a common monetary
policy through the franc area; reciprocal preferential trade relations, extended by the 1963 Yaoundé convention to include the
EEC, which also provides financial assistance through the European development fund whilst French aid is channelled through
the aid and cooperation fund; and technical and cultural cooperation, mainly through the provision of personnel. The transitory
Community, although it survives meaninglessly in the constitution, is just an indistinct memory, but the relations of unilateral
dependence upon France have remained.

Twelve of France's former colonies, plus Cameroun and Togo
(previously UN trusteeship territories) remain in monetary union
with France through the franc area. The currencies of member
countries are mutually convertible at fixed parities in unlimited
amounts. Foreign exchange receipts are pooled, all central banks
holding their reserves in French francs in French treasury accounts.
Foreign exchange dealings are made through the Paris money
market, giving it an international standing that it would not
otherwise have. These countries offer reliable and expanding
markets for French goods, France's favourable trade balance with
them being compensated by their excess of exports to other
countries, providing the common foreign exchange pool with a
useful injection of funds. The advantage of securing a French
guarantee for their currency and the reward of French aid
involves acceptance of French influence over their internal monetary policies, exercised notably through Frenchmen sitting on
the boards of their central banks. Furthermore, franc area
countries suffer the indignity of having their currencies devalued
by the French government without consultation. Whereas the
1963 Jeanneney Report on Cooperation Policy stated that the
maintenance of the protected franc area was no longer in France's
interest once she had demonstrated that she could increase her
trade in the competitive European community, a 1970 report
to the economic and social council on the franc area suggests that
its survival still benefits France on balance.

The work of conducting 'cooperative' relations with France's
satellite states operates at two levels : overtly, through a minister
(reduced in 1966 to a junior minister within the foreign ministry)

who conducts the formal relations between governments; covertly, through the secretariat for African and Malagasy affairs, attached to the president of the republic, through which the more important informal relations between heads of state are conducted. The junior minister is responsible for cultural and technical cooperation with all sub-Saharan French-speaking countries but has to compete with two divisions of the foreign ministry which are also concerned with the same functions. It is through this agency that cooperation agreements are signed and aid missions set up to organize a substantial programme of assistance through the provision of personnel; judicial, police and administrative officials in the early 1960s, predominantly secondary and higher education teachers since then. The main beneficiaries have been the Ivory Coast – which alone accounts for 25 per cent of all technical assistance teachers – Malagasy and Senegal. Cultural centres, financed by the aid and cooperation fund, have been established in the capitals of former French colonies, helping to foster the 'cultural presence' to which France and the local Frenchtrained élite attach great importance. In 1970 a French-speaking countries cultural and technical cooperation agency was established in Paris by twenty-one countries, including (in addition to nine of the twelve former Community states and France) Belgium, Burundi, Cameroun, Canada, Luxembourg, Monaco, Ruanda, Togo, Tunisia and South Vietnam. France supplied 45 per cent of its modest budget, Canada 33 per cent, Belgium 12 per cent, the remaining 10 per cent being shared amongst the other signatories of the agreement. Despite its French-Canadian secretary-general's exertions, the agency has not fulfilled its projected ambitious role. Its birth was characterized particularly by the struggle over whether Quebec should be recognized as an equal signatory with the other member states, a problem resolved by the equivocal compromise of counter-signature.

'Cooperation has become an integral part of our foreign policy,' asserted France's former foreign minister, Couve de Murville. 'There is such an interconnection between our political relations and our cooperation relations that it would be impossible to separate the two. . . .'[22] During the de Gaulle period, there were especially close links between Jacques Foccart, head of the general secretariat for African and Malagasy affairs, and the president. Foccart reported daily to de Gaulle, in his capacity as the president's adviser both on African affairs and on secret service matters. Foccart has been described as 'the president's right-hand man in the arcane cloak-and-dagger upper reaches of French politics and the trusted confidant of a dozen African presidents, many of whom owed more to him than they did to their electorates.' In addition to the 'day-to-day supervision, execution and quite often initiation' of policy in relation to France's ex-colonies, Foccart's secretariat rather than the foreign ministry was the communications centre for these matters. This was due to the fact that in addition to numerous unofficial sources of information, 'many key ambassadorial posts in black Africa were held by non-career diplomats, many of them Foccart's colleagues and leading Gaullists'.[23] Furthermore, Foccart was able to place advisers on the personal staff of several African presidents and in at least one case the person in question was at the same time a member of Foccart's secretariat. After a brief eclipse during the interregnum following de Gaulle's resignation, Foccart was restored to office by President Pompidou, a testimony to his standing both in the Gaullist hierarchy and with France's African client states. On his visits to these countries, Pompidou has stressed the continuity of French policy, Foccart being both a symbol and a guarantee of this continuity.

The Algerian rebellion played a decisive role in the decolonization process. It accelerated the movement towards independence in Black Africa after de Gaulle had established a Community that he hoped might preserve Algeria within the French fold. The 1962 peace agreement, whereby France granted independence to Algeria in return for a commitment to cooperate with France and guarantee the rights of the French settlers, was quickly undermined. The mass emigration of the French settlers was due in part to their own extremists and partly to the pressures of the Algerian government wishing to get rid of all the vestiges of French colonialism as soon as possible. Throughout the 1960s the Algerian government gradually eliminated France's economic and military presence in Algeria. It took advantage of the importance the French government attached to relations with Algeria, regarded as a passport to good relations with the developing countries in general and the Mediterranean countries in particular.[24] So, despite measures of nationalization without compensation and the cancellation of two-thirds of Algeria's debt to

France, Algeria continued to receive a large share of French aid, nearly as much in 1970 as the aid granted to the whole of French-speaking Black Africa. One-fifth of Algeria's national income in 1970 derived from the remittances of about 650,000 Algerian workers in France (a total which does not include the 150,000 Muslims who chose to retain French citizenship and were repatriated to France along with the 1·5 million Europeans who returned from French North Africa). France's main remaining stake in Algeria was oil, ownership of which was vital to its national fuel policy as well as its defence and foreign policy, but this too was drastically curtailed following the Algerian government's acquisition of majority control in 1971. Responsibility for Algerian affairs passed from the prime minister to the foreign minister in 1966, indicative of the reversion of Algeria's status to being that of just another country.

A small part of France's overseas empire has survived as an integral part of the republic. These imperial residues are of two types: overseas departments and overseas territories, the joint responsibility of a junior minister in the French government. The former consist of two Caribbean islands – Martinique and Guadeloupe – French Guiana on the South American mainland and the island of Réunion in the Indian Ocean. They are represented by ten deputies and eight senators in the French parliament and the official fiction is that they are treated in all respects as though they were part of metropolitan France. The attempt to assimilate them has resulted in absurd consequences, notably an inflated administration, a lopsided economy and an inappropriate educational system, which renders them financially dependent on metropolitan France. The local leaders are torn between political pressures favouring autonomy and economic pressures requiring integration. So, despite the occasional eruption of violence and repression, France will continue to enjoy the use of the Kourou rocket launching site and space centre in Guiana, while an electorally corrupt Réunion will continue to provide a safe seat for defeated metropolitan politicians such as Michel Debré. The seven overseas territories, whose population amounts to half a million people, have varying degrees of autonomy but share the characteristics of being remote from and economically dependent upon France. French Polynesia is militarily important as the location of the Pacific Experimental Centre at which

France explodes her nuclear bombs. The economies of New Caledonia and the Wallis and Futuna islands are dominated by the Rothschild-controlled firm *Le Nickel*. Finally, the New Hebrides is the picturesque product of the encounter of two empires : an Anglo-French condominium over sixty thousand Melanesians inhabiting eighty islands.

While French ministers make great play with the size of French aid to developing countries – notably that in 1970 French aid amounted to 1·24 per cent of her gross national product, France being second only to the Netherlands and well ahead of the United States – they generally omit to mention that this figure includes aid to French overseas departments and territories, which absorb nearly one-fifth of the total. It also includes military aid and capital loaned or invested by private firms. In 1970 public aid accounted for 54 per cent of all aid; 89 per cent of public aid is bilateral, which can be exploited politically but generally neglects the recipients' economic priorities. The beneficiaries submit annual investment programmes to the local aid and cooperation mission, then to the cooperation officials of the foreign ministry and finally to the French assistance and cooperation fund which allocates the aid. Although France has increased the share of aid going to countries outside the franc area to over one-third of the total, three-fifths of French aid in 1970 was allocated to countries with under 1 per cent of the underdeveloped world's population. In 1970 a committee was set up to re-examine the French policy of cooperation with the developing countries. The 1971 Gorse Report was so critical of French aid, on grounds such as the deliberate neglect of industrialization, arguments which had been advanced a decade earlier by Réné Dumont in *False Start in Africa*, that it has remained unpublished. Chapter 6 of Dumont's book was entitled 'Independence is not always "decolonization" '. Appreciation of this fact has led to demands from some of France's client states to renegotiate their 'cooperation agreements'.

The French government has engaged in both covert and overt military intervention in Africa. French military aid to Biafra's breakaway attempt from July 1968 strengthened her secessionist resolve at a crucial moment, temporarily reprieving her from defeat and prolonging the Nigerian civil war but falling decisively short of ensuring victory. De Gaulle's motivation was political :

especially a desire to end the contrast between a large Anglophone federation and a congeries of fragmental Francophone states as well as to frustrate the great powers, all pro-federal Nigeria. Personal influence also played a part: the persuasion of Houphouet-Boigny, president of the Ivory Coast and de Gaulle's most respected African ally coupled with Foccart's desire to extend French influence into English-speaking Africa. Foccart was 'the driving force behind France's Nigeria policy', helping the Biafrans even before secession in an 'indirect, limited and pain-stakingly clandestine' way.[25] France never recognized Biafra officially, waiting in vain for enough African countries to follow the example of Gabon and the Ivory Coast, the countries through which French arms were principally channelled. Non-recognition and restraint were urged by the foreign ministry but it was power-less in the matter compared to Foccart, who had the president's support. However, de Gaulle was able to preserve diplomatic relations with Nigeria to safeguard the French position should Biafran secession fail. This safeguard worked successfully, Franco-Nigerian relations rapidly returning to normal at the end of the civil war. In the case of poor and landlocked Chad, France – in fulfilment of her defence treaty commitments – has employed a small force in supporting the black African southerners in a long and bitter civil war against the Arab nomads of the north. Whereas a 1964 intervention in Gabon quickly restored a government over-thrown by a military coup, Chad has not merely had to be rescued; it appeared to need to be propped up indefinitely by the French military, a factor likely to dissuade French governments from similar interventions in the future.

National defence and nuclear deterrence

Although a combination of indecisive government and colonial war led to a military usurpation of civil power under the fourth republic, the re-emergence of General de Gaulle in 1958 was to establish strong government, terminate the Algerian war and restore civil control over the military. The disastrous 1940 experi-ence of confiding the conduct of war to the army convinced de Gaulle that the chiefs of staff should be reduced to advisers of the civilian authorities and he embodied this principle in the decrees of 1946 and 1959 determining defence organization. Despite the importance he attached to military power as the instrument of national independence (declaring at the *Ecole Militaire* in 1959 that France and Germany had never achieved anything great without a large measure of military participation), de Gaulle did not have a flattering opinion of the political capacities of his former comrades in arms. In any case, 'national defence' was not just a euphemism for the old title 'war' or a concession to the need to coordinate the three services. The traditional distinction between peace and war had been blurred by involvement in prolonged colonial wars and in the 'cold war' in Europe, communism being both the domestic and foreign enemy. Given the 'total' nature of modern warfare, defence embraced civil as well as military matters, necessitating wide-ranging interministerial cooperation. This involved the ministry of the interior for civil defence, police and the prefects, the finance and industry ministries on the economic side – especially important as the cost of modern weapons escalated – and the scientific and technological research necessary to perfect this weaponry. National defence of such a comprehensive kind could not safely be entrusted to the military, who formed a world apart, with their own law and courts, their peculiar values and professional code, frequently incomprehensible if not repugnant to the civilian population.

The uneasy relationship between the civil government and its military subordinates is reflected in the fact that from 1945 to 1965 there were twenty-five major reforms of defence organization. All accepted the spirit of St Just's assertion in 1793 : 'There must be only one will in the state, the lawmaker must command war operations.' But who was the 'lawmaker'? In 1946 de Gaulle asserted the unity of defence by eliminating separate service ministries and placing defence firmly in the premier's hands. Within a year of de Gaulle's resignation, the logic of the fourth republic led to the delegation and dispersal of power to other ministers, to the assembly and to the generals. Apart from the integration of French defence with NATO, and the denial to the French defence minister of responsibility for the Indochina and Algeria war efforts which weakened political control, the confusion and paralysis within the interministerial defence committee produced by quarrelling coalition partners left the way open for the military leaders to take the political initiative, choosing whom to obey as between ministers and finally refusing to obey at all.

A situation in which a general could declare : 'Each party, each politician has a clientèle and candidates in the army' was ripe for revolt, particularly when members of the defence minister's personal staff were plotting to overthrow the republic.[26]

The French system of total integration of the three services within a single ministry, combined with the elimination of separate junior ministries for each service, instituted by de Gaulle in 1958, has its advantages and its disadvantages. It has facilitated budgetary economies at a time when military technology renders this especially necessary, as well as undermining the independence of the three services. However, owing to the inability of a single minister effectively to control all aspects of defence, the military are likely to enjoy greater political autonomy unless there is strong administrative backing to the ministerial integration. During de Gaulle's presidency, the armed forces minister, as he was called – to denote his more limited function – was a non-politician, whose role was simply to implement the president's policy. The key 1959 Defence Ordinance was deliberately vague, to allow maximum scope for regulatory discretion in defence organization. Following up Article 20 of the constitution, which describes the prime minister as 'responsible' – a strong but vague epithet – for defence, the 1959 Ordinance entrusts the making of defence policy collectively to the government but policy coordination and implementation as well as the oversight of military operations is confided to the prime minister. However, if the prime minister is generalissimo on paper, de Gaulle saw to it that the president embodies the indivisibility of military power in practice. Using his chairmanship of the defence council, President de Gaulle assumed control of defence policy, reducing his prime minister and defence minister to executants of his edicts.

In the early 1960s, by a combination of presidential practice and of decrees, the prime minister's defence powers were delegated to the armed forces minister for day-to-day matters and to the president of the republic for major decisions.[27] Prime Minister Pompidou reduced Debré's large military *cabinet* to one officer and was content to leave his defence functions to the armed forces minister who was directly answerable to the president. The 1962 decrees increased the role of the defence council – composed of the president, prime minister, foreign, interior, finance and armed forces ministers, responsible for general defence policy, including diplomatic, economic and nuclear matters as they relate to defence – and the defence committee (concerned with more detailed matters such as military plans and the allocation of forces), but this was not a return to collective decision-making on the fourth republic pattern. The president treated these bodies as he did the cabinet. The main function of the secretariat general of national defence (SGND) was to prepare the monthly meetings of the defence council and committee and see that their decisions were implemented. It worked to presidential directives rather than for the prime minister to whom it was formally attached. Should anyone have doubted the president's dominance over defence policy, the 1964 decree giving him control over France's strategic nuclear deterrent provided a formal acknowledgement of the realities of power. Military predominance in the SGND – sixty out of its seventy top officials, including its head, are officers – made it amenable to armed forces influence even before it was attached to the defence minister in 1969. The SGND was de Gaulle's instrument for the general oversight of defence policy and had responsibilities in international defence negotiations, the collection and communication of political, economic, scientific as well as military intelligence and the export of arms. Consequently, when Debré secured the SGND's transfer to the defence ministry, he achieved a major shift in power.

Although Debré's resumption of the fourth republic title of defence minister and his acquisition of a junior minister (until 1972) seemed to mark the reversal of the policy of confiding defence policy nominally to the prime minister and in fact to the president, the ground had been prepared by the twenty-three decrees reorganizing the armed forces ministry in 1961. The minister emerged with his capacity to secure information and exert direct control substantially increased. Not only did he acquire control over promotion through his direct responsibility for military personnel. Through the new general supervision of the armed forces corps, he obtained a super-inspectorate over all administrative and financial matters. Legislative and regulatory proposals having administrative, economic or financial consequences had to be approved by members of this body, which could only be overruled by the minister. However, the minister's authority was based on three main pillars : the secretary-general (administration), the ministerial delegate (armament), and the chiefs of staff committee. Unlike the secretary-general in the foreign ministry, the defence secretary-general has only a partial coordinating role and was created to achieve unity of administrative and financial management to counterbalance the power of the service chiefs and of the armaments delegate. The secretary-general (administration) works in close contact with the minister, the director and members of the minister's *cabinet*. He is the minister's main adviser on budgetary matters. About half the secretary-general's time is spent with the division directors, coordinating budgetary, personnel and purchasing policy. He is an important factor in securing civilian control over defence.[28]

The chiefs of staff committee, with the minister in the chair, advises him on the conception and implementation of defence policy, notably in the controversial matter of budget allocations. In addition to the three service chiefs of staff, there is a chief of the armed forces general staff (AFGS) but he is not their hierarchical superior. Until 1969, the chief of AFGS acquired authority at the expense of the minister and the other chiefs of staff, given de Gaulle's preference for a united military command under his control. De Gaulle used to meet all four chiefs of staff regularly. With the decline in presidential interest under Pompidou, and the arrival of an assertive defence minister in the shape of Debré, there was a weakening in the position of the chief of AFGS, the minister preferring to allow greater autonomy to the service chiefs while reserving to himself the power to choose between their rival views. Debré's conflict with the navy chief of staff in 1970 led to the latter's resignation over the sacrifice of the surface fleet (notably aircraft carriers) to the priority accorded by the government to nuclear missile submarines. In 1972, partly to placate unrest in the navy, the defence council approved a fifteen year 'Blue Plan', which stated that in addition to its nuclear deterrent role, the navy was still required to support traditional gunboat diplomacy, as well as providing supply and communications protection. Debré's abrasive interventionism also led to conflicts with ministers peripherally concerned with defence, irritated by Debré's tendency to send them notes demanding that action be sanctioned in line with his own schemes. His strength lay in the fact that President Pompidou felt it necessary to humour a Gaullist leader who commanded the support of the intransigent wing of the UDR.

The 1961 creation of the ministerial delegation (armament) initiated a McNamara-style centralization of authority over the military research and development programme, all the more remarkable because until then the separation between science and defence was – with the exception of nuclear research and development – almost complete. It established, alongside the secretary-general (administration) and the service chiefs, a ministerial delegate responsible for the management and coordination of arms research and production who would supply French-designed weaponry rather than rely on American arms. The delegation's research and testing directorate brought university scientists, engineers and officers together for the first time within one organization to achieve a highly centralized focus for science research policy-making, notably through the selective award of research grants and contracts. Thus the French space programme – third only to those of the United States and Soviet Union – is like the proverbial iceberg, the civilian component being the tip, the hidden portion being made up of the delegation's military projects. On the nuclear deterrent, the delegation works closely with the atomic energy commissariat's military applications division. In the belief that it will encourage a 'spillover' into the civil economy and alter its 'unproductive' image, French military research, development and production is being contracted out to private firms. While as yet there has been little evidence of 'spin off', the policy of subsidizing advanced technology industries with military funds is encouraging the development of a mini industrial-military-scientific complex on the American pattern.[29] This process is facilitated by the increasing number of retiring senior officers who take up important positions in arms manufacturing firms, for example Dassault, who recruited as one of his business associates General Gallois, France's most ardent advocate of a national nuclear force. Dassault's contacts in the air force helped his firms secure three-quarters of the funds voted for aerospace under the first statutory programme establishing the *force de frappe*.

Arms exports are primarily the responsibility of the delegation's internal affairs division, which makes the preliminary appraisal of 'whether a proposed export sale falls within France's *armaments* policy'. If it does, the matter goes to the interdepartmental arms exports committee, serviced by the defence secretariat, which meets under the chairmanship of a defence secretariat official, with the foreign and finance ministries represented. If the decision is not unanimous, the matter is referred to an interministerial arms exports committee, which 'determines whether the proposed sale fits into France's *political* policy. If the sale is a particularly delicate one, the request will end up at the Elysée Palace for decision.'[30] The president, defence and foreign ministers are the main people involved in a policy which was primarily politically motivated under de Gaulle – to diminish Anglo-American influence compared to that of France – but has switched to a more economic emphasis under Pompidou. While France re-established herself as a major arms exporter under the fourth republic, her sales increased fourfold (in money terms) between 1958 and 1968. The combination of diplomatic and economic motives in weapons exports is exemplified by the change in French middle east policy in 1967, the embargo on sales to Israel – previously France's leading arms customer – reflecting a desire to secure a political and economic breakthrough into a two hundred million Arab market compared to Israel's mere three million. Economic factors are more exclusively evident in the French exploitation of the United Nations embargoes on arms sales to South Africa and Rhodesia. These factors led to a tripling of French arms exports in 1970, bringing France to third place after the United States and the Soviet Union, her sales being double those of Britain. Arms (especially aircraft) represented 7·3 per cent of all French exports, two-thirds as much as the purchases of the French armed forces, and gave employment to one hundred thousand workers in 1970. Because this export drive is essential if the burden of French arms expenditure is to be shared with foreign purchasers, the defence minister instructed the chiefs of staff and armaments delegation to equip French forces, as far as possible, with weapons that could also be exported. The government also guarantees to take delivery for the French forces of arms intended for export but not sold.

In a world threatened by total destruction and in a country as divided as France, it has proved impossible to devise a form of national defence organization which is both sufficiently intimidating to deter potential enemies and sufficiently democratic to reassure her own citizens. One may question whether France has achieved the power to deter despite paying the price in loss of democratic accountability. The capacity of the assembly defence committee to influence defence policy has been drastically curtailed. Its record under the fourth republic is not calculated to make this a matter of regret. Attracting a disproportionate number of fire-eating diehards, it lobbied effectively on behalf of the military, securing the restoration of separate service junior ministers in 1956 after they had been abolished by Mendès-France. Under the fifth republic it set up working groups for each of the three services, symbolic of its rearguard battle to resist integration. In 1972 its chairman, Alexandre Sanguinetti, pleaded that defence proper should not be sacrificed to the nuclear deterrent and outbid Debré's insistence that the military budget should not fall below 3·5 per cent of the gross national product – it was only 3·15 per cent in the 1972 budget – raising the target to 5 per cent. Parliament's control over military expenditure on equipment – decided in defence council* – is minimal, particularly as it is voted in medium-term statutory programmes, in whose preparation the forecasting and evaluation centre (transferred from the research and testing directorate directly to the defence minister in 1965) plays an important part. The Third Military Plan (1971–5) coincides with the duration of the Sixth National Plan, the first two military statutory programmes having covered the decade 1960–70. Each year, when it debates the defence budget, parliament also receives the annual Report on the implementation of the Military Plan. It is confronted by a tale of gross underestimation of costs leading to underfulfilment in the planned provision of equipment. President Pompidou sought to stem the tide of public reluctance to accept the cost of defence by speaking of the need to 'recreate patriotism without an enemy' but he did not find the answer to this intractable problem. Meanwhile, he insisted that the military share of public expenditure should not be allowed to decline further.

In 1967, Messmer (de Gaulle's armed forces minister from 1960–69 before becoming Pompidou's prime minister in 1972) exposed the unreality of ministerial accountability to parliament over defence expenditure when he declared : 'There are military secrets which are reflected in budgetary silences.' In no area of the military budget is this admission more relevant than in the

* See above, p. 175 on the ministerial discussion of defence estimates and pp. 187–8 on the defence application of RCB methods.

matter of the nuclear deterrent. While it is not surprising that nuclear weapons policy should be secretive, the striking contrast between France and either Britain or the United States is that the French atomic programme was militarized in the 1950s by a series of incremental steps in which the political leaders responded to technocratic pressures rather than made deliberate decisions. 'Guidance and direction for nuclear policy came not from the French government or the French parliament, but from a small, dedicated group of administrator-technocrats, politicians and military officers' whose activities centred on the atomic energy commissariat. '. . . it was the commissariat cadre which provided the element of continuous advice and support for a military atomic programme and which assured continuity in French nuclear progress, even in the face of disinterested or unsympathetic political leadership.'[31] The interplay between the techno-bureaucrats and the politicians, with individual army officers and industrialists playing an accessory role, is most instructive about the way policy is made in situations where the government is divided and insufficiently interested and therefore indecisive, allowing those with a clear objective to get their way.

The atomic energy commissariat, established by de Gaulle in 1945, enjoyed the unique situation of state financial support without supervision by any ministry or budgetary surveillance by the finance ministry. The explanatory memorandum creating it explained that it would be attached to the prime minister so that it would be 'very close to the government and, so to speak, mingled with it, and nevertheless vested with great freedom of action'. It had two heads, a high commissioner on the research side and an administrator-general who as 'government delegate' was the link with the prime minister's office. Although in the first, pure research, phase of the commissariat's work, it was the high commissioner who was in effective command, the removal in 1950 of Joliot-Curie on the grounds of his communist affiliations and his refusal to accept the possibility of a military orientation of the commissariat's work prepared the way for dominance by the administrator-general on the classic French pattern. This in turn led to a change in the early 1950s towards an industrial and military emphasis, as the pacifist and left-wing scientists were purged and administrative leadership was assumed by *Polytechniciens* with Gaullist sympathies. In 1951 *Polytechnicien* Louis

Armand refused the succession of *Polytechnicien* Raoul Dautry and suggested *Polytechnicien* Pierre Guillaumat who accepted the post of administrator-general. Guillaumat held this post from 1951 to 1958, when he was appointed armed forces minister by de Gaulle, which was both a tribute to his pre-eminent past role in fostering the development of a French nuclear deterrent and an indication of the central role it was to play in defence policy.

The combination of a military and engineering *Ecole Polytechnique* training naturally inclined its products to think in terms of giving nuclear power a military application. Guillaumat was well aware that the majority of senior officers were wedded to reliance upon the American deterrent within the NATO alliance and he successfully prevented subordination of the commissariat to military control. To help him achieve his aims, he nevertheless used well-placed *Polytechnicien* army allies such as Charles Ailleret, in charge of special weapons at the defence ministry from 1952–8 and subsequently armed forces chief of staff and exponent of the ultra-Gaullist doctrine of 'all-round defence' in 1967. Another strategically situated ally was *Polytechnicien* General Lavaud, nuclear arms adviser to the defence minister, Bourgès-Maunoury, in the Mollet government of 1956–7, who worked with Guillaumat as armed forces minister and became armed forces chief of staff in 1959. The *Polytechnicien* old boy network[32] extended to politicians like Bourgès-Maunoury, who played a key role as minister for atomic affairs, defence and as prime minister. With premier Félix Gaillard (a former atomic affairs minister) he provided the political support that was indispensable if the techno-bureaucratic influence of a Guillaumat was to be effective. It was pressure within his cabinet, as well as from the commissariat and the assembly defence committee, that led Mollet to turn a blind eye to the development of an independent nuclear deterrent under his premiership. Nor must one forget Gaullists such as General Koenig. As president of the assembly defence committee from 1951 to 1954 and especially as defence minister in 1954 and 1955, Koenig was able to smuggle into the 1956 budget substantial 'hidden' funds for the atomic programme, helped by Gaston Palewski, atomic affairs minister in 1955 (who was to succeed Guillaumat as atomic energy minister in 1962). It is significant that when it was necessary to find Gaullist Olivier Guichard a post in 1955, he was appointed press attaché to the atomic energy commissariat.* So, the continuity between the nuclear policy of the fourth and fifth republics was not a matter of chance. The latter unveiled and exploded a deterrent that had been furtively prepared by its predecessor.

The advent of the fifth republic was to lead to a decline in the influence of the atomic energy commissariat as the nuclear deterrent became officially the centrepiece of French defence strategy. With the policy of diplomatic independence accepted, the commissariat – formerly a state within the state, with Gaullists taking advantage of its technocratic status – could recede into the subordinate role of implementing government policy. De Gaulle kept close personal control over the commissariat through frequent contacts with the administrator-general, the high commissioner and director of the military applications division. In the mid-1960s, 60 per cent of the commissariat's budget came from the defence ministry and three-quarters of its expenditure went on the nuclear weapons programme but by 1969 a shift in emphasis led to its transfer from the prime minister to the minister of industrial and scientific development. It was no longer so necessary to pretend that France's nuclear energy programme could only be achieved with military assistance, whereas in fact this was not true. The military justification for nuclear weapons came after their production, the real motivation being to influence allies rather than to dissuade enemies. The conflict between civil and military objectives was obvious in the 1957 second five-year atomic energy programme, with the crucial decision to create a factory for separating isotopes at Pierrelatte implying a 'willingness to make enormous sacrifices in order to ensure national independence in the production and use of fissile material'. When completed in 1967, Pierrelatte proved to be 'the most expensive factory ever to be built in France' but 'too small and limited to serve a civilian programme' as well.[33] Yet in military terms, by 1975 when the French nuclear deterrent force was to become fully operational, its striking power would amount to the load of one American B52 bomber. With delivery systems divided between the three services

---

* One of Guillaumat's successors as administrator-general, *Polytechnicien* Robert Hirsch, pushed his Gaullist political sympathies as far as standing as candidate for mayor of Le Havre in the 1971 local elections, although by then he had moved on to administer *Gaz de France*.

to minimize professional jealousy, the thirty-six Mirage 4 bombers (first generation), the eighteen land-based medium-range missiles (second generation), and three nuclear missile submarines (third generation), the *force de frappe* has been dismissed as 'only a nuclear paper tiger' whose military nuisance value was bought at the expense of conventional forces, resulting in 'deterrence without defence'.[34]

However, the French nuclear deterrent makes greater sense if seen as a political symbol of national independence from America rather than as a military weapon directed at Russia. De Gaulle declared at the *Centre des Hautes Etudes Militaires* in 1959, in a statement which he quoted in his *Memoirs of Hope*, that 'France defends herself, by herself, for herself and in her own way'. He nevertheless appreciated that confronted by one super-power, France would have to rely on the support of the other; but such alliances were 'incidental not axiomatic' and to tie oneself simply to America would be fatal to French independence.[35] The French nuclear deterrent was the only hope of resisting a joint Russo-American hegemony and utilizing the United States to discourage any threat from the Soviet Union, while looking to the latter to prevent a resurgence of German (nuclear) militarism. Even the refusal to join in arms limitation talks makes sense, as the value of the French deterrent will be increased if other countries impose restrictions which France can ignore. Because French nuclear policy is a logical corollary of French foreign policy, it is idle to hope that the former will change unless and until the latter does. This is what makes Anglo-French nuclear cooperation so difficult, disagreement over military integration in NATO reflecting a difference of opinion over western Europe's relationship to the United States. French nuclear policy having been ambiguously described as irreversible and adaptable by Chaban-Delmas when he was premier, the second term may be expected to assume greater importance as domestic and foreign pressures assert themselves. The abandonment in 1968 of the policy of 'all-round defence', the military expression of a foreign policy of armed neutrality in which France having no specific enemy would be prepared to meet an attack from any direction, marked a return to modesty even before de Gaulle gave way to Pompidou. Further movement in this direction is probable.

Public opinion, which cannot be expected to consider defence problems in depth, and accords a lower priority to military as against civil public expenditure, may well exert some influence but one can easily overrate the electoral importance of defence policy. Table 35 indicates that while de Gaulle was still in power there was a notable increase in support for an integrated NATO defence policy, support being strongest on the right (with the UDR bringing up the rear) but including 20 per cent of communist votors! Specifically on the *force de frappe*, table 36 demonstrates how divided French public opinion was in the 1960s, with a movement against it on two counts. Compared with 1964, opinion shifted by 1968 from equilibrium to hostility on the French nuclear deterrent's capacity to protect her security, and from support to scepticism on the issue of independence. In spring

Table 35
Which Defence Policy Should France Pursue? (%)*

Defence Policy	September 1967	November 1968
NATO	34	42
European defence alliance without the United States	25	17
Neutralist like Switzerland or Sweden	18	22
No reply	23	19

	November 1968	
According to Party Vote	NATO	*Neutralist*
All	42	22
Communist	20	40
Socialist	46	26
Centre	57	17
Independent republican	54	15
UDR	52	16

* Source: *Sondages*, 1969, nos 1–2, p. 42.

Table 36
Does France's Independent Nuclear Deterrent
Protect Her Security or Independence? (%)*

	Yes	*No*	*No Reply*
(i) France's security: October 1964	38	38	24
September 1968	37	43	20
(ii) France's political independence: October 1964	38	33	29
September 1968	37	38	25

* Source: *Sondages*, 1969, nos. 1–2, p. 43.

1970, 42 per cent of Frenchmen believed that all defence was futile and should be abandoned (45 per cent disagreed and 13 per cent abstained); 53 per cent disagreed with France having an independent nuclear force (36 per cent agreed and 11 per cent abstained); while 75 per cent agreed that France could not alone defend itself and had to form part of a wider alliance (12 per cent disagreed and 13 per cent abstained).[36] French élite opinion has remained sceptical about the credibility of the French deterrent, while the left-wing opposition favours the conversion of France's nuclear forces to peaceful uses; it is not clear whether this would be done unilaterally. There has been no mass movement comparable to the British Campaign for Nuclear Disarmament but after what was stated above concerning the role of *Polytechniciens* in creating the French nuclear deterrent, it is only fair to mention that one of its leading opponents, the veteran socialist leader Jules Moch, was also a *Polytechnicien*. Given public apathy and parliamentary acquiescence, it is only if the French president decides that his country cannot or should not pursue an independent foreign and defence policy that France will give up its membership of the nuclear club.

9 Political Stability and the Industrial Imperative

Speaking at the National Defence Advanced Studies Institute in January 1968, de Gaulle described the Japanese as 'united, numerous, docile and endowed with a nationalist élite'. These epithets can be taken to reflect a regret that the French nation lacked such advantages in the international rivalry for political, military and economic power. Japan also represented the most remarkable demonstration of the rapid success with which the 'industrial imperative' could be accepted by a society that had been highly traditionalist and agriculturalist, achieved by a selective adoption of certain aspects of the American model of an industrialized polity. While de Gaulle could not himself be expected to embrace this vision of France's future, holding firmly to his view that the political sovereign could preserve an adapted but distinctively French society, the mass of Frenchmen have been fascinated by America as 'a prefiguration of what they yearn to be and dread becoming'.[1] The political and economic élite, alway better disposed to the United States than de Gaulle, were quick to seize the opportunities offered by his departure in 1969 at the behest of the disunited and insufficiently docile French people. With President Pompidou at the helm, the fascination with the yardstick of profitability as the main indicator of performance in the context of international market rationality took precedence over the repugnance at the numerous changes in traditional French society that such a commitment entailed.

However, it is important to appreciate that the French advocates of the industrial imperative are not economic liberals who believe that state intervention should be minimized. Consequently, they do not come into head-on conflict with the traditional French conception of authority, although they wish the government to rely less on civil servants and leave more of the initiative to

269

businessmen. In his January 1971 press conference, Pompidou said that his objective was to double French industrial production in the 1970s. While keeping political power firmly in his hands, his intention was to let industrial development render certain changes appear inevitable rather than seek to force reforms through politically before France was ready to accept them. This oblique and prudent approach contrasted starkly with that of Chaban-Delmas, whose 1969 programme adopted a much more overtly modernizing image, with the government acting as the pacemaker of change from stalemate society to 'new society'. The former prime minister was very conscious that it was necessary to placate the interests that might resist the drive towards industrial society, concentrating his attention on the industrial workers; whereas Pompidou was more concerned to placate the farmers, small shopkeepers and craftsmen whose votes were necessary to keep political power in the hands of the industrializers, although some crumbs of consolation should be thrown to the workers, to blunt the edge of their discontent. Pompidou's appointment of Giscard d'Estaing as finance minister in 1969 indicated that whatever the political rivalries separating him from the leader of the independent republicans, they shared a common view of the direction in which the political economy should be steered. Although Giscard has given a more liberal gloss to the type of industrial polity envisaged for France, reflected in the book by his industrial policy adviser called *L'Impératif Industriel*,[2] the need not to leave his party's traditionalist electorate too far behind and coalition necessities have kept him in step, leaving his party's general secretary (Michel Poniatowski) to give full vent to his master's unspoken sentiments.

Despite widespread public disgruntlement with the standard of living and the equity with which increasing national wealth has been shared, by 1970 France's per capita gross national product ($2,920) had far outstripped that of the United Kingdom ($2,170) and Italy ($1,693) and was rapidly overhauling Federal Germany ($3,180) although the United States ($4,380) was still well out of reach. Nevertheless, a strong sense of insecurity persists in France and the state is regarded as the institution to which recourse is necessary even though the groups who feel most threatened have a sense of alienation from government, conceived as remote and insensitive. The state as the instrument of a 'general interest' still enjoys a remarkably great measure of public support, although in practice there is an acceptance that the agents of the state's will are partisan and that leading politicians are as likely to act out of self-interest as anyone else. The French have a very passive view of citizenship, conceived as obedience to the law, fulfilment of the duty to vote and the payment of taxes or simply a withdrawal into private life; they do not regard the citizen as necessarily a well-informed person, still less an active participant in a trade union or political party.[3] The fact that successive finance ministers have instituted tax privileges which allow large numbers to escape taxation, while the state is defrauded of an estimated 15 per cent of its income tax revenue, puts this conception of *civisme* into perspective. Perhaps the attainment of her industrial society goal will, by drastically diminishing the number of self-employed people, increase fiscal justice in France. However, even before France has attained the industrialization targets so fashionable in the 1960s, the 1970s switch of emphasis from industrial modernization to environmental conservation suggests a new objective at the head of the political agenda. The Seventh Plan (1976–80) will probably mark a shift away from planning for national power through industrial competitive strength to planning for national happiness through stress on the quality of life. The Americanization inseparable from the industrial imperative may therefore be replaced by a revival of French *dirigisme* and high public investment and expenditure to preserve what is valuable in France's traditional way of life.

Conscious that except in times of desperate crisis the French detest change, President Pompidou has patiently and pragmatically sought to appease and reconcile rather than risk conflict, to assert his supreme power rather than use it to carry out an ambitious programme of reform. While proclaiming on his 1972 visit to Lorraine that 'thanks to the supreme arbitrament of the head of state, France is able to have a policy at home and abroad', Pompidou prefers to regularize changes that others have brought about rather than expose the impressive but fragile superstructure of political authority to the strains and hazards of heroic innovation. However, this diffidence in action is combined with a determination to concentrate power as never before in the hands of the president, so that all power flows from the top and all decisions are referred to the top. His replacement of the prime minister in

July 1972 at the start of a parliamentary recess, without bother-
ing to offer any explanation of his action, was eloquent testimony
to his desire to stress the purely discretionary and non-accountable
nature of presidential power in relation to parliament, political
parties and the people. Although he prefers to react rather than
act, he is able to monitor all the important stages of the decision-
making process (thanks to his personal staff and the men he has
placed in key positions) and to decide the opportune moment at
which to intervene personally. The partial exceptions to this
generalization are the finance and defence ministers, Giscard
d'Estaing and Debré. They each represent an important and
independent power base which allows them to enjoy a measure
of autonomy. These ministers are irritations that the president
would undoubtedly like to eliminate. Of the two, Debré's position
as the guardian of Gaullist intransigence is less of a threat than the
dynamic conservatism of Giscard d'Estaing because the passage
of time is likely to weaken the diehards more than the liberal conservatives. (Debré left the April 1973 Messmer government.)

Georges Pompidou has been an extremely popular president.
While many identify his presidential style as close to that of de
Gaulle, others recognize a more conciliatory type of leadership,
especially in the sphere of foreign policy but also in the spheres of
industrial relations and law and order. He is regarded as having
been most successful in foreign policy (except for relations
with Algeria) and least successful in economic policy (especially
prices and wages) and educational policy. He was not noticeably
hurt personally by the series of financial scandals in which a
number of his supporters were involved in 1971, thanks to his
ability to exert his control surreptitiously. This has enabled the
president to allow others to take the blame for mistakes, his role
being to put things right subsequently as the great adjudicator.
Because a majority of the French public still seem to favour a non-
partisan 'president of all the Frenchmen', Pompidou's unobtrusive assertion of power enables him to combine comprehensive
control with minimum risk of being held responsible when the
administered became discontented with the government. In June
1971, two years after he was elected to the presidency and five
years before the end of his term of office, 54 per cent of the public
(76 per cent of supporters of the government) hoped he would
eventually stand again; 12 per cent would have preferred another

candidate from the ranks of the governing coalition (e.g. Giscard d'Estaing); while 34 per cent abstained from stating a preference. Compared with the de Gaulle presidency, the French public are more inclined to express satisfaction with the role of President Pompidou (57 per cent compared with 43 per cent) and much less desirous of reducing his importance (13 per cent compared with 33 per cent).[4] Pompidou has made it easier for past opponents of the fifth republic's presidentialism to become reconciled to this key feature of the new institutions.

On 1 January 1972, at the traditional ceremonies in which the president of the republic receives the good wishes for the New Year from the government, parliament and the administrative corps, Pompidou took the opportunity to reassert the public philosophy of the fifth republic, centred on 'the identity of France and the state'. As against those who conceived the French and their state as locked in a permanent and bitter conflict, he claimed that

. . . history reveals that our people, naturally inclined to division and the most extreme individualism, has only been able to constitute the French nation through the action of the state. Successively the kings, the republic, the empire, then once again the republic have, patiently and relentlessly, built and rebuilt the institutions and administration of the state as the guardian of our unity, of our independence, of our liberty. . . . A stable and strong state appears to be the only guarantor of liberty and creator of justice.

Despite the changing character of French society – perhaps partly *because* of the strains which such changes impose upon the political system – the political élite in France remains attached to what we have seen to be an ancient public philosophy. Although the centralization of power which it involves has been diagnosed as a major cause of resistance to change, the French public appears to welcome President Pompidou's use of his extensive powers to control the pace of change to a rate compatible with social peace, even when they have strong reservations about the direction of change. As France ceases to be a pre-industrial society and enters the era of post-industrial society without having properly become an industrial society, she seems to have had appreciable success in carrying out 'change without changing'.[5] In an insecure world, the state remains the institution to which almost all

Frenchmen instinctively turn for protection and assistance. Although resented as is all authority, the One and Indivisible Republic still retains some of its original revolutionary impetus in combination with the mature capacity to negotiate rather than sweep aside obstacles. Periodically rocked by crises, France has found a way of either containing or surviving conflict, even if it must from time to time make the concession of changing the number of the republic.

Notes

Chapter 1   The Unwritten Constitution

1   A. de Tocqueville, *Democracy in America* (1st edn 1835), World's Classics edition, 1959, ch. 4, p. 51.

2   See Blackwell edition of *Six Books of the Commonwealth* (1st edn 1576), book VI, chapter 4, p. 197, and book II, chapter 1, p. 52.

3   *Ibid.*, book III, chapter 13.

4   E. J. Sieyès, *What is the Third Estate* (1st edn 1789), 1963 English edn, p. 80; E. Thompson, *Popular Sovereignty and the French Constitutent Assembly 1789–91*, 1951, p. 6.

5   Quoted by J. Roels, *La notion de représentation chez Roederer*, 1968, p. 83; cf. E. Thompson, pp. 50–53. For J. de Maistre's castigation of the sovereignty of the nation concept, see his 'Considerations on France' of 1796, published in J. Lively (ed), *The Works of Joseph de Maistre*, 1965, pp. 68–9.

6   Quoted in G. G. Van Deusen, *Sieyès. His Life and his Nationalism*, 1932, p. 130.

7   Reprinted in B. Constant, *Cours de Politique Constitutionnelle*, 1861 edn, vol. I, pp. 203–4.

8   *Ibid.*, pp. 9–10; cf. *On Liberty*, chapter 2.

9   *Ibid.*, p. 11. See also J. de Maistre, 'Study on Sovereignty', in *The Works of Joseph de Maistre*, p. 93.

10   *Ibid.*, p. 12.

11   S. Hoffmann, 'Protest in Modern France', in M. A. Kaplan (ed.), *The Revolution in World Politics*, 1962, p. 69; cf. also pp. 72–4.

12   P.-J. Proudhon, *Idée Générale de la Révolution au XIX⁰ Siècle*, 1851, epilogue.

13   P. Avril, *Politics in France*, 1969, part 1, chapter 2.

14   In S. Hoffmann *et al.*, *France, Change and Tradition*, 1963, p. 8.

15   *The Old Régime and the French Revolution* (1856), 1955 English edn, p. 202.

16   *The Old Régime*, pp. 210–11. It was Victor Hugo who so dubbed Louis Napoleon in his book on the 1851 coup.

17 S. Hoffmann, 'Heroic leadership, the case of Modern France', in L. J. Edinger (ed.), *Political Leadership in Industrialized Societies*, 1967, p. 127 and *passim*.

18 M. Crozier, *The Bureaucratic Phenomenon*, 1964, p. 196; cf. Charles de Gaulle, *Le fil de l'épée* (1944), 1962 edn, pp. 53–7.

19 S. Hoffmann, 'Heroic Leadership', p. 117.

20 Crozier, *The Bureaucratic Phenomenon*, p. 287; cf. p. 196.

21 R. Aron, *The Elusive Revolution*, 1969, p. 18. The translation of de Gaulle's comment has been amended slightly.

22 *Journal Officiel. Assemblée Nationale. Débats*, 12 December 1968, p. 5409.

Chapter 2   Modernizing Centralism and Traditional Localism

1 Quoted by G. G. Van Deusen, *Sieyès. His Life and his Nationalism*, 1932, pp. 85–6, 95.

2 *De la Capacité Politique des Classes Ouvrières* (1st edn 1865), quoted in the Rivière *Oeuvres Complètes* edition of 1924, p. 286.

3 G. Schubert, *The Public Interest*, 1960, p. 93.

4 E. Pisani, *La Région . . . pour quoi faire?*, 1970, p. 54.

5 C. Roig, 'Théorie et réalité de la décentralisation', *Revue Française de Science Politique*, June 1964, pp. 463–4, and C. Roig, 'L'administration locale et les changements sociaux', in *Administration Traditionnelle et Planification Régionale*, 1964, pp. 13, 19–20, 33, 45. See also P. Grémion, *La structuration du pouvoir au niveau départemental*, 1969, pp. 29–32.

6 B. Chapman, *Introduction to French Local Government*, 1953, p. 225, and B. Chapman, *The Prefects and Provincial France*, 1955, p. 16; cf. P. Grémion and J.-P. Worms, 'La concertation régionale, innovation ou tradition', in *Aménagement du Territoire et Développement Régional*, vol. 1, 1968, p. 38.

7 V. F. Gruder, *The Royal Provincial Intendants*, 1968, p. 3; cf. B. Chapman, *The Prefects and Provincial France*, pp. 12–13.

8 B. Chapman, *The Prefects and Provincial France*, pp. 145, 164, 173.

9 P. Grémion, *La structuration du pouvoir au niveau départemental*, pp. 45–7; cf. P. Grémion and J.-P. Worms, *Les institutions régionales et la société locale*, 1968, pp. 227–8.

10 B. Gournay et al., *Administration Publique*, 1967, p. 142; cf. M. Kesselman, *The Ambiguous Consensus*, 1967, chapter 9 *passim*.

11 M. Kesselman, *The Ambiguous Consensus*, p. 173; cf. B. Chapman, *Introduction to French Local Government*, pp. 124 ff.

12 J.-C. Thoenig and E. Friedberg, 'Politiques urbaines et stratégies corporatives', *Sociologie du Travail*, 1969, no. 4, pp. 389–92; cf.

M.-F. Souchon, *Le Maire, élu local dans une société en changement*, 1968, pp. 240–1, 246–7.

13 B. Chapman, *Introduction to French Local Government*, p. 42.

14 M. Kesselman, *The Ambiguous Consensus*, p. 75. See also L. Wylie (ed.), *Chanzeaux: A Village in Anjou*, 1966, chapter 12.

15 B. Chapman, *Introduction to French Local Government*, p. 64; cf. S. Tarrow, 'The urban-rural cleavage in political involvement. The case of France', *American Political Science Review*, LXV, June 1971, p. 341 ff.

16 Club Jean Moulin, *Les Citoyens au pouvoir*, 1968, pp. 71, 136; C. Alphandéry *et al.*, *Pour nationaliser l'Etat*, pp. 175–6.

17 J. E. S. Hayward and V. Wright, 'The 37,708 microcosms of an Indivisible Republic : The French Local Elections of March 1971', *Parliamentary Affairs*, XXIV, Autumn 1971, p. 284 ff. See also the articles in *Revue Française de Science Politique*, XXII, April 1972.

18 S. P. Huntington, 'Political Modernisation : America vs. Europe', *World Politics*, April 1966, pp. 378–9, 405–6.

19 Article in *Revue Française de Science Politique*, April–June 1956, p. 309, special issue on 'Aménagement du Territoire'; cf. M. Debré, *La mort de l'Etat républicain*, 1947. On the historical background to the development of regionalism, particularly the numerous third republic regional reform proposals in parliament, see the well documented study by M. Bourjol, *Les institutions régionales de 1789 à nos jours*, 1969.

20 Article in same issue of the *R.F.S.P.*, pp. 298–9.

21 *Ibid.*, 'Administration de gestion, administration de mission', pp. 316, 321; cf. p. 325.

22 G. Delaunay, 'Plaidoyer pour une infante attendue', *Direction*, September 1964, pp. 825–6.

23 S. Hoffman, 'Areal division of powers in the writings of French political thinkers', in A. Maas (ed.), *Area and Power. A theory of local government*, 1959, pp. 121–2.

24 J. E. S. Hayward, 'From functional regionalism to functional representation in France, the Battle of Brittany', *Political Studies*, March 1969, p. 59 ff; cf. A. Baccigalupo, 'La participation des forces démocratiques à l'expérience française de planification régionale', *Canadian Journal of Political Science*, March 1972, pp. 1–27; P. Grémion, *La mise en place des institutions régionales*, 1965, *passim*; P. Grémion and J.-P. Worms, 'La concertation régionale', pp. 49–50; P. Grémion and J.-P. Worms : *Les institutions régionales et la société locale*, 1968, *passim*; R. Mayer, *Féodalités ou démocratie?*, 1968, pp. 53, 60–7, 75.

25 *Journal Officiel. Débats. Assemblée Nationale*, 14 December 1968, p. 5466.
26 *Ibid.*, 12 December 1968, p. 5334; cf. H. Simmons, 'The Planner's Dilemma. Regional Reform in France', *The Canadian Journal of Political Science*, September 1971, pp. 388–9.
27 P. Grémion and J.-P. Worms, 'La concertation régionale', p. 60.

Chapter 3   The Representative Mediators

1   M. Crozier, *The Bureaucratic Phenomenon*, pp. 204–5.
2   J. Gretton, *Students and Workers*, 1969, p. 47.
3   L. Wylie, *Village in the Vaucluse*, 1961, p. 330.
4   F. Bourricaud, *Esquisse d'une théorie de l'autorité*, 1961, p. 313.
5   H. W. Ehrmann, 'French Bureaucracy and Organized Interests', *Administrative Science Quarterly*, vol. V, no. 4, 1961, p. 541; cf. 545–6.
6   Y. Weber, *L'Administration Consultative*, 1968, p. 3 (quoting Chenot, who as a minister had access to the index in the prime minister's office), and G. Mignot and P. d'Orsay, *La Machine Administrative*, p. 92; cf. J.-M. Diemer, 'L'administration consultative à l'échelle départementale', *Revue Administrative*, 1964, p. 118 ff.
7   *La Vie Bretonne*, July 1962, p. 11.
8   F.-H. de Virieu, *La fin d'une agriculture*, 1967, pp. 73–4; cf. Y. Tavernier, 'Le syndicalisme paysan et la politique agricole du gouvernement', *Revue Française de Science Politique*, September, 1962, p. 599 ff.
9   M. Crozier, 'White-Collar Unions—the case of France', in A. Sturmthal (ed.), *White Collar Trade Unions*, 1966, pp. 121, 126.
10 H. Finer, *Representative Government and a Parliament of Industry. A Study of the German Federal Economic Council*, 1923, p. 229.
11 H. Daalder, in J. LaPalombara and M. Weiner (eds.), *Political Parties and Political Development*, 1966, pp. 46, 54–6.
12 J. Charlot, *The Gaullist Phenomenon*, 1971, p. 17. For a more cautious view, see J. S. Ambler, 'The Democratic Union for the Republic : to survive de Gaulle', *Rice University Studies*, vol. 54, no. 3, summer 1968, esp. pp. 34–9.
13 W. Bagehot, *The English Constitution* (Nelson edition), p. 262.
14 *The Old Régime and the French Revolution*, p. 145.
15 P. Williams, *The French Parliament (1958–1967)*, 1968, pp. 21, 12.
16 P. Williams, *Crisis and Compromise. Politics in the Fourth*

Republic, 1964, p. 242; cf. R. K. Gooch, *The French Parliamentary Committee System* (1935), 1969 edn pp. 219–21.

17 P. Williams, *The French Parliament*, p. 38.

18 N. Wahl, 'The French Parliament. From last word to afterthought', in E. Frank (ed.), *Lawmakers in a Changing World*, 1966, p. 52; cf. pp. 49–63.

Chapter 4   Making and Implementing Government Policy

1 P. Avril, *Le Régime Politique de la Ve République*, p. 205.

2 C. de Gaulle, *Memoirs of Hope*, 1971, p. 324; cf. 31–2. For the Bayeux speech, the de Gaulle press conference and the Pompidou apologia, see M. Harrison, *French Politics*, 1969, pp. 28, 52, 75. On the de Gaulle presidency, see M. Anderson, *Government in France*, 1970, chapter 2.

3 J.-L. Parodi, 'Sur deux courbes de popularité', *Revue Française de Science Politique*, February 1971, p. 129 ff.

4 C. Debbasch, *L'Administration au pouvoir*, 1969, pp. 50–1; cf. pp. 44–56.

5 C. E. Lindblom, 'The science of "muddling through" ', *Public Administration Review*. Vol. XIX, no. 2, spring 1959, p. 80, note and passim; cf. C. L. Schultze, *The Politics and Economics of Public Spending*, 1968, chapter 3.

6 E. Pisani, article in *Revue Française de Science Politique*, April–June, 1956, p. 325; cf. pp. 316, 324; C. Debbasch, *L'Administration au pouvoir*, pp. 114–19; and P. Racine, in Institut Français des Sciences Administratives, *La Coordination Administrative en matière économique et sociale*, 1967, pp. 48–51.

7 Quoted in J. H. McArthur and B. R. Scott, *Industrial Planning in France*, 1969, p. 286. For opinion poll evidence, see *Les Français et l'Etat*, pp. 90–3.

8 Professor Wallon, quoted in J.-J. Ribas, *L'Ecole Nationale d'Administration et la formation des fonctionnaires*, 1946, p. 81.

9 Emile Boutmy, quoted by T. B. Bottomore, *Elites and Society*, 1964, p. 82.

10 See J. Siwek-Pouydesseau, *Le personnel de direction des ministères*, 1969, p. 73, based on calculations for twelve ministries.

11 E. G. Lewis, 'Social background of French Ministers, 1944–1967', *Western Political Quarterly*, vol. XXIII, no 3, September, 1970, pp. 567–8. For details on the fifth republic ministers, see C. Debbasch, *L'Administration au pouvoir*, pp. 50–1.

12   J. E. S. Hayward and V. Wright in *Parliamentary Affairs*,
     Autumn 1971, p. 292.

Chapter 5   Public Order and Civil Liberties

1   *Traité de Droit Constitutionnel* (1911, 3rd edn 1927), vol. II, pp.
    756–7.
2   Whilst Georges Vedel (*Droit Administratif*) is the leading con-
    temporary exponent of the Hauriou view, André de Laubadère
    (*Traité Elémentaire de Droit Administratif*, 5th edn 1970, vol.
    I, pp. 41–51, 554) is closer to Duguit's standpoint.
3   SOFRES, *Les Français et l'Etat*, 1970, pp. 55–6, 66–8.
4   71 per cent regarded the abolition of press freedom and 68 per
    cent described the abolition of judicial independence as 'very
    serious', whilst fewer so described the abolition of parliament
    (61 per cent) and political parties (42 per cent). (SOFRES poll
    published in *Le Figaro*, 10 November 1969, p. 6).
5   L. Favoreau, 'Le Conseil Constitutionnel, régulateur de l'activité
    normative des pouvoirs publics', *Revue du Droit Public*, 1967,
    p. 62; cf. pp. 5–120; M. Duverger, *Institutions Politiques et
    Droit Constitutionnel* (1963 edn), pp. 643–4.
6   B. Chenot, *Etre Ministre*, 1967, p. 101; cf. 99–100; and C. de
    Gaulle : *Memoirs of Hope*, p. 317. See also J. P. Négrin, *Le
    Conseil d'Etat et la vie publique en France depuis 1958*, 1968,
    pp. 123–9.
7   G. Braibant, 1 July 1960, *Recueil Dalloz*, 1960, p. 692, quoted in
    Négrin, *Le Conseil d'Etat . . .*, pp. 152–3.
8   Négrin, p. 141 (note), quoting R. Drago, *Sociologie du con-
    tentieux administratif*, 1967, pp. 76–9.
9   C. Laroche-Flavin, *La Machine Judiciaire*, 1968, p. 106.
    Laroche-Flavin is a pseudonym for a number of French judges.
10 See the comments by a group of judges, *ibid.*, pp. 101–4; cf.
    90–1 and the testimony of a former police commissioner and
    senior official of the ministry of the interior writing under the
    pseudonym of J. Lantier, *Le Temps des Policiers*, 1970, pp.
    280–1, 289–90.
11 P. M. Williams, *Wars, Plots and Scandals in Post-War France*,
    1970, p. 3 ff. and chapter 6 for a discussion of the Ben Barka
    Affair. On the Casamayor Affair, which arose out of a judge's
    defence of the independence of the judiciary involving criticism
    of the minister's hushing up of the Ben Barka Affair, leading to
    a reprimand by the high council of the judiciary which is sup-
    posed to protect judicial independence, consult C. Laroche-
    Flavin, *La Machine Judiciaire*, pp. 139–40.

12 Laroche-Flavin, p. 29.

13 Y. Lévy, 'Police and Policy', *Government and Opposition*, July-September, 1966, p. 507; cf. 491 ff.

14 See C. Angeli and R. Backmann, *Les Polices de la Nouvelle Société*, 1971, pp. 36–42.

15 D. Langlois, *Les Dossiers Noirs de la Police*, 1971, p. 164 and chapter 5 *passim*.

16 B. Chapman, *Police State*, 1971, p. 81; cf. p. 93.

17 J. Lantier, *Le Temps des Policiers*, p. 102; cf. chapter 3 *passim* on 'The police and the army'.

18 J. S. Ambler, *Soldiers Against the State. The French Army in Politics*, 1966 (1968, ed. pp. 7–9, 25). Military personnel still cannot belong to a political party except for two weeks before an election in which they stand as a candidate. Officers require the permission of the ministry of defence to write articles on current military policy.

19 Quoted in *ibid.*, p. 41.

20 SOFRES, *Les Français et l'Etat*, 1970, pp. 103–4.

21 See the account in P. M. Williams and M. Harrison, *Politics and Society in de Gaulle's France*, 1971, pp. 287–91.

22 SOFRES, *Les Français et l'Etat*, pp. 105–6.

23 A. de Laubadère, *Traité Elémentaire*, vol. 3, pp. 304–8.

24 Speech by Raymond Marcellin, minister of the interior, reported in *Le Monde*, 27 July 1971.

25 J. Chevallier, 'Le problème de la réforme de l'ORTF en 1968', *L'Actualité Juridique. Droit Administratif*, April 1969, pp. 218, 224.

26 Rapport Paye, pp. 24–5, 104–5.

Chapter 6   Economic Policy: By Whom and How It Is Made

1 P. Huvelin, quoted in L. Stoleru, *L'impératif industriel*, 1969, pp. 151–2.

2 P. Bauchard, 'Les intendants du Général', *La Nef*, no. 38, February-April 1968, special issue on 'Dix années du Gaullisme', p. 133. On Pompidou's strengthening of the prime minister's power relative to the finance minister, see P. Rouanet, *Pompidou*, 1969, pp. 105–11.

3 F.-L. Closon and J. Filippi (eds), *L'Economie et les Finances*, 1959, pp. 131–60.

4 See P. Lalumière, *Les Finances Publiques*, 1970, p. 404; cf. 401 ff. and J. Rivoli, *Le budget de l'Etat*, 1969, p. 23.

5 F. Bloch-Laîné and P. de Vogüé, *Le Trésor Public et le mouve-

ment général des fonds, 1960, pp. 169–70; cf. Closon and Filippi, *L'Economie et les Finances*, p. 196.

6   Quoted in F. Bloch-Laîné and P. de Vogüe p. 167; cf. Lalumière, *Les Finances Publiques*, pp. 371–5. On the relations between the treasury and Bank of England, see R. A. Chapman, *Decision Making*, 1968, chapter 5.

7   J. G. S. Wilson, *French Banking and Credit Structure*, 1957, p. 296; cf. 285 ff.

8   F. D'Arcy, 'La Société Centrale pour l'Equipment du Territoire', in *Aménagement du Territoire et Développement Régional*, vol. II, 1969, pp. 80–6, 101–3. See also A. Chazel and H. Poyet, *L'Economie Mixte*, 1963, chapter 3.

9   Bloch-Laîné, Postface to R. Priouret, *La Caisse des Dépôts*, 1966, pp. 426, 429; cf. p. 396 ff. See also P. Lalumière, *Les Finances Publiques*, pp. 334–6.

10 J. H. McArthur and B. R. Scott, *Industrial Planning in France*, pp. 321–4; cf. J. and A.-M. Hackett, *Economic Planning in France*, 1963, pp. 65–8.

11 S. S. Cohen, *Modern Capitalist Planning. The French Model*, 1969, pp. 101–3; cf. 112–15.

12 B. Pouyet, *La Délégation à l'Aménagement du Territoire et à l'Action Régionale*, 1967, pp. 8, 59–63, 118–26, 134–5.

13 The minister of education was M. Sudreau, September 1962, quoted in Lalumière, *Les Finances Publiques*, p. 448; the agriculture minister M. Edgar Faure, in his *Ce que je crois*, 1971, p. 20.

14 See E. Faure, 'Quand le dormeur s'éveillera', *Le Monde*, 16 November 1971; cf. R. Charvin, 'L'évolution du rôle des Commissions des Finances', *Revue de Science Financière*, January–March 1969, p. 122 ff. On parliament and the 1968 budget, see P. M. Williams and M. Harrison, *Politics and Society in de Gaulle's Republic*, pp. 314–21.

15 P. Lalumière, *Les Finances Publiques*, p. 226; cf. 204 ff.

16 On INSEE, consult F.-L. Closon and J. Filippi, *L'Economie et les Finances*, chapter 3. See also the extended interview of Ripert in *L'Express*, 8 February 1971, pp. 68–74 and M. Bosquet, 'L'INSEE', in *Le Nouvel Observateur*, 7 October 1968, pp. 22–3. On FIFI, see M. Aglietta and R. Courbis, 'Un outil pour le plan, le modèle FIFI', *Economie et Statistique*, no. 1, May 1969, pp. 45–65, and Atreize, *La planification française en pratique*, 1971, pp. 310–24.

17 Atreize, p. 52. On the forecasting division, see F.-L. Closon and J. Filippi, *L'Economie et Les Finances*, chapter 2, chapter 4 being devoted to the finance ministry and planning. On the

'economic budget' see E. Mossé, *Comment va l'economie?* 1965, chapter 6 *passim*.

18 *Sondages*, 1966, no. 2, pp. 55–6.

19 On the role of the ESC in plan preparation, see J. E. S. Hayward, *Private Interests and Public Policy*, 1966, p. 65 ff. On the role of parliament, see P. Corbel, *Le Parlement français et la planification*, 1969, pp. 163–78, 278–81.

20 Cour des Comptes, *Rapport au Président de la République suivi des réponses des administrations, 1964*, 1966, pp. 33–4; cf. pp. 31–5, 142–5.

21 J. H. McArthur and B. R. Scott, *Industrial Planning in France*, p. 136 (note).

22 P. Huet, in 'Rationalisation des Choix Budgétaires', *Notes et Etudes Documentaires*, no. 3815–6, 20 September 1971, p. 5.

23 M. Anshen, in D. Novick (ed.), *Program Budgeting*, 1965, p. 19; cf. p. 289. Consult C. E. Lindblom, 'The science of "muddling through" ', *Public Administration Review*, XIX, no. 2, spring 1959, pp. 79–88, and C. L. Schultze, *The Politics and Economics of Public Spending*, 1968, especially, chapters 2–3.

24 See the special issue of *RCB, Bulletin interministériel pour la rationalisation des choix budgétaires*, 1971, on 'La RCB et les administrations'. See also an article by the director-general of the RCB Mission, P. Huet, on 'The Rationalization of Budget Choices in France', *Public Administration*, autumn 1970, pp. 273–87.

25 L. Sfez, *L'Administration Prospective*, 1970, pp. 150–61.

Chapter 7 Elusive Autonomy: Education and Public Enterprise

1 Quoted by H. Taine, *Les Origines de la France Contemporaine. Le Régime Moderne*, vol. 2, 1894, pp. 157–8.

2 C. Roig and F. Billon-Grand, *La socialisation politique des enfants*, 1968, pp. 64–5, 115–18, 163; cf. appendix 4 on civic education.

3 W. D. Halls, *Society, Schools and Progress in France*, 1965, p. 3; cf. W. R. Fraser, *Reforms and Restraints in Modern French Education*, 1971, pp. 58, 120.

4 A. Darbel and D. Schnapper, *Les Agents du Système Administratif*, 1969, p. 94 ff., esp. pp. 102–3 and 158.

5 J. Fournier, *Politique de l'Education*, 1971, p. 44; cf. pp. 43–9. See also P. Bourdieu and J.-C Passeron, *Les Héritiers*, 1964, esp. appendix 1; P. Bourdieu, 'La transmission de l'héritage-culturel', in Darras, *Le Partage des Bénéfices*, 1966, p. 387 ff., 409 ff; P. Bourdieu and J.-C. Passeron, *La Reproduction. Eléments pour*

une théorie du système d'enseignement, 1970, p. 176 ff. and appendix.

6   R. Gilpin, *France in the Age of the Scientific State,* 1968, p. 111; cf. p. 86 ff.

7   G. Bonnot, 'Kafka règne au Ministère de l'Education Nationale', *L'Express,* 23 June 1969, p. 37; cf. J. Minot, *L'Entreprise Education Nationale,* 1970, pp. 197–202, 332–3.

8   Guichard's statement, attached as appendix 1 to the OECD *Reviews of National Policies for Education. France 1971,* pp. 152–3; cf. Minot, *L'Entreprise Education Nationale,* pp. 203–9.

9   J.-L. Crémieux-Brilhac (ed.), *L'Education Nationale,* 1965, p. 315. See also J. M. Clark, *Teachers and Politics in France,* 1967.

10 J. Minot, *L'Entreprise Education Nationale,* pp. 207, 403–10; W. R. Fraser, *Reforms and Restraints . . .,* pp. 109, 115; OECD *Reviews,* pp. 87–93, 133–7, 152.

11 C. Frankel, in OECD *Reviews,* p. 27; cf. M. Crozier, *The Bureaucratic Phenomenon,* pp. 239–43, and M. Crozier, *La société bloquée,* 1970, p. 145 ff.

12 J. de Chalendar, *Une loi pour l'université,* 1970, pp. 235–45; cf. pp. 31, 122–4, 164–5. See also P. M. Williams and M. Harrison, *Politics and Society . . .,* pp. 326–31.

13 J. Capelle, *Tomorrow's Education—The French Experience,* 1967, pp. 210, 208.

14 C. Debbasch, *L'Université désorientée,* 1971, pp. 37–40; cf. p. 103 ff. But see E. Faure, *Ce que je crois,* pp. 191–4.

15 *Sondages,* 1968, no. 1, pp. 39–41, and no. 2, p. 35.

16 IFOP in *Les Informations,* 25 September 1972, pp. 28–9.

17 *Rapport sur les Entreprises Publiques,* 1968, p. 20; cf. pp. 17–19. Known as the Nora Report, it was presented to the government in April 1967 but not published until the autumn of 1968. The appendices, examining particular public enterprises, were not published.

18 J. Sheahan, *Promotion and Control of Industry in Post-War France,* 1963, p. 123; cf. pp. 116–25, 197–8, 208.

19 M. Debré, *Au Service de la Nation,* 1963, pp. 258–60.

20 Nora Report, p. 80; cf. B. Chenot, *Les Entreprises Nationalisées,* 1959, pp. 98–105.

21 On the problem of a tripartite board, see M. Byé, in M. Einaudi *et al., Nationalization in France and Italy,* 1955, pp. 98–104; cf. pp. 29–31, and A. de Laubadère, *Traité . . .,* vol. 3, pp. 545, 560–1.

22 N. Delefortrie-Soubeyroux, *Les Dirigeants de l'Industrie Française,* 1961, pp. 120–1, and P. Lalumière, *L'Inspection des Finances,* pp. 128, 154–8; cf. D. Granick, *The European*

Executive, 1962, chapters 5 and 19 *passim*, B. Chenot, *Les Entreprises Nationalisées*, pp. 108–11, 118–19, and A. G. Delion, *L'Etat et les Entreprises Publiques*, 1958, pp. 78–80, 156–8.

23 J. Baumier, *Les Grandes Affaires Françaises*, 1967, pp. 192–3; cf. p. 185 ff. See also J. Sheahan, *Promotion and Control . . .*, p. 190, and A. Griotteray, 'La République des Féodalités', *Le Monde*, 23 October 1971, p. 34 and the summary of the 1972 Griotteray Report in *Le Monde*, 28 June 1972. The danger of a nationalized industry '*République de Techniciens*', was pointed out by Camus' *Combat* as early as 14 February 1944. See A. Werth, *France 1940–1955*, 1956, p. 231.

Chapter 8   National Independence and International Mission

1 C. de Gaulle, *Memoirs of Hope*, 1971, p. 39; cf. pp. 36, 48.

2 F. S. Northedge, *The Foreign Policies of the Powers*, 1968, p. 37.

3 C. de Gaulle, *Memoirs of Hope*, pp. 28–9.

4 M. Couve de Murville, *Une Politique Etrangère, 1958–69*, 1971, pp. 9–10.

5 P. Rouanet, *Pompidou*, p. 99; cf. R. Buron, *Le Plus Beau des Métiers*, pp. 219–21.

6 P. de Forges, 'Les Secrétaires Généraux de Ministères', Colloquium of the Institut Français des Sciences Administratives, *Les Superstructures des Administrations Centrales*, 1973, pp. 106, 109–13, 119.

7 J. Baillou and P. Pelletier, *Les Affaires Etrangères*, 1962, pp. 83–4.

8 J. Charlot, *L'U.N.R., Etude du pouvoir au sein d'un parti politique*, 1967, pp. 157, 160, 165. On the third and fourth republic foreign affairs committees, see R. K. Gooch, *The French Parliamentary Committee System*, 1935, pp. 241–7, and A. Grosser, *La IV République et sa politique extérieure*, 1961, pp. 84–90.

9 *Memoirs of Hope*, p. 291 and 289; cf. p. 290.

10 SOFRES, *Les Français et l'Etat*, 1970, p. 28.

11 *Sondages*, nos 1–2, 1971, p. 157, and C. Roig and F. Billon-Grand, *La Socialisation . . .*, pp. 120, 131–7.

12 A. Grosser, *French Foreign Policy under de Gaulle*, 1967, p. 143.

13 *Memoirs of Hope*, pp. 182, 194–5; cf. M. Couve de Murville, *Une Politique Etrangère*, pp. 292–8, 347 ff., and PEP, *France and the European Community*, Occasional Paper No. 11, January 1961, pp. 10–12, 26–35.

14 *Memoirs of Hope*, p. 196; cf. p. 170 ff. On Franco-German

relations, see A. Grosser, *French Foreign Policy under de Gaulle*, chapter 5 and pp. 90–5; Couve de Murville, chapter 7.

15 Pompidou interview in *L'Express*, 4 September 1967, p. 9.

16 L. Scheinman, in R. S. Jordan (ed.), *International Adminis-tration*, 1971, pp. 219–20, cf. p. 194 (note); cf. J. Dromer, 'Le Comité Interministériel pour les questions de Coopération Economique Européenne', in the Institut Français des Sciences Administratives symposium on *La Coordination Administrative en matière économique et sociale*, 1967, pp. 33–9.

17 *Une Politique Etrangère*, p. 303; cf. pp. 301–4.

18 H. S. Wallace, 'The impact of the European Communities on National Policy-Making', *Government and Opposition*, autumn 1971, p. 537; cf. p. 523 ff. See also P. Gerbert, 'La préparation de la décision communautaire au niveau national français' in P. Gerbet and D. Pepy (eds), *La Décision dans les Communautés Européennes*, 1969, pp. 195–205. J. Baillou and P. Pelletier, *Les Affaires Etrangères*, pp. 174–6, 339, 345–51.

19 *Sondages*, no. 1, 1969, pp. 49–50, and J. Rabier, 'Europeans and the Unification of Europe', *Government and Opposition*, autumn 1971, p. 485.

20 *Sondages*, nos 1–2, 1971, pp. 23–5.

21 A. Peyrefitte, in *Le Monde,* 18 September 1960, republished in PEP, *France and the European Community*, pp. 36–7. See also Couve de Murville, *Une Politique Etrangère*, pp. 366, 384.

22 *Une Politique Etrangère*, p. 449.

23 J. de St. Jorre, *The Nigerian Civil War*, 1972, pp. 211–12; cf. 323. See also G. Chaffard, 'Foccart et les fonds secrets', *Le Nouvel Observateur*, 3 November 1969, pp. 52–8.

24 G. de Carmoy, *The Foreign Policies of France, 1944–1968*, 1970, pp. 232–40; A. Grosser, *French Foreign Policy Under de Gaulle*, pp. 35, 46–50 and chapters 3 and 4.

25 J. de St. Jorre, *The Nigerian Civil War*, pp. 211–15; cf. J. Stanley and M. Pearton, *The International Trade in Arms*, 1972, pp. 185–7.

26 General de Monsabert, quoted by B. Chantebout, *L'Organisa-tion générale de la défense nationale en France depuis la fin de la Seconde Guerre Mondiale*, 1967, p. 177; cf. p. 98 ff.

27 Chantebout, p. 224; cf. p. 192 ff.

28 P. de Forges in *Les Superstructures . . .*, pp. 104, 108–9, 117–18.

29 R. Gilpin, *France in the Age . . .*, p. 264; cf. pp. 257–81, 291–5, and Chantebout, p. 426. See also W. L. Kohl, *French Nuclear Diplomacy*, 1971, pp. 202–4.

30 G. Thayer, *The War Business. The International Trade in Armaments*, 1969, p. 270; cf. pp. 269–77. See also J. Stanley and

M. Pearton, *The International Trade in Arms*, pp. 31–2, 85, 94–6, 117, 126–7, 171–7, 196 ff., and Stockholm International Peace Research Institute (SIPRI), *The Arms Trade with the Third World*, 1971, chapter 6.

31 L. Scheinman, *Atomic Energy Policy in France Under the Fourth Republic*, 1965, pp. 215, 212; cf. XVI–VII, 94–5, 210–15. On parliament and the nuclear force in 1960, see J. S. Ambler, *The Government and Politics of France*, 1971, pp. 188–91.

32 W. Mendl, *Deterrence and Persuasian. French nuclear armament in the context of national policy, 1945–1969*, 1970, p. 200; cf. pp. 144, 155, 181–4, 188–200, and Scheinman, pp. 66, 97.

33 Mendl, pp. 147, 151, 180; cf. pp. 178–9, 224–5 and R. Gilpin, *France in the Age . . .*, p. 283 ff.

34 Mendl, pp. 209, 225; cf. pp. 111–12, and W. L. Kohl, *French Nuclear Diplomacy*, p. 376.

35 Mendl, pp. 61, 77; cf. p. 78 ff., and *Memoirs of Hope*, p. 204.

36 SOFRES, *Les Français et l'Etat*, pp. 32–4. On élite opinion, see K. W. Deutsch *et al.*, *France, Germany and the Western Alliance*, 1967, chapters 5–6, and D. Lerner and M. Gorden, *Euratlantica. Changing Perspectives of the European Elites*, 1969, chapter 4.

Chapter 9   Political Stability and the Industrial Imperative

1 J. Ardagh, *The New France*, 1970, p. 680; cf. D. Lerner and M. Gorden, *Euratlantica*, chapter 1.

2 L. Stoleru, 1969.

3 SOFRES, *Les Français et l'Etat*, pp. 98–100; cf. pp. 79–80.

4 *Sondages*, 1971, nos. 1–2, pp. 25, 41; cf. pp. 23–4, 40.

5 See the Plan et Prospectives Sixth Plan study group report *1985, la France face au choc du futur*, 1972, p. 146 and chapter 5 *passim*. For a roseate assessment of France's economic present and future, see the Hudson Institute report by E. Stillman *et al.*, *L'Envol de la France, portrait de la France dans les années 80*, 1973, passim.

Further Reading

General

For an invaluable historical perspective, Alexis de Tocqueville's *The Old Régime and the French Revolution* (1856, 1955 English version, Doubleday, Garden City, New York) is still unequalled. Eric Cahm has provided a very broad documentary history in *Politics and Society in Contemporary France, 1789–1971* (1972, Harrap, London), but for a more specifically political collection of strictly contemporary readings, one should turn to Martin Harrison's *French Politics* (1969, Heath, Lexington, Mass.). The best study of the 1946–58 period is Philip Williams' *Crisis and Compromise, Politics in the Fourth Republic* (1964, Longmans, London). On social, economic and political change, Stanley Hoffmann *et al.*, *France: Change and Tradition* (1963, Gollancz, London) has not been superseded by more recent works like John Ardagh's informative *The New France* (1970, Penguin, Harmondsworth) or Harvey Waterman, *Political Change in Contemporary France, the Politics of an Industrial Democracy* (1969, Merrill, Columbus, Ohio), the latter being marred by trying to fit France into a post-industrial, end of ideology framework. Michel Crozier's *La Société Bloquée* (1970, Seuil, Paris) is a very stimulating analysis of resistance to change, also treated in Mark Kesselman's 'Overinstitutionalization and political constraint. The case of France', *Comparative Politics*, III, no. 1, October 1970.

On the early years of the fifth republic, the testimony of Charles de Gaulle's *Memoirs of Hope* (1971 English version, Weidenfeld and Nicolson, London) should be supplemented by other sources, notably Philip Williams and Martin Harrison, *Politics and Society in de Gaulle's Republic* (1971, Longmans, London), who carry the record judiciously to the Pompidou succession. Anthony Hartley's *Gaullism, the Rise and Fall of a Political Movement* (1972, Routledge and Kegan Paul, London) sums up the de Gaulle era; while P. Rouanet's *Pompidou* (1969, Grasset, Paris) provides a subtle analysis of his career up to his election as president. For detailed general studies in French of the fifth republic, Pierre Avril's *Le Régime Politique de la Ve République* (1964, 2nd edn 1967, Librairie générale de droit et de jurisprudence, Paris) and François Goguel's *Institutions Politiques Françaises* (3 vols, 1967–8, Les Cours du Droit, Paris) can be recommended. Avril's treatment is more critical of the régime and should not be confused with his *Politics in France* (1969, Penguin, Harmondsworth). For an administrative emphasis, one may turn to A. de Laubadère's classic *Traité Elémentaire de Droit Administratif* (3 vols, 5th edn 1970, Librairie générale de droit et de jurisprudence, Paris). Those who find organization charts useful should consult Georges Dupuis *et al*, *Organigrammes des Institutions Françaises* (1971, Colin, Paris).

Local and regional politics and administration

For excellent worm's eye views of rural France, one should consult Laurence Wylie's *Village in the Vaucluse* (1957, Harvard University Press, Cambridge, Mass.) and Wylie *et al.*, *Chanzeaux, a Village in Anjou* (1966, Harvard University Press, Cambridge, Mass.). For a penetrating treatment of rural politics, see Mark Kesselman's *The Ambiguous Consensus: A Study of Local Government in France* (1967, Knopf, New York), which should be supplemented with Sidney Tarrow's 'The urban-rural cleavage in political involvement. The case of France', *American Political Science Review*, LXV, June 1971. Somewhat dated but still valuable descriptions are provided by Brian Chapman's *Introduction to French Local Government* (1953, Allen and Unwin, London) and *Prefects and Provincial France* (1955, Allen and Unwin, London). The interconnection between local and national politics is discussed in J. E. S. Hayward and V. Wright, 'The 37,708 microcosms of an indivisible Republic', *Parliamentary Affairs*, XXIV, autumn 1971. Two French political sociologists, Pierre Grémion and Jean-Pierre Worms, have made a number of remarkable studies of local and regional politics. See especially their contributions to a special issue of *Sociologie du Travail* (1966, no. 3) devoted to 'L'administration face aux problèmes du changement'; Grémion's *La mise en place des institutions régionales* (1965, Copédith, Paris) and Grémion and Worms, *Les institutions régionales et la société locale* (1968, Copédith, Paris). For a more formal and official analysis, see J. Monod and P. de Castelbajac, *L'Aménagement du Territoire* (1971, Presses Universitaires de France, Paris).

Interest groups, parties and parliament

Jean Meynaud's *Les groupes de pression en France* (1957, Colin, Paris) still remains the only full-length general description of French interest groups. Somewhat dated but useful discussions of particular interests are provided by Henry W. Ehrmann, *Organized Business in France* (1957, Princeton University Press, Princeton, New Jersey), a study of the CNPF; Gordon Wright's *Rural Revolution in France, The Peasantry in the Twentieth Century* (1964, Oxford University Press, London) and Jean-Daniel Reynaud's *Les Syndicats en France* (1963, Colin, Paris). A more up to date discussion is provided by John Gretton, *Students and Workers, an analytical account of dissent in France, May–June 1968* (1969, Macdonald, London), one of the best books to have come out of the 'events'. For a description of the participation of the major interest groups in a functionally representative third chamber, see Jack Hayward's *Private Interests and Public Policy, the experience of the French Economic and Social Council* (1966, Longmans, London), while their relations with the civil service are admirably discussed in H. W. Ehrmann's 'French bureaucracy and organized interests', *Administrative Science Quarterly*, V, no. 4, 1961.

Peter Campbell's *French Electoral Systems and Elections since 1789* (2nd edn 1966, Faber, London) provides the best succinct description of France's many experiments with electoral systems, while Philip Williams' *French Politicians and Elections, 1951–1969* (1970, Cambridge University Press, Cambridge) gives one the feel of what the elections were actually like. Jean Charlot has provided the best analysis of *The Gaullist Phenomenon, the Gaullist Movement in the Fifth Republic* (1971, Allen and Unwin, London), which should be supplemented with his study of the UDR's earlier incarnation, *L'U.N.R. Etude du pouvoir au sein d'un parti politique* (1967, Colin, Paris) and J.–C. Colliard's study of the UDR's main ally, *Les Républicains Indépendents V. Giscard d'Estaing* (1971, Presses Universitaires de France, Paris). For the left, one should consult Annie Kriegel's admirable survey of *The French Communists* (1968, English version 1972, University of Chicago Press, Chicago) and Harvey G. Simmons, *French Socialists in Search of a Role, 1956–1967* (1970, Cornell University Press, Ithaca, New York). Philip Williams has provided a brief but excellent study of *The French Parliament, 1958–1967* (1968, Allen and Unwin, London).

The executive

The seminal analysis of the values and behaviour characteristic of the French style of authority has been provided by Michel Crozier in *The Bureaucratic Phenomenon* (1963, English version 1964, Tavistock Publications, London). The best general discussions of the executive in English are those of Malcolm Anderson, *Government in France, an introduction to the Executive Power* (1970, Pergamon,

Oxford) and F. F. Ridley and J. Blondel, *Public Administration in France* (1964, 2nd edn 1969, Routledge and Kegan Paul, London), although neither of them uses the insights afforded by the Crozierian analysis. On the role of ministers, we must turn to part three of Robert Buron's *Le Plus Beau des Métiers* (1963, Plon, Paris) and to Bernard Chenot's *Etre Ministre* (1967, Plon, Paris).

For general discussions of the French civil service in a comparative context, Brian Chapman's *The Profession of Government* (1957, Allen and Unwin, London) remains interesting but should be supplemented with F. F. Ridley (ed.), *Specialists and Generalists, a comparative study of the professional civil servant at home and abroad* (1968, Allen and Unwin, London). On the recruitment of the senior civil service, one should consult the *Rapport de la Commission d'étude des problèmes de l'Ecole Nationale d'Administration* (April, 1969, La Documentation Française, Paris) and Henry Parris, 'Twenty years of l'Ecole Nationale d'Administration', *Public Administration,* winter 1965, the same issue containing A. Dutheillet de Lamothe's excellent study of 'Ministerial Cabinets in France'. On the role of the *grands corps,* see F. F. Ridley, 'French technocracy and comparative government', *Political Studies,* XIV, no. 1, February 1966; Charles Debbasch, *L'Administration au Pouvoir, fonctionnaires et politiques sous la Ve République* (1969, Calmann-Lévy, Paris) and P. Escourbe, *Les Grands Corps de l'Etat* (1971, Presses Universitaires de France, Paris). For a penetrating criticism of French civil service studies, see E. N. Suleiman, 'The French bureaucracy and its students, towards the desanctification of the state', *World Politics,* XXIII, no. 1, October 1970.

Public order and civil liberties

Brian Chapman's brief *Police State* (1970, Macmillan, London) provides a suggestive introduction in a rather neglected area. Roger Errera's *Les Libertés à l'Abandon* (1968, Seuil, Paris) documents the inroads on civil liberties made by successive governments. For a general critique of the judicial system by an anonymous group of French judges, consult C. Laroche-Flavin, *La Machine Judiciaire* (1968, Seuil, Paris). On the council of state, it is still worth reading C. J. Hamson's classic *Executive Discretion and Judicial Control, an aspect of the French Conseil d'Etat* (1954, Stevens, London). Margherita Rendel's *The Administrative Functions of the French Conseil d'Etat* (1970, Weidenfeld and Nicolson, London) draws mainly on examples prior to the fifth republic, so for a more general and up-to-date treatment one should also consult J.–P. Negrin, *Le Conseil d'Etat et la Vie Publique en France depuis 1958* (1968,

Presses Universitaires de France, Paris), which is far more useful than the more ambitious study by M.–C. Kessler, *Le Conseil d'Etat* (1968, Colin, Paris).

In a class by itself is the sinisterly entertaining collection of articles by Philip Williams entitled *Wars, Plots and Scandals in Post-war France* (1970, Cambridge University Press, Cambridge). This sets the scene for an insider's pseudonymous study of the political organization and utilization of the police by J. Lantier, *Le Temps des Policiers* (1970, Fayard, Paris) and a collection of articles by two well-informed left-wing journalists, R. Backmann and C. Angeli, *Les Polices de la Nouvelle Société* (1971, Maspero, Paris). On the domestic role of the French military, the best study is J. S. Ambler's *Soldiers Against the State, the French Army in Politics* (1966, 1968 edn Doubleday, Garden City, New York). On newspapers, consult 'La Presse Française', *Notes et Etudes Documentaires* (no. 3,521, September 1968, 'La Documentation Française', Paris) for factual information; while for comment a special issue of *Esprit*, February 1971, is devoted to 'Le Journal et ses lecteurs'. On the perennial problem of state radio and television, see the very brief but useful collection of facts and views in G. Dupuis *et al.*, *L'O.R.T.F.* (1970, Colin, Paris).

Economic policy

The best general introduction remains Andrew Shonfield's *Modern Capitalism, the changing balance of public and private power* (1965, Oxford University Press, London) although a more up-to-date assessment is provided by Jack Hayward's 'State intervention in France, the changing style of government–industry relations', *Political Studies*, xx, no. 3, September 1972. For a dated but still useful description of the finance ministry, consult F.–L. Closon and J. Filippi (eds), *L'Economie et les Finances* (1959, Presses Universitaires de France, Paris). On the working of financial control, see Pierre Lalumière's *Les Finances Publiques* (1970, Colin, Paris), the same author having earlier studied *L'Inspection des Finances* (1959, Presses Universitaires de France, Paris). On the budgetary process one may consult M.–C. Kessler, 'Pour une étude du système budgétaire français, problématique', *Revue Française de Science Politique*, xxii, no. 1, February 1972, but the best study is Guy Lord's *The French Budgetary Process* (1973, University of California Press, Berkeley).

On state intervention in industry, John Sheahan's *Promotion and Control of Industry in Postwar France* (1963, Harvard University Press, Cambridge, Mass.) can still be read with profit but the key work in this field is J. H. McArthur and B. R. Scott, *Industrial Planning in France* (1969, Harvard University Press, Cambridge, Mass.). Lionel Stoleru's *L'Impératif Industriel* (1969, Seuil, Paris) should also be read as indicative of French official thinking. J. and A.-M. Hackett's *Economic Planning in France* (1963, Allen and Unwin, London) is an excellent institutional description but somewhat dated, while Stephen S. Cohen's *Modern Capitalist Planning, the French Model* (1969, Weidenfeld and Nicolson, London) is more political in emphasis but refers to an earlier period than its publication date would suggest. They should therefore be supplemented by a symposium produced by thirteen French planners : Atreize, *La Planification Française en pratique* (1971, Editions Ouvrières, Paris). The minimal role of parliament is exhaustively treated in P. Corbel, *Le Parlement Français et la Planification* (1969, Editions Cujas, Paris). On the main agency shaping regional planning, see B. Pouyet, *La Délégation à l'Aménagement du Territoire et à l'Action Régionale* (1967, Editions Cujas, Paris). On innovation in the administration of the economy the best study is that by Lucien Sfez on *L'Administration Prospective* (1970, Colin, Paris).

Education and public enterprise

An excellent description of the education ministry's organization is provided in J. Minot, *L'Entreprise Education Nationale* (1970, Colin, Paris) while education policy is dealt with in J. Fournier's *Politique de l'Education* (1971, Seuil, Paris). There are useful discussions of French education in W. D. Halls *Society, Schools and Progress in France* (1965, Pergamon, Oxford) and the more up to date study by W. R. Fraser, *Reforms and Restraints in Modern French Education* (1971, Routledge and Kegan Paul, London) but the most penetrating discussion available is in the OECD *Reviews of National Policies for Education, France* (1971, OECD, Paris). One may also consult J. M. Clarke, *Teachers and Politics in France, a pressure group study of the Fédération de l'Education Nationale* (1967, Syracuse University Press, Syracuse, New York) and A. B. Fields, *Student Politics in France, a study of the Union Nationale des Etudiants de France* (1970, Basic Books, New York). A judiciously inconclusive discussion of the eight main explanations of the May 1968 events is provided by P. Bénéton and J. Touchard, 'Les interprétations de la crise de mai–juin 1968', *Revue Française de Science Politique*, xx, no. 3, June 1970, while Jacques de Chalendar provides an insider's testimony on the preparation of the 1968 University Guidelines Act in *Une Loi pour l'Université* (1970, Desclée de Brouwer, Paris).

The best discussions of public enterprise: Maurice Byé, in M. Einaudi *et al.*, *Nationalization in France and Italy* (1955, Cornell University Press, Ithaca, New York), A. G. Delion's *L'Etat et les Entreprises Publiques* (1958, Sirey, Paris), and B. Chenot's *Les Entreprises Nationalisées* (1959, Presses Universitaires de France, Paris), are now rather out of date. They should therefore be supplemented with *Rapport sur les Entreprises Publiques*—the Nora Report— (1968, La Documentation Française, Paris) and the badly translated chapters by Roland Drago and D. G. M. Lévy in W. G. Friedmann and J. F. Garner (eds), *Government Enterprise, a comparative study* (1970, Stevens, London).

Foreign and defence policy

For a (dated) description of the foreign ministry one should consult J. Baillou and P. Pelletier, *Les Affaires Etrangères* (1962, Presses Universitaires de France, Paris). Alfred Grosser has provided masterly discussions of the content of French foreign policy under the fourth and fifth republics in *La Quatrième République et sa Politique Extérieure* (1961, Colin, Paris) and *French Foreign Policy under de Gaulle* (1965, English edn 1967, Little, Brown, Boston). For an official apologia, see Maurice Couve de Murville's *Une Politique Etrangère, 1958–1969* (1971, Plon, Paris) while G. de Carmoy's *The Foreign Policies of France, 1944–1968* (1970, Chicago University Press, Chicago) provides a more critical assessment of Gaullist policy abroad. W. L. Kohl's *French Nuclear Diplomacy* (1971, Princeton University Press, Princeton, New Jersey) closely links foreign and defence policy, as does Wolf Mendl's *Deterrence and Persuasion, French nuclear armament in the context of national policy, 1945–1969* (1970, Faber, London). Lawrence Scheinman skilfully disentangles the threads of clandestine policy-making in *Atomic Energy Policy in France under the Fourth Republic* (1965, Princeton University Press, Princeton, New Jersey). The only thorough discussion of defence organization is B. Chantebout's *L'Organisation de la Défense Nationale en France depuis la fin de la Seconde Guerre Mondiale* (1967, Librairie générale de droit et de jurisprudence, Paris).

Index